MILLIONAIRE
REAL ESTATE
MENTOR

ADVANCE PRAISE FOR *MILLIONAIRE REAL ESTATE MENTOR*

"We all need a 'millionaire mentor' and Russ Whitney is the man. I've read more than a dozen real estate wealth-building books, and this is the book I'm putting to practical use in my life. For the first time, Russ Whitney exposes the secrets that make real estate investors thrive and prosper. Read this book, then read it again as you follow the step-by-step road to wealth. You'll have fun while you're making money, and that is the key to ultimate success."

—Steve Crowley, Former Money Editor, *Good Morning America*, and Author of *Money for Life*

"After interviewing hundreds of the top entrepreneurs in the world, I've isolated one profound secret! They've all had a mentor! If you want to make money in real estate, there's no mentor better then Russ Whitney. In *Millionaire Real Estate Mentor*, he proves why."

—Mike Litman, Coauthor of *Conversations with Millionaires: What Millionaires Do to Get Rich, That You've Never Learned About in School!*

"How often has a mentor made a difference in your life? Turning points can often be traced to the guidance provided by a trusted friend. Consider Russ Whitney, and his brilliant work, *Millionaire Real Estate Mentor*, as your personal real estate mentor who will take you by the hand and teach you practical, easy-to-understand ways to profit from real estate. Russ and his proven methods for success are with you every step. Read *and* apply what you find in this book, and I am sure you will Make it Big!"

—Frank McKinney, Author of *Make It BIG! 49 Secrets for Building a Life of Extreme Success*

"Russ Whitney unquestionably knows more ways to help individuals create wealth in real estate from a standing start (with or without any beginning capital) than any other expert in the field. I've personally watched him transform 250 people in a day from absolute real estate greenhorns to creative real estate Green Berets. His ideas are ABSOLUTELY worth learning."

—Jay Abraham, Marketing Expert, Strategic Growth Advisor

MILLIONAIRE
REAL ESTATE
MENTOR

THE SECRETS TO FINANCIAL FREEDOM
THROUGH REAL ESTATE INVESTING

RUSS WHITNEY
AND HIS WEALTH TEAM

Dearborn™
Trade Publishing
A **Kaplan Professional** Company

Vice President and Publisher: Cynthia A. Zigmund
Editorial Director: Donald J. Hull
Acquisitions Editor: Mary B. Good
Senior Managing Editor: Jack Kiburz
Interior Design: Lucy Jenkins
Cover Design: Design Solutions
Typesetting: the dotted i

Published by Dearborn Trade Publishing
A Kaplan Professional Company

Library of Congress Cataloging-in-Publication Data

Whitney, Russ.
      Millionaire real estate mentor : the secrets to financial freedom
    through real estate investing / Russ Whitney and his wealth team.
            p.   cm.
      Includes index.
      ISBN 0-7931-6686-1 (pbk.)
      1. Real estate investment.   2. Real estate investment—United States.
    I. Title.
    HD1382.5 .W45 2003
    332.63′24—dc21   2002154242

DEDICATION
In Memory of Richard Brevoort, 1937–2002

Richard was a man of extraordinary brilliance, dedication, and loyalty. His contributions and commitment to our students, trainers, and staff are a very small part of his wonderful legacy. The wisdom, inspiration, and compassion he shared so unselfishly will be a living monument to a man whose priorities were teaching, helping, and serving. I am both proud and humbled that he called me his friend.

ACKNOWLEDGMENTS

Though there may be just one name on the cover, no book can be written by only one person. From conception to organization and research through the actual process of writing to editing, production, and finally publication, books are a collective effort. And I would like to thank the people who assisted me in this one.

Of course, tremendous appreciation goes to the Wealth Team: Jim Aviza, Don Burnham, Shawn Casey, Robert Demes, David Gilmore, Kevin Haag, Jean Lapoint, Glenn Purdy, David Shamy, Jim Shead, Larry Simons, Gary Tharp, Pete Youngs, and Tony Youngs. My personal friendship with each of them is enhanced by their willingness to share the knowledge that has made them millionaires.

There are no words to express my gratitude to my students, for they are the purpose of Whitney Education Group. I feel an immense amount of responsibility for each of them, and I am humbled that God has given me the chance to serve in such a meaningful way. In particular, I would like to recognize the students who shared their stories for this book: Steve Bias, Carlos and Melissa Budet, Dan Davis, Joe Fucheck, Debbra Greig, Chuck and Sherri Hastings, Karen Herrera, Glenn and Michelle Kuperus, Jay and Kasey London, Beverly Martin, Anthony and Joan Peters, Steve and Carolyn Rawlings, Rosanna and Michael Reilly, Con Reynolds, Lorne and Angie Saltsman, Rita Swanson, Lester Theiss, Bobby Threlkeld, Ron Watke, and Carroll and Melisa Wimett.

By virtue of their contribution to the company, every member of the Whitney Education Group staff has helped with this book, but some deserve special recognition: Marian VanDyke, who coordinated the initial planning and information gathering; Susan Carrillo, my ever-patient assistant; Valerie Gaines; Melody Babineau; Lisa Marino; Morsa Spidle; Joe Gnapp; Teresa Sells; John Kane; Ron Simon; and Marie Code. Though not an actual employee of Whitney Education Group, Don Abbott of Abbott Productions, who oversees all of the video products we offer, plays an important role both in marketing our company and in creating the high-quality products our students expect and deserve.

Thanks also go to my agent, Michael Baybak, who found the right publisher to showcase this work.

Special thanks go to Jacquelyn Lynn, who assisted me in writing this book. I appreciate her tireless efforts and, in particular, the time she took to learn the techniques, strategies, and mindsets of all the people who contributed to this project. It was her special talent that made this more than "just another book."

Finally, I want to acknowledge Richard Brevoort, to whom this book is dedicated. Officially, he served as the president of Whitney Information Network, Inc.™, and Whitney Education Group, Inc.™ More important, he was a dear friend and trusted advisor. He had been instrumental in the growth of the companies as well as in helping thousands of our students and staff realize their potential and achieve their dreams. Richard's generosity and compassion extended deep into the community, and he believed we all have a responsibility to public service. The lives that benefited from the gentle but firm guidance provided by Richard Brevoort, a consummate teacher and mentor, are too numerous to count. He was a major contributor to this book and was involved throughout its research and writing, making substantial contributions to the content and presentation. Just a few weeks after the manuscript was completed in 2002, Richard lost his hard-fought battle with cancer. Though we are deeply saddened by his death, we are all richer for having known and worked with him.

■ CONTENTS

■ PREFACE

You can become wealthy. You can build a fortune that will allow you to enjoy the lifestyle you've always dreamed about without ever worrying about the future. It doesn't matter where you are in life or what you've done so far. You may be fresh out of school and trying to decide what to do. You may be a baby boomer fed up with your job or even facing a layoff. Or you may be a senior citizen who is either not ready, or can't afford, to retire. Whatever your particular circumstances, you can change your life for the better.

I know, because I've done it. I was a high school dropout working in a slaughterhouse when I started looking for my ticket out. I found a start in a $10 how-to book about investing in real estate. The information it contained allowed me to make $11,000 in just three weeks—pretty good money for a kid whose job killing hogs started at $5 an hour (although I was up to $6 an hour when I made that investment). And that was just the start. I immediately reinvested that money and began building my portfolio. By the time I was 23, I was financially independent, and my wife and I were able to quit our jobs. At the age of 27, I had become one of America's youngest self-made millionaires.

I was so excited about what I was doing that I started telling my friends about it, and soon I was helping them do the same thing. Sure, some were skeptical and not all of them took my advice, but the truth was clearly in front of them. And of course I made some mistakes, but that didn't stop me from working toward my goals.

Today, my wife and I live in our 16,000-square-foot dream home on Florida's Gulf Coast near the headquarters of our worldwide business operations. One of the businesses I started years ago is now a publicly traded corporation and the parent company of a wide range of other businesses. Through those operations, we have helped thousands of people become wealthy—people who started out just as I did, people like you who had the drive and the courage to change their life for the better.

How did I do it? I started with real estate and then diversified into a number of other businesses, including, among others, construction, mortgage services, publishing, business consulting, software development, education, and even a chain of resort recreation equipment rental shops. Were all of those ventures successful? No. Most were, but even the things I tried that failed taught me valuable lessons that made my other businesses even more profitable. I think you learn as much, if not more, by studying what didn't work so you know what *not* to do as you learn by studying what works so you know what *to* do. And I'm going to share many of those lessons with you in this book.

Even though I have an interest in many companies, the foundation of my wealth is still real estate, which is not unique. Many major corporations have substantial real estate holdings. Celebrities better known for entertainment wisely invest in real estate—such as Robert Redford's Sundance and Oprah Winfrey's holdings that include residential and commercial real estate. Ted Turner is more than a media mogul; he's one of the largest landowners in the United States. At the opposite end of the spectrum are individual working people whose biggest chunk of their net worth will likely be found in their home—real estate.

Investing in real estate is not a get-rich-quick scheme. Yes, you can make a considerable amount of money in a very short time if you know what you're doing. Yes, you can become rich if you are willing to put forth the effort to develop the skills necessary to build a real estate business.

Think about this: By making real estate your business, you can provide safe, clean housing to young families, senior citizens, and others who might not otherwise be able to afford a decent place to live. You can help people avoid foreclosure. You can help others buy their first homes or recover from economic difficulties. You can contribute to the revival of distressed areas in your community by increasing the value of properties and getting them back on the tax rolls. You'll create jobs and assist the overall economy. And in the process, you can make millions of dollars.

No other business I know of lets you do so much for so many while making money for yourself and your family and creating freedom for you to enjoy life on your own terms. Think of the legacy you can build. Your children will see what you're doing and will understand that the financial security you have created for them has been built on helping people. They can carry on your work and pass it along to their own children. Can you think of a better way to be remembered?

Look around your community. Who are the real movers and shakers? It's the wealthy businesspeople who make things happen. When they speak, people listen. When they command, people act. They may come from varied backgrounds, but I can guarantee you that, with few exceptions, they own real estate. If it works for the wealthy, it can work for you.

There are so many ways to make money in real estate that regardless of what you like to do, you can find a way to do it in this book. Beyond basic real estate—buying, selling, renting, managing your own properties—is a wide range of related businesses that are easy to start, require little or no capital, and can quickly grow to generate hundreds of thousands of dollars a year in revenue.

You'll learn about those businesses and much more in this book. You'll see how, as a wealth-building vehicle, real estate has created more fortunes than any other investment. But it's more than just buying, selling, and renting houses. You'll learn how to build a business, negotiate deals, cultivate relationships, manage your finances—all the elements that are critical to success in any endeavor.

When I first started my real estate business, my only guide was that one $10 how-to book. Even though it contained some valuable information, I quickly realized I needed to know more. I read more books, I asked questions, and then I had to sift through all the information I had gathered to figure out what was useful and what wasn't.

As I figured things out, I began to teach my friends how they could do what I was doing. I realized that this information wasn't being taught in schools, but it's important for people to know. So I wrote my first book in an effort to reach a wider audience than I could have by just helping people one-on-one.

I wrote more books and began conducting training camps but still faced the same challenge: There was only one of me but thousands of people who wanted and needed to hear what I had to share. So I created the Whitney Education Group and assembled a teaching team of self-made millionaires with tremendous knowledge and expertise in all areas of real estate, business, and wealth building. These are down-to-earth people who, as I did, built their own fortunes after starting with little or nothing, and they have the ability to explain in simple, easy-to-follow language how they did it and how you can do it, too. Across the country every weekend, one or more of them teach an intensive training program for Whitney Education Group that focuses on their particular area of expertise.

I've asked these friends of mine, who are all self-made millionaires, to work with me on this project to give you all the information you need to understand these techniques, be able to apply them immediately, and see profitable results right away.

The structure of this book is simple and easy to understand. We begin with an overview of real estate as an industry and how it serves as the foundation for wealth. Then I'll discuss what you need to know to set up your own business. After that, I'll go through specific wealth-building techniques that you can use either separately or collectively to build your own personal fortune.

If real estate were taught in college, this book could be the model for a four-year degree except that it is fun and exciting and can change your life. Even better, the only tests are the ones you give yourself when you put the techniques to work—and you can start using each technique as soon as you learn it. College students don't remain ignorant for four years and then suddenly become smart the day they receive their degree. They learn as they go along, and so will you.

Many of the techniques here can be applied to various situations—thus, you might learn something in the chapter on foreclosures that you can use in doing lease-option deals. So be sure to read the entire book, even if you don't read each chapter in order. Also, each chapter contains real-life examples of how our instructors and students have successfully used the techniques to become wealthy. I know you'll find their stories inspiring and motivating.

One final point before we begin: I wrote this book to be your own personal millionaire mentor. It tells you how to use real estate and other businesses to build your own personal fortune, but it isn't just about making money—it's about changing your life. You bought this book because you want more out of life than you're getting now. I understand, because I've been there. And I'm going to show you how to get where you want to be. So let's get started.

CHAPTER 1

Planting Your Own Money Tree

Money may not grow on trees, but it does grow out of the ground. Just look around at all the houses, apartment complexes, office buildings, retail centers, and industrial facilities that are making their owners very rich. Think about being able to pick your share of "fruit" from those brick-and-mortar "trees."

Most millionaires have a significant portion—if not the majority—of their wealth in real estate. Why? It just makes sense. The supply of real estate is limited—what we have on the earth is all we're ever going to have; no one is making more of it. Real estate will always be in demand because no matter what happens to the world in terms of politics or economics, people will need places to live, businesses will need places to operate, and governments will need places to function. And the value of real estate has been consistently rising for more than 200 years. Of course, we have seen both up cycles and down cycles in the real estate market, but the down cycles don't last long and real estate always comes out a winner.

As an investment, real estate puts you totally in the driver's seat. When you buy stocks, you don't have control—you're investing your money in a company, but it's the officers and directors who decide how the company will operate. When you invest in precious metals, gems, or collectibles, you're at the mercy of the market. But when you invest in real estate, *you* have control. *You* make the decisions. And *you* make the money.

What it boils down to is this: Real estate is one of the best vehicles we have for building wealth and creating financial security. It's a tool that has been used successfully by people who have virtually no resources, by average Americans who have some money to work with, by highly educated professionals looking to diversify, and by businesses ranging from very small to multinational corporations. What category do you fit into?

Maybe you're having trouble picturing yourself as a real estate investor. Believe me, not all real estate investors are high-profile, flashy celebrities like the ones who so often appear in the gossip tabloids. Of course, if that's what you want, real estate can get you there. It can also provide you and your family financial security and a higher standard of living, no matter where you live or what you're starting with. Even better, you don't have to quit whatever you're doing now to start learning about and making big money in real estate. You can start part-time—that's how I did it, and that's how most of the successful investors I know did it.

The advantage that you'll have is the knowledge I'm sharing in this book. You'll have learned clear and specific strategies that will allow you to generate cash and build wealth. This book is modeled after the training programs my company offers: It's easy to understand and apply; it's reality based; it's as close to hands-on learning as a book can possibly be; and it is absolutely "doable" by anyone who really wants to learn.

Most of the math skills you'll need are no more difficult than eighth-grade arithmetic. The techniques and strategies are no more complicated than middle school history or science memorization. You don't have to memorize dates, but you will have to understand how to find the right investment properties and what to do with them. These aren't complicated theories; they are basic, real-world techniques that work and that you can use over and over to generate profits and build wealth.

Words of Wisdom

All distractions and excuses are equal. It doesn't matter what's keeping you from achieving your dreams—you just need to ignore your distractions, tear up your excuses, and get to work making success and security a part of your life.

■ The Difference between Income and Wealth

Having a large income doesn't necessary mean you are wealthy. I know doctors and lawyers who make $300,000 a year but can't afford to go to dinner with my wife and me because they don't have two nickels to rub together at the end of the month. Why? Because they make a decent income, but they don't understand the financial strategies that wealthy people use. They buy cars that are too expensive and houses with payments beyond their means; their kids are in expensive private schools; and they're busy trying to keep up with the Joneses. They may have income, but they don't have wealth. When you live paycheck to paycheck, it's not the amount that matters; it's the lifestyle.

It's not how much you make but what you do with it that counts. If you earn $1 million and spend $1.2 million, you don't have wealth. And if you're using credit to buy depreciating assets—that is, clothes, jewelry, electronics, or anything else that goes down in value—you're digging yourself into a hole that's going to be very hard to climb out of. Based on advice from his father, who was a financial failure, Charles Dickens wrote in *David Copperfield:* "Annual income, twenty pounds; annual expenditure, nineteen pounds; result, happiness. Annual income, twenty pounds; annual expenditure, twenty-one pounds; result, misery."

The challenge most people face is that consumers are programmed to buy depreciating assets. Everywhere you turn, you see advertising messages urging you to buy such things as cars, furniture, and clothes that will only go down in value—and it doesn't matter if you don't have the cash, because the sellers are happy to either extend you credit or accept your credit cards. You're left with too much debt and a pile of useless goods that you couldn't sell for pennies on the dollar if you had to.

I'm not saying that debt is always bad—it isn't. When you use debt to buy things that increase in value and generate profits, you are thinking and operating like a wealthy person. The idea is to spend as much of your money as possible (after you pay for your necessities) on *appreciating assets,* such as real estate or any business that will go up in value and generate profits. That will start you on your way to true wealth, and then you can enjoy the luxury of buying *depreciating assets* because you know you can afford to pay for them.

Wealth isn't necessarily a number. Wealth is living within your means with most of your money coming from passive sources so you don't have to work if you don't want to. Wealth begins with financial independence—and financial independence is freedom and the first step to achieving true wealth.

■ Who Should You Listen To?

Too many people have been programmed to believe they can never become rich. How is this programming acquired? From people who are not rich.

Think about it. Who is best qualified to give you financial advice? Is it someone who is struggling along from paycheck to paycheck, or is it someone who has worked smart, built a business, and achieved the status of millionaire?

You will hear from your parents, your siblings, other relatives, the people you work with, your neighbors—and they'll all tell you that your goals are just pipe dreams and you'll never become wealthy. I often hear this from the students in my training programs. Some don't tell anyone they're investing in their education because they're afraid they'll be laughed at. Some don't even tell people that they're buying their first few investment properties for the same reason.

I understand that, and if you're afraid of being laughed at, you're not alone. My advice for how to deal with this is simple: Don't take financial advice from poor people. Instead, take your advice from people who have started from nothing and built substantial fortunes. That's the kind of material you'll get in this book.

■ Your First Goal: Financial Independence

Dreams of wealth, a luxurious lifestyle, and multimillionaire status may be driving you now, but if you're going to make them come true, you need to establish a few simple goals. And your first goal should be financial independence.

The definition of financial independence is having enough money coming in every month to make your mortgage and car payments, put food on the table, have a little luxury money left, and not need a full-time job. For me, financial independence came at the age of 23, when I had properties generating a net income of $1,400 a month. That may not sound like much today, but remember that at the time I was making $6 an hour working in a slaughterhouse—$240 a week—so $1,400 a month was nearly double my take-home wages. That's when I was able to quit my job and concentrate on building my real estate business.

That's what *you* want: Have enough passive income coming in every month so you can pay your mortgage and car loan, handle your other expenses, and have a little bit left over for pleasure without a full-time job. For most people today, that means $3,000 to $5,000 a month. Basically, you want to replace your salary with revenue from your investments, which is not hard to do; in Chapter 4, for example, you'll learn several strategies for doing this within a very short time frame. That's financial independence, and it's the first step to becoming a millionaire. Once you achieve this step, where you go from there is entirely up to you.

Wealth Secrets

Use credit (borrowed money) to invest in things that go up in value and will generate positive cash flow so you can service your debt and increase your net worth.

■ But Is It Safe?

Can you lose money in real estate? If you tried really hard to do everything wrong, I'm sure you could. But as an investment and a business, real estate is the simplest, easiest, most stable vehicle available. Consider this: When the stock market drops, investors pull their money out and put it in real estate. Why? Because when you buy real estate, using the sound business principles you'll learn in this book, it's the safest place to invest. The key is to buy smart and manage your holdings wisely, and I'm going to show you exactly how to do that.

The methods for buying, selling, managing, and making *huge* profits in real estate that I'm going to explain are time tested and proven. They are sound formulas that have been working successfully for decades and some for centuries. They're not complicated, they're not difficult—they're simple techniques that you can easily learn and do. They've already worked for people from all walks of life who have been willing to learn and apply my strategies. Just follow the advice I'm sharing here, and you'll make one smart, profitable investment after another.

Words of Wisdom

Commit time and money to educate yourself. Top athletes don't just start playing at the championship level. They study, practice, and get better. Doctors don't take a few courses and are then qualified to perform surgery. Why would you expect your career to be any different?

SUCCESS STORY

You're Never Too Old

Widowed and in her 70s, Rita Swanson was living on Social Security when she decided to start investing in real estate. Her first property was a "fixer-upper" that she rehabbed and sold. She quickly bought five more houses and a condo that she rents for the cash flow.

Rita's next investment was a 35-unit apartment building she bought with a partner; then she bought a larger complex. Today, her holdings are worth well in excess of $2 million. She says, "Being able to acquire cash flow real estate doesn't take any special status in life. All it takes is some training and determination. Some people have asked me, 'What can you do at your age?' And I say, 'Anything I want!'"

SUCCESS
STORY

Getting Fired Got Him Fired Up

Joe Fucheck was facing eviction from his one-bedroom apartment, his wife was pregnant, he had about $1,000 in the bank, and he'd been fired from his job. Depressing? You bet. But instead of diving into a pit of despair, Joe learned how to invest in real estate at a Whitney training program and quickly put more than $300,000 in his bank account.

"I am my own boss and have people working for me. That's the American dream," he says. "I have nobody to answer to but myself."

Joe enjoys being the boss but more important are the benefits his family receives. "Let's face it: If you have problems paying the bills, it has an adverse effect on your family," he says. "How much I want to earn is directly proportional to how much I want to work. Real estate has absolutely and unequivocally taken the stress out of paying my bills."

His advice: "Get the resources and then read them over and over again until you understand how it's done, and then go out and put your knowledge to use."

■ If One Is Good, Several Are Better

Owning your home is one of the best personal investments you'll ever make. So if owning one piece of property is good, it makes sense that owning more is better.

Think about this: You buy your home, pay off the mortgage after 20 or 30 years, and you then have an asset that is likely worth substantially more than you paid for it. If you did that with just two or three more houses that you bought, rented out (which means you will pay your mortgage with the money your tenants pay you), what would you have? You'd have enough to make a major difference in your retirement lifestyle, or enough to send your kids to college, or enough to do all those other things you've dreamed about but thought you couldn't afford.

Look around your community at houses that were selling for $50,000 just 20 or 30 years ago. What are they going for now? $175,000? $200,000? More? The people who bought those houses for $50,000 and paid them off are sitting on a very impressive and valuable asset right now. Maybe you know someone who has done that. Maybe you've done it yourself with your own home. If so, chances are you didn't have a serious investment strategy in mind at the time. So pretty much by accident, you ended up with a house you own free and clear that's worth several times what you paid for it. If you can do that without planning for it, imagine what you'll be able to do when you learn the secrets in this book to making big money in real estate.

There's little difference between owning and caring for your own home and owning and caring for rental property. You have to maintain rental property, which means keeping it painted and in good repair. You have to fix things when they break, which means doing what you can yourself and paying someone else to do what you either can't or don't want to do. Sure, you have to find and screen tenants and collect the rent, but that doesn't take a lot of effort in relation to the amount of positive cash flow and profits you can make.

Think of it this way: If someone offered to make your mortgage payments if you'd just spend 30 to 40 hours *a year* doing administrative and minor fix-up chores, would you do it? Of course you would. Owning rental property is no different. You use the rent from your tenant to make the mortgage payment on the property. That means you're building equity in the property and increasing your net worth each month as you deposit the tenant's rent check and write your own check to the lender. And if you can do it with one house, why couldn't you do it with two or three or four or however many it will take for you to reach your financial goals?

Words of Wisdom

We all pay for our education one way or another. You can either spend the money to take classes and read books (like this one) to learn from experts with the hands-on experience to teach you, or you can lose money on deals. Which is the better choice?

■ What Kind of Real Estate Business Should You Start?

This book shows you a wide variety of real estate businesses, so you can choose based on what you like to do. Real estate is an industry with so many aspects that anyone can find something to do within the industry that is suited to his or her particular talents and interests.

Should you specialize in a particular area? You can, but you don't have to. My own personal strategy has always been to specialize in the types of real estate that generate positive cash flow, whether single-family houses, apartments, rooming houses, or whatever. I know successful investors who take the same approach I do, and I know successful investors who find a particular niche they like and focus exclusively on that. You may choose to start with one type of real estate—particularly if you're operating with limited capital—and then expand into other areas as you generate cash and equity. My advice is to read this entire book at least once before deciding whether to specialize and, if so, in what area.

For example, do you like to work with your hands? Then you might choose to buy cosmetically distressed properties, fix them up, and either sell or rent them. You don't have to do all the fix-up work yourself, but you can if you want to. Or if fix-up work is not your thing, you can hire people to do it for you while you focus on the buying and selling side of the business.

There's No Security in Having a Job

When you are your own boss, you never have to worry about being unappreciated or getting laid off. It was those concerns that drove Constance Reynolds into real estate investing.

After 13 years on the job as a word processor for a law firm, Constance was devastated when she received an unexpected—and, she felt, undeserved—poor performance review. At the same time, her husband was worried about being laid off from his corporate job. Constance decided something had to be done to achieve financial independence, so she bought my book, *Building Wealth,* and decided to start investing in real estate.

"My husband, a business major and engineer by education, cautioned me not to get into real estate—too risky," she told me. "I ignored him, believed you, and one year later we had seven income properties netting $3,500 a month [after expenses]."

Constance is adding to their portfolio at the rate of one property a month, and she and her husband no longer worry about bad reviews or corporate layoffs.

Maybe you don't want to own property. That's fine—there are still plenty of ways to make money in real estate without ever buying property. You can use options (explained in Chapter 5) to control property and profit from it without owning it. Or you can find deals for other investors using wholesale techniques (taught in Chapter 4). Another alternative is to deal in privately held mortgages by buying, selling, and brokering the paper that secures real estate loans (the subject of Chapter 13).

If you like helping people in trouble, foreclosures could be for you. You can help people stop a foreclosure, find a home they can afford, and profit from the transaction. Or if you prefer a more sophisticated client base, get into commercial real estate.

In addition to these direct real estate businesses, you can pick from a wide range of ancillary services that can create revenue streams of hundreds of thousands of dollars each year.

The opportunities in real estate are endless, and most of the techniques you'll learn here will work in just about any market. There are some variables, of course, which is why I'll show you how to evaluate your local market for the realistic potential of each technique.

Words of Wisdom

Create your business based on something you enjoy, something you'll look forward to doing every day. Do things you enjoy that will also reward you financially.

■ What's Stopping You?

Many people believe they can't be successful because of long-held misconceptions about what it takes to succeed. Are any of these beliefs stopping you?

Misconception: Some people can't be successful because of their background, education, or other factors beyond their control.

Reality: Anyone who wants to can be successful. It's a matter of having the desire, learning what to do and how to do it, and then doing it.

Misconception: You've got to work 60, 70, or 80 hours a week to be successful.

Reality: Though you have to work hard to achieve success, it's not a matter of quantity but rather of quality. Doing the right things will lead to success.

Misconception: Successful people don't make mistakes.

Reality: Successful people make plenty of mistakes. What they also do is learn from those mistakes so they don't repeat them.

Misconception: If you have help, it's not success.

Reality: Few people make it on their own without any help at all. Learn how to build a Power Team that will help you. I'll show you how to do that in Chapter 2.

Misconception: It takes luck to be successful.

Reality: Luck has nothing to do with it. Success takes finding the right opportunity, educating yourself about how the opportunity works, and then taking action while you continue to learn.

■ The First Step

I have built my fortune based on three things: the hands that I shake, the decisions that I make, and the actions I take. You can do the same.

Obviously, the hands that you shake are the people you know. This is more than just networking. What you need is a Power Team—a group of people who have a vested interest in your success, who will work with you and for you, and who will help you build your own fortune. That's what we're going to talk about in the next chapter.

MILLIONAIRE MENTOR Money Tree Highlights

- ■ Real estate is the best vehicle for building wealth and creating financial security.

- ■ Use debt to buy appreciating assets—that is, things that will increase in value and generate profits.

- ■ Take your financial advice from wealthy people.

- ■ Your first goal should be financial independence. Get enough money coming in from your real estate investments so you don't have to work a full-time job. Then decide where you want to go from there.

CHAPTER 2

Creating a Power Team

If you're going to be wealthy, you must think and function like a wealthy person, which doesn't mean buying flashy cars and passing out $100 tips to the parking valets. It does mean applying the concepts of teamwork and mastering the art of delegation.

When I first started building my own fortune, I thought I could do it all by myself. I'd read a few books, and I saw no reason to spend my hard-earned money paying other people to do things I could do myself. It didn't take me long to understand the error of that thinking.

Even though it's possible to do everything yourself, it isn't practical or effective. You have to focus your energy and efforts on the things that will increase your wealth. Hire others to handle the menial, mundane, non-revenue-generating tasks—you have better ways to spend your time. For professional services and other critical support issues, find and use top talent—an approach that will get you to your goals much faster.

How do you do this? By assembling your own Power Team, a team of professionals who will get the results you want. Essentially, this is your brain trust, the team of people committed to your success who provide the human foundation for your operations. Your Power Team includes such people as your real estate broker, mortgage broker, banker, and others who will work for you absolutely free because they want you to succeed. Why? Because when you succeed, they make money. Your real estate broker earns a commission from the property seller; your mortgage broker earns a commission from the lending source; your banker makes money on the interest you pay on the loan; your insurance agent is paid by the insurance company; and so on. What I really loved about real estate when I first got started was that I had all these knowledgeable, skilled professionals working hard for me, and someone else paid them—it fit right into my budget.

You'll have to go looking for some of these people; others will come to you through circumstances. Here's a great example. Karen Herrera was a shy single mother, heavily in debt, struggling to send her daughters to school, when she came to work as the receptionist in our corporate offices. She sat in on some classes, learned how to buy property, and now coordinates our Intensified Real Estate Training Program when she's not managing her own real estate holdings. She was in the process of building her Power Team when she got a call from someone at a mortgage brokerage that was just a few years old and marketing for new clients. Somehow the company found out Karen was investing in real estate, and one of its brokers called her. The next time Karen needed financing, she called that broker, who did that deal and a few others. When Karen had a large deal involving 32 units, the owner of the firm handled it. Karen now has a knowledgeable, experienced mortgage broker on her team—someone she can call for advice, for information, for referrals, and, most important, for funding. You could find yourself in this same situation. I'll explain more about how mortgage brokers work later on in this chapter, but they're always on the lookout for new clients because that's how they get paid. If you're borrowing money, they want to know you.

There's no telling where you'll meet members of your Power Team—it might be on the golf course, at a party, in church, or even in line at the grocery store. The point: Pay attention when you meet people so you don't miss any opportunities.

I began putting together my Power Team within a year of buying my first investment property. Of course, I didn't realize at the time what I was doing—had I understood the concept, I would have done it even sooner. I don't mind paying people well for their expertise, and I don't mind when people make a lot of money from the deals I'm involved in because when the members of my Power Team are making money, I'm making money too.

■ Potential Choices for Your Power Team

The makeup of your own Power Team will vary according to the particular type of business you choose to start. I'm going to tell you about the Power Team members I consider essential as well as others that you may or may not need, depending on your particular business. In some cases, the functions may overlap.

Let's take them one at a time.

Words of Wisdom

Don't let an incomplete Power Team stop you from getting started. You'll find the people you need as you go along. In fact, the initial members of your team will likely refer you to others as your relationship with them strengthens.

Banker

Bankers *want* to loan you money. If you've been turned down for loans time and time again, you may not believe this, but it's true. Bankers don't make money unless they are making loans—but they want to make good loans, loans that they believe will be repaid on schedule.

Banks are businesses, and they need to make a profit to stay in business. What's more, they are heavily regulated businesses, so they are accountable to regulatory entities as well as their shareholders. This means there are times when a banker may genuinely want to make a loan but can't because the regulators won't let him, and it will have nothing to do with you or your deal. When this happens and you don't have a personal relationship with the banker, you'll never find out the real reason why you were turned down. But if the banker is on your Power Team, he'll tell you the truth and probably help you find another source for your funding.

Another interesting point about banks: Some banks (and other types of lenders) place a maximum on the amount of money they will lend to any one person, regardless of that individual's income, credit, or collateral. Others limit the number of separate loans, regardless of the dollar amount. If you reach that arbitrary amount, you can't borrow any more money from that institution. Having a banker on your Power Team provides insight into various lending restrictions, no matter how logical or how absurd, and what you can do to work with them.

Building a relationship with a banker to the point that you can consider her a member of your Power Team is a process that takes time and effort. The best approach is to interview several bankers until you find one or two with whom you feel comfortable, who clearly want to work with you, and who have the lending authority to accomplish what you need. You don't need to be arrogant, but be confident and professional. Remember, you're not asking for favors—you're offering them the opportunity to make a profit on your business. If they don't seem enthusiastic about your plans, move on.

You may be tempted to start with the bank where you currently have your personal accounts. This may not work, because that banker already has a first impression of you. He already knows what you do for a living and how much money you have. It may be difficult for him to see you as a real estate investor, so you will probably have greater success starting fresh with some-one who doesn't know you.

Chapter 15, which discusses using credit as a wealth-building tool, has more information about issues that will help you when dealing with bankers, such as how to put a loan package together and understanding credit scores. Be sure to read that chapter before approaching a banker for the first time.

Words of Wisdom

You've heard the old cliché about not putting all your eggs in one basket; the same rule applies to money and banks. Don't put all your deposits in, and make all your loans with, one bank. If another bank acquires that bank, your ability to obtain loans and other services may be affected. By distributing your deposits and loans among several institutions, you'll always have a banking backup available.

■ National Banks versus Community Banks

Because the banking industry is changing at an unprecedented pace, it's getting harder and harder to recognize the players. Traditional banking is going the way of the horse and buggy—in fact, the major banks are now calling themselves "financial services" firms and are offering a range of investing services, real estate, insurance, and more. Although these services may sound attractive, my advice is to deal with a community bank, especially when you're first starting in business. Let's take the time to understand the difference between a large national or international bank and a community bank.

Large national banks have names you recognize: Bank of America, Wells Fargo, Wachovia (which recently merged with First Union), SunTrust, CitiGroup, and J. P. Morgan Chase & Co. They are found in many locations and spend heavily on advertising. They often promote low loan rates, but when you consider their overall terms, the package may not be as attractive as it initially seemed, so you will often be better off going to a smaller bank or different type of lender. When it comes to commercial loans, big banks are looking for big-dollar deals, generally in the area of seven figures or more.

By contrast, community banks usually incorporate the name of the area they serve in their own name. They typically have one main location and perhaps a few branches, depending on the size of the city. What makes them attractive to you is their local ownership and management, which allows you to deal with the decision makers. They're generally more flexible—which doesn't mean they want to make bad deals, but they have the ability to be more creative than a larger, more rigid operation. Most important, they want to build relationships. Community bankers want to finance projects for you today, next year, ten years from now, and beyond. They want to handle your other banking needs and help you grow because they know that's how they'll get more business.

Insurance Agent

The properties you buy have to be insured for two primary reasons: first, because lenders require it and, second, because you want to protect your investment. Basically, you need property and liability coverage and thus need a good commercial insurance agent to help you get the best deal.

A good insurance agent can provide you with a wealth of knowledge that you don't have to pay for, because the agents are paid by the insurance companies. Your best candidate is an independent agent with strong experience in commercial lines—not necessarily the same person who has been selling you coverage for your home and personal automobile. The agent should have other clients who do what you do and should be willing to take the time to conduct risk assessments with you so you can make the best decision about what types of coverage and limits you need.

When you do any deal where any of the parties are requiring you to purchase insurance, your agent should let you know exactly what you'll need to buy and how much it will cost *before* you sign the contract. That may sound intimidating, but it's not. It can usually be accomplished in two phone calls—you call to tell the agent the details, and the agent calls you back with the rates. What's most important to remember about insurance is that you don't buy it until you have a profitable deal, and then the deal pays for it.

If you decide to invest in commercial real estate, something else a good agent can help you with is selecting the type of, and limits on, insurance you want to require your tenants to have.

Government Grant and Loan Expert

I'll talk about government grants and loans in greater detail in Chapter 9, but you need one or more people on your Power Team who understand the complexities and challenges of tapping into the gold mine of government funds. Most large banks and many community banks have a government loan expert on staff. This person is responsible for making sure the financial institution is in compliance with the Community Reinvestment Act (CRA, also explained in Chapter 9), a big part of which is making loans that will benefit the community—and your deals, of course, will benefit the community. To find a government grant and loan expert, start by calling several banks and ask to speak with the CRA officer.

You will also find assistance at your area economic development agency. The names of these agencies vary, although they usually include such phrases as *Economic Development* and *Growth*. They can be a government agency, a private operation, or a public-private partnership. In general, their mission is to improve the community through business development, making it more attractive so businesses will move into the area, stay and expand. If they don't have a staff person who can assist you with various government funding options, they should be able to refer you to someone who can.

■ Do You Need an Accountant?

Once you begin making money, you're going to have to start thinking about such issues as tax planning and reporting. In the beginning, what's most important is that you keep good records—track every penny of income and all your expenses. You can do it by hand in a notebook, or you can use one of the many popular computer software programs on the market; choose what you're comfortable with.

When you're ready to file your first business tax return, you're probably going to need to hire an accountant. But that's OK, because by then you'll be making money, and a good accountant should be able to save you more in taxes and time than the accountant's fee.

Keep in mind that not all accountants are created equal. You need one who understands your business and supports your financial goals. Your accountant must be able to speak your language, whether you're investing in real estate or operating a restaurant or running a manufacturing plant. As a tax advisor, your accountant must know state and federal tax laws that affect you and must be a strategic thinker so you can factor tax issues into your decision-making process. Finally, you have to be comfortable with your accountant; you have to share a high level of mutual trust and respect.

Finding the right accountant is not difficult—look around for people who are in the financial situation you aspire to, and ask them who they use. Ask your banker, real estate broker, and other members of your Power Team for referrals. Then interview several before making a selection.

Warning

Stay away from mortgage brokers who ask for a lot of up-front fees. You want a broker who closes deals, not one who is paid merely to push papers around.

Mortgage Broker

Mortgage brokers are another tremendous resource. They will do your loan shopping for you, and the lenders pay their commissions. They'll help you build your own stable of funding sources that are just waiting to give you money.

Mortgage brokers are in business to bring borrowers and lenders together, and they don't make money until a loan closes. Good mortgage brokers take the time to know you and understand your investment strategy and goals. They know how to match you and your deal with the right lender, and they'll help you put the package together. I show you how to find the right brokers—ones who don't care if you have cash because they know they can make just as much profit on no-money-down deals as they can on loans with down payments.

Before you start making offers, you need to know what kind of financing you'll be able to get so you can look for properties that fit your qualifications and structure your offer accordingly. Sit down with a mortgage broker and let her pull your credit report to see your overall situation so she can figure out where you stand and what you are going to be able to qualify for. Even if you have no cash and poor credit, you can still qualify for loans from certain lenders, but you want to be sure the mortgage broker you choose has access to those lenders.

Other Investors and Business Owners

Be sure your Power Team includes at least one other real estate investor or business owner. You need someone who does what you do, someone off whom you can bounce ideas, who you can brainstorm with, and who in general offers mutual support.

A Power Team in Action

Karen Herrera, formerly our corporate receptionist who attended our training and now is an investor and program coordinator, had been actively investing in real estate for about a year when she discovered the incredible strength of her Power Team. She owned about 20 rental units and had just closed on an 8-unit deal when her mortgage broker showed her an ad for 16 duplexes that were for sale by the owner.

"It was almost a dare," Karen recalls. "So I picked up my cell phone and called." The 32 units were a perfect match for Karen's investment strategy, so she issued a challenge to the mortgage broker: "I said, 'Okay, you got me into this. Now get me the loans. And remember, no money out of my pocket.'"

The mortgage broker came through, structuring the deal with a combination of new loans, assumable notes, seller financing, and second mortgages that allowed Karen to buy $850,000 worth of income-producing properties with no money down. "That's how I use my Power Team," Karen says. "I don't know what I would have done if I'd had to structure that deal by myself. But I've got a great mortgage broker working with me. He's taught me a lot, he looks out for me, and we both profit from our relationship."

■ Get the Most out of Your Realtor

When you think of Realtors, what comes to mind? Yard signs, access to the Multiple Listing Service (MLS), and standard commissions. And that's fine for the average homebuyer or seller who has no plans to become wealthy. As an investor, your relationship with your Realtor will be far from traditional. Here are some tips to make your Realtor a truly effective member of your Power Team.

First, recognize a real estate agent's or broker's expertise. Once you have used my advice for finding the right Realtor, take advantage of what he knows and can do for you. Realtors are a lot like exercise equipment—they do you no good if you don't use them. Remember that they make their living by brokering real estate deals. They *want* to help you close deals, because that's how they make money. The Realtor you choose should know how to write contracts that will protect you, how to present offers, and how to negotiate win-win deals.

When you find a property yourself using the techniques you'll learn here, let your Realtor do the legwork to research the property, find the owners, determine the value, consult with you to come up with an offer amount, put together an offer, and then present it. While your Realtor is doing that, you can be out looking for more property.

Your Realtor doesn't have to make a commission on every single deal he helps you with. You just need to explain why it's worth his while to do a little *free* work for you. For example, let's say you found a for-sale-by-owner property that's distressed, and the seller is absolutely adamant about not paying a commission. Your response is, "No problem, there's no commission." Because your Realtor is going to spend a few hours helping you close this deal, then you're going to fix the house up and put it back on the market—and with whom are you going to list it? Your Realtor, of course.

Any sensible Realtor is going to jump at an arrangement like this, because you've done the hard work, which is finding the property. The Realtor has merely put together the paperwork, done a bit of research on the computer in his nice air-conditioned office, and now has a listing on which he's going to make a nice commission. If a real estate agent doesn't want to help you this way, you don't have the right Realtor for your Power Team.

When you list the property, of course you'll pay a commission when it sells. That's no problem, because you'll know how to make sure the property will be profitable after all your costs are considered, and a sales commission is one of those costs.

Speaking of commissions, your listing contract should provide for a reduced commission if you find a buyer without the assistance of your Realtor. It's fair to offer 1 percent and expect the Realtor to help the buyer with the offer, assist the buyer with obtaining financing, and supervise the entire transaction. Such an agreement gives the Realtor incentive to find a buyer before you do. It also provides the Realtor with a customer he didn't have before.

Another point on commissions is that just because the standard commission in your area is 6 percent or 7 percent or whatever doesn't mean that's what you have to offer. Be creative. Offer a percentage point above the norm—don't you think that will have every Realtor in town showing your property because they can make more money on it? Or do a nonstandard commission split. Instead of 50/50, you might offer the listing agent 2 percent and the selling agent 5 percent. Again, that's going to get your property shown more. Or offer a bonus if the property sells within a certain period of time. Anything you do to make your property stand out with the real estate agents in the area is going to increase the chances of a quick sale. Be sure your Realtor promotes the special commission structure or bonus in the MLS listing.

You may also want to negotiate a deal whereby you pay for a portion of the advertising your Realtor does for your property. Of course, the terms are that you pay only if and when the property sells, so this is risk-free for you. Offer to pay half the cost of ads featuring your property that you approve during the listing period up to a certain amount. That amount could be $500 or $1,000, depending on the profit you expect from the sale.

What it all comes down to is this: Make your Realtor your partner—not necessarily in the legal sense (although I have partnered with my Realtors on some great projects) but in a working sense where you share the common goal of mutually profitable deals.

Realtor/Real Estate Broker/Real Estate Agent

When you're buying property, Realtors work for you free, so why not take advantage of this tremendous resource? Let them find properties, make offers, and help negotiate your deals—and get paid by the sellers, so their services don't cost you anything.

If you're going to be investing in various types of real estate, you may want to have more than one Realtor on your team. Good real estate brokers specialize in particular property types and geographic areas. I have one Realtor who handles my high-end residential development projects, another who handles moderate residential investment properties for me, and a third who handles my commercial deals.

Just because someone has a real estate license doesn't automatically make her the right agent for you. In fact, probably 90 percent of the licensed real estate agents out there are wrong for you. The average real estate agent in the United States makes less than $6,000 a year. Do you want someone who can't do any better than that trying to help you become wealthy? Of course not. What about the top producers, the real estate agents who earn six-figure incomes? It may surprise you to know that they're not the answer either. The agent making that kind of money isn't likely to have the time to work with you personally; she's probably busy with her own deals and with the investors she's already built relationships with over the years. What you want is the agent who will eventually become that top producer.

Here's how to find a Realtor who belongs on your Power Team. Select the area or areas in which you want to invest. You'll learn how to do that with the specific types of real estate discussed in later chapters. Drive through the area and write down the name on every real estate sign you see. Pick the top three offices and call them. Tell the receptionist you are a real estate investor and want to speak to the broker (or owner of the office).

When you get that person on the phone, say, "I'm in the market for income-producing real estate. Give me the name of a good, aggressive agent, someone who has been with you at least a year—don't give me the floor agent." In real estate offices, the agents take turns with floor duty, which means they handle the calls that come in from signs, ads, and other sources.

Sometimes the person on floor duty—the floor agent—is very competent; at other times, the floor agent is new or doesn't have the experience you need. Dealing with the floor agent is a gamble you don't have time to take.

Once you get an experienced agent's name, call her to set up an appointment for an introductory interview. This interview needs to be in person. Sure, you could do it faster over the phone, but you'll be wasting your time, not saving it. A face-to-face meeting allows you to do more than get answers to your questions. You'll be able to see the agent's working environment, get a sense of her operating style, and decide if the two of you can work together compatibly.

Remember, you're not locked into working with one real estate agent for life. If you are going to be investing in different types of property, you'll want agents who specialize in each area. And if you have been using an agent who has a change in attitude for whatever reason and you're no longer satisfied with her service, let her know how you feel and start looking for someone else.

■ What to Ask

When you sit down for your introductory interview with a real estate agent, here's what to ask:

How long have you been in the real estate business? In most cases, three to five years is a good range because it indicates experience and a track record, and an agent who is probably still flexible in her approach.

Do you specialize in any type of real estate and/or any part of town? Successful real estate agents specialize, and you want one who specializes in the type and location of the real estate you want to buy.

Do you depend on real estate to make a living? You don't need a part-timer who is just doing real estate on the side for pocket change; you want someone who is hungry and depends on commissions to pay his bills.

Will you give me references? Talk to a few of the agent's other clients to find out how the agent is to work with.

Are you willing to put in the time to help me find the right property? How much time do you have? Listen to the nonverbal answer as well as what is actually said, and decide if the agent is really willing to invest his time in you.

Do you have any banking or other funding connections? Find out if the agent can help you with getting your deals financed.

Is this a good time to buy? Why? What is your opinion of which way the market is headed? It's always a good time to buy, but the answers to these questions tell you a lot about the agent's general attitude and overall market knowledge. A negative agent is poison; you want an agent who is positive but also realistic.

Do you own any real estate? He should. If he doesn't, why should you trust his "expertise" on buying and selling property?

How many properties do you currently have listed? You don't want a "listing specialist"; you want someone who closes deals. The ideal agent for you shouldn't have more than 12 to 15 listings, and if the market is hot and properties are selling fast, it's OK if he has none.

How many properties did you sell last year? The agent should be closing on three or four a month.

Can you be flexible in how you work with your broker? Find out if the broker will listen to new ideas and try different approaches in finding, negotiating, and closing deals.

Title Company

You need a solid relationship with a title company. It will handle your title searches, provide title insurance to protect you, and serve as a neutral place for your closings. And in most states the seller pays for the title insurance, which means you get the title company's services at no charge.

Because much of what title companies do is handle closings, their offices are usually equipped with at least one nicely furnished conference room—sometimes more. When it doesn't conflict with other business, they may let you use those conference rooms for meetings with potential buyers and sellers as you work out details of deals, thus providing you a professional image without the need to invest in your own office.

Born to Do This Business

Carroll and Melisa Wimett have real estate in their blood—his on the building side and hers as the daughter and sister of real estate agents. When they married in 1982, they started with little more than shared ambition. "We had a wonderful wedding thanks to my parents, but our marriage began with one car, a rented house, $65 in cash, and everyday jobs," Melisa recalls. Carroll worked as an interior trim carpenter and Melisa as a hairdresser. They saved their money and bought their first house on their first wedding anniversary. They continued working, and Melisa returned to college at night.

Four years later, they bought five acres of land with a three-acre lake and built their dream house. That house was such a dream that just a year later, someone offered them the full appraised value of $150,000 for the house that had cost them only $74,000 to build, so they sold. "We took the money, quit our jobs, and started W&W Development Builders," Melisa says. They built spec houses and sold them, built another home for themselves, and Melisa continued in school, eventually earning a master's degree in early childhood education.

Then Carroll learned about foreclosures and wanted to buy some properties to resell, so the couple bought two houses one summer at foreclosure auctions. They paid $64,144 for the first one and sold it for $87,000 less than a month later after cleaning it up and painting one bathroom. The second house cost them $67,710; after painting the interior, installing new carpet, and installing a new roof, it sold eight weeks later for $90,900. They made more money that summer with two houses than Melisa had made all year teaching. Today, working together full-time in real estate investing, Carroll and Melisa continue to buy and resell properties but also own rentals that generate $8,427 a month in positive cash flow.

"I think it's very important to have a Power Team," says Melisa. The Wimetts' team includes a Realtor, a contractor, attorneys, an accountant, an insurance agent, an appraiser, several bankers, a mortgage broker, other investors, a magistrate, the magistrate's office staff, the property tax clerk and record room clerk at the courthouse, and the consulting team at Whitney Education Group, Inc.™ (We have a staff of consultants available to our students to assist them with their real estate investments.)

Even more important is what the real estate business has done for the Wimetts. "It has given us more time together as a family," Melisa says. "I'm thankful that I get to work with my husband on a daily basis. I've been able to enjoy my daughter's company as she has grown up. All my children love the investment business and have each picked out at least one house we have purchased. It has become a family hobby."

Professional Associations

A professional association obviously isn't a person who can join your team, but it is a rich resource of information and referrals that costs you very little. Most produce a range of publications that keep you current on what's going on in the industry. Many offer benefits, such as group insurance, that can save you money. And many also have local chapters that provide you with personal networking opportunities. The resources section at the back of this book provides the names and contact information for a number of national associations for real estate investors, property owners and managers, and others. You can find out more about local groups by checking the business section of your daily newspaper, your weekly business paper, or the local library.

Another great networking resource that is absolutely free is the <www.russwhitney.com> community bulletin board on the Internet. Logging on is a quick and easy way to put my professional staff and thousands of my students on your Power Team at no cost to you.

Words of Wisdom

Ask people you respect and admire for referrals as you're building your Power Team. Successful people will be happy to refer you to other successful people who are able to help you reach your own financial goals.

Handypersons and Craftspeople

Whether you're a licensed contractor or have ten thumbs, you need people to handle repairs and fix-up work (carpeting, painting, other cosmetic improvements). Even if you know how to do these repairs and enjoy it, you won't have time to do it all—and your time will be better spent finding and closing deals. If you're buying distressed properties, a good handyperson can help you estimate the time and cost of repairs before you make an offer.

These people don't need to be employees. Establish an independent contractor relationship with them, so you just pay them when you need them.

■ The Process of Assembling Your Team

Putting together and maintaining a Power Team is an ongoing process. Once you get one or two people on your team, the rest will come in a very natural, logical flow. Begin with a Realtor, a mortgage broker, and a banker. These three people are key for real estate investing, because they help you find and purchase property. Then network your way to the rest.

Your team should never be static. Over the years, people drop off and you'll meet new people who will make strong additions. Always be aware of the importance of your Power Team; cultivate it, nurture it, and keep it working hard for you.

■ Who Doesn't Belong on Your Power Team

Now that we've talked about who should be on your Power Team, let's finish up with who *shouldn't* be on it. Reject anyone who thinks you can't achieve your dreams. That includes the well-meaning friends and relatives who tell you that owning your own business is a nice fantasy, but maybe you should get a job and work for someone else for a while. It includes anyone who implies that you don't have what it takes. It includes all of those—no matter how much you care about or trust them—with a negative attitude who want to keep you in the hole they've dug for themselves.

Your Power Team is your support network, your best information resource, your brain trust—don't pollute it with naysayers and dream busters.

MILLIONAIRE MENTOR Power Team Highlights

- Build a Power Team that will support you and help you maximize your efforts.

- Spend your time on the things that will make money for you; hire others to handle menial, mundane, non-revenue-generating tasks.

- A typical Power Team for a successful real estate investor includes a real estate agent or broker, a mortgage broker, a banker, an insurance agent, a government grant and loan expert, a title company, other investors, contacts made through professional associations, and handypersons and craftspeople.

- Always be alert to potential new members for your Power Team—you never know where you may meet them.

- Remember that your Power Team will change over time. As your needs change, you will lose some people and add others.

- Do not allow anyone with a negative attitude on your Power Team.

CHAPTER 3

An Overview of the Real Estate Business

Real estate happens to be my favorite business; it's what I started with, and it's a business to which I still devote much of my time. Like many longtime real estate investors, I had to figure things out the hard way. But because I did, building a successful and profitable real estate investment business will be much easier for you than it was for me. When I got started, traditional schools didn't treat this business as a profession that deserved attention in their curriculum (most still don't), and training organizations like the one I eventually founded didn't exist.

One of the most important things I've learned and that I teach my students is that making money in real estate is not a gamble nor does it depend on luck or chance. If you are properly trained, have developed a working system, and understand the basic rules, you'll make money consistently, no matter where you live. Every industry has its characteristics, the basic realities that are unchangeable and unarguable. In this chapter, I share some key fundamentals about investing in real estate and being in business. These truths apply virtually all the time, no matter the circumstances.

■ No Money Down: It's Real and It Works

One of the things I hear most often from skeptics is that you can't really buy real estate with no money down. Or that "it used to work but it doesn't anymore." Try telling that to my students—people like Karen Herrera, who owns more than 50 rental units, all purchased within the past three years without her putting a nickel down on any of them.

As I discuss specific types of real estate in later chapters, you'll see how you can use no-money-down techniques in different situations. The secret to successful no-money-down deals is to understand the necessary ingredients in terms of the property itself and the seller's needs so you can structure the transaction. If you know what to look for, you'll find it. And I'm going to tell you what to look for.

Here are six basic ways to structure a no-money-down deal:

1. *Have the owner provide all of the financing.* If the seller owns the property free and clear and is willing to hold the mortgage, she may also be willing to sell it without a down payment. You may suggest structuring the deal with two notes—one for 80 to 90 percent of the price over a long term and the other for 10 to 20 percent for a short term—which can essentially be the down payment.

2. *Assume the first mortgage and have the seller carry a second.* Show the seller an amortization schedule so she'll clearly see the total payoff of the second mortgage, which will be substantially more than if you had made a cash down payment.

3. *Create a wraparound mortgage.* The existing mortgage will continue to stand, but you create a new mortgage that "wraps" around that one so that you make the payments to the seller, who continues to make the payments on the original mortgage.

4. *Obtain financing from a hard money lender.* This type of funding source lends at high interest rates based on the property's value without concern for the creditworthiness of the borrower (see glossary). Typically, this type of lender lends 50 to 70 percent of the appraised value at rates higher than does a bank with its three to ten points. In most cases when

you use a hard money lender, you'll also have to ask the seller to carry a second mortgage until you can arrange for new financing to replace both loans.

5. *Arrange a lease option.* Instead of buying the property outright, rent it with an option to buy after a specified period with a portion of your rent credited to the purchase price, thus creating a down payment. This technique is explained in detail in Chapter 5; it's a powerful and exciting way to buy real estate with no cash.

6. *Obtain a new first mortgage from a community bank or through a mortgage broker and have the seller carry a second mortgage.* This works only if you have a decent credit rating and the seller can manage without cash at closing.

Even better than a no-money-down deal is to walk away from the closing table with cash. To do this, the circumstances have to work for the seller as well as for you. It needs to be win-win, with both parties protected.

One way to get cash back at closing is with a repair and redecorating allowance—that is, money the seller gives you to pay for fix-up that she didn't do. It's easy to structure a transaction this way when the property is selling for less than the appraisal price. Here's how it would look. You find a cosmetically distressed house that would appraise for $110,000; the seller has agreed to accept $95,000. You have secured a 90 percent loan that allows you to borrow $99,000; so you offer to pay the seller $99,000 with a $4,000 repair and redecorating allowance. That $4,000 is paid to you at closing from the loan proceeds. The seller is getting the price she wants, you're getting the property and the cash you want, and the lender's terms are met—everybody is getting want they want from the deal.

There are plenty of other ways to do no-money-down and cash-back-at-closing deals. Carroll and Melisa Wimett, whom you met in the previous chapter, tell me that they can get more financing than they can do deals. Although they have cash if they need it, they still do most of their transactions on a no-money-down basis and frequently walk away from closing with cash.

Once you understand how lenders work and how sellers think, you'll know how to structure your deals creatively so everybody gets what they want. As I show you each technique, I explain what motivates the sellers in specific situations and how lenders want to handle the loans. After you've purchased a few properties using the methods you'll learn from this book, seeing these opportunities and knowing how to profit from them in a way that benefits everyone involved will become second nature to you.

Russ's Law of Scared Money

Good luck comes only to people who don't need it. When you're scared and in a panic, feeling as though you absolutely have *to make money on a deal or the world will come to an end, that's when it's unlikely that the deal will work. The world won't come to an end, but your deal probably will. Desperate people rarely attract good deals. Sellers sense the desperation and lose confidence in you. But when you're not chasing "scared money," when you're comfortable and confident in your knowledge and ability, and when it doesn't really matter if a deal goes through because you've got so many others in the pipeline, sellers are more motivated to work with you. Good luck usually comes only to those who don't need it, and they don't need it because they understand that there's really no such thing as luck—it's actually preparation meeting opportunity.*

■ Go Where the Money Is

This book is full of ways that you can make substantial profits in real estate using little or none of your own cash. But even though the cash might not be yours, it takes money to buy real estate. If you don't have money, I'm going to tell you where to find it. If you do have money, I'm going to show you how to use it for maximum profits and return on investment.

Lots of people want to invest in real estate but don't want to do the work involved in finding the properties and putting the deals together. They may be retired investors who have worked long enough and want to spend their time relaxing, or they may be working professionals (doctors, lawyers, etc.) who want a secure investment with a good return, or they may be anyone who understands the value of investing in real estate. They're willing to fund the deals of people like you who are out there doing the work. They make money and you build wealth—it doesn't get much better than that!

Kevin Haag, a real estate broker who is a personal friend and also a member of my Power Team, knows a couple of brothers here in Cape Coral who clean carpets for a living. They saved their money but instead of putting it in mutual funds or stocks, they now lend it to people who want to buy real estate. Essentially, they have become the bank, earning a healthy rate of interest, and their investment is completely secured by the property. When the loans are repaid, they find somebody else to whom they can lend money. These two guys have built a net worth of hundreds of thousands of dollars for themselves, and they've helped countless other real estate investors buy property on which the investors made a profit.

How do you find investors like these brothers? It's easier than you might think. Often, they advertise in the real estate section of the paper (look under "Money to Lend" or "Mortgages"). Or you can place an ad saying that you're looking for investors. Put it in the financial or real estate section, and keep the text simple. Here's a sample: "Investor wanted. $60K, secured by real estate. Call 304-555-9876."

It's also quite common for mortgage brokers to have a supply of private investors; just ask. You will also be surprised by what happens when you start networking with your friends and colleagues, letting them know you have a great deal that they can make money on if they're willing to invest with you. Lester Theiss, a student of mine who you'll learn more about in later chapters, tells me he got his own doctor to commit to more than $100,000 in one real estate deal—and the doctor was thrilled to have the opportunity to put his money in a secure investment with a substantial return.

You may think you don't know anyone who has money to invest, but you could be surprised to find that you really do.

Did You Know?

Jim Seneff, chairman and chief executive officer of CNL Financial Group, Inc., started his first business in 1973 with a $5,000 loan. He went on to build a real estate empire of both privately held and publicly traded companies with more than $5 billion in assets that spans retail businesses, hotels, restaurants, retirement homes, real estate developments, and finance entities.

■ Why Do Sellers Hold Second Mortgages?

What would motivate a seller to agree to hold a second mortgage—or even a third mortgage—so you can buy their property with no money down? Possible reasons abound.

The seller may be in a tax situation where making payments over several years is more attractive than making a lump sum payment. Or the seller may be retired and looking for an income stream to supplement Social Security payments and a pension.

If the seller doesn't need the cash for immediate expenses and is planning to invest it anyway, holding a second mortgage is an excellent investment vehicle. The interest rate is good, and the note is protected by the property.

In cases where the property is distressed and needs a considerable amount of fixing up or the property has been on the market a long time, the seller may be motivated to be more flexible and creative about financing options. These are just a few of the ingredients to a successful no-money-down purchase or a transaction with other terms favorable to you.

Before you make a no-money-down offer, you need to understand the seller's situation so you can structure and present your offer in a way that demonstrates how advantageous it is for everyone involved. You'll learn how to do that as I discuss various types of real estate transactions in each chapter.

■ How to Determine What to Pay for a Property

Most sellers price their property emotionally—especially if they've occupied a house for a long period. They think about what it has meant to them over the years, how much they've spent on it, or how much cash they need for a variety of reasons. This is *not* how you decide what you'll pay. Investor-sellers tend to be more realistic and reasonable, but they, too, can be influenced by various emotional issues. Certainly the seller's needs should be factored into your calculations and you'll consider their emotions in how you present your offer, but you'll decide what to pay based on the market, the condition of the property, and the cash flow and profit it will generate for you.

This is not chance or guessing. It's just knowing what to do and what information you need before you can make a decision.

Have you ever bought a used car? Would you have paid $153,000 for a ten-year-old Saturn? Of course not. But how would you have known whether the seller was asking a fair price? You'd study the market. You'd know what similar new cars cost. You'd know the book value of the car you're considering. You'd check the ads to see what similar vehicles are selling for. You'd test-drive the car and maybe have your mechanic look it over. Then you'd be able to decide if the price was fair and reasonable.

The process is similar when you're buying real estate. Start with determining what you could sell the property for after you've done any necessary repairs and fix-up. Calculate the fire sale price—that is, a number slightly under the market that would guarantee a quick sale. From that, subtract your sales and closing costs (advertising, commission, title insurance, documentary stamps, etc.). Then subtract the amount you think it will cost you to put the property in a salable condition—and always overestimate this figure, because fix-up usually costs more than you think it will, especially when you're getting started. (Chapter 10 discusses techniques for fixing up properties and price ranges for specific items.) Next, subtract the amount of profit you want to make. The figure you have left is what you'll pay for the property.

You should use this formula whether you're buying property for a quick flip (meaning you buy and immediately sell) or to hold. A good rule of thumb is to never pay more than this for a property unless there are extenuating circumstances that justify a higher price. For example, if the property has the potential for a higher and better use, you may decide to pay more.

Converting a single-family home to a rooming house is a good illustration of higher and better use. Let's say you've found a four-bedroom house in a moderate-income area that would rent for $750 a month. Assuming the house has the proper zoning, renting those rooms separately for $100 a week (including utilities) would take your monthly gross revenue to $1,600 a month. You complete your price determination worksheet (see the sample worksheet in Figure 3.1) and come up with a price of $68,000, but the seller wants $70,000. Under these circumstances, paying the extra $2,000 could be worth it. Or you might find a residential property that you know is going to be rezoned to commercial. When that rezoning occurs, the value of the property will increase substantially. (You'll learn about this aspect of

FIGURE 3.1

■

Price
Determination
Worksheet

Date _____

Address _____

City _____ State _____ Zip _____

Owner_____ Phone _____

Agent _____ Phone _____

Listing price $_____

Fire sale price $_____ (after fix-up)

Closing costs for buyer on purchase $_____

Fix-up estimate $_____

Describe work to be done _____

_____

_____

Sales costs $_____

(includes advertising and other sales-related expenses; closing costs for seller)

Desired profit $_____

From fire sale price, subtract closing costs for purchase, fix-up costs, sales costs, and desired profit. That number is

Price you'll pay $_____

commercial real estate in Chapter 12.) In that situation, you might pay more than the price determination worksheet recommends. But what's important to keep in mind is that the extenuating circumstances must clearly justify the higher price; if they don't, go by your numbers and be willing to walk away from the deal if the seller wants more than you can profitably pay.

Once you've determined the price you're willing to pay, then you can figure out how you need to structure the financing so that you can be assured of positive cash flow during the time you own the property.

Russ's Law of Cause and Result

Money is a result, not a cause. If you get into business solely for the money, chances are you will never be great at what you're doing. That's why so many people fail at network marketing businesses—they're attracted by the promise of big profits, but then they realize they have to sell soap or vitamins or lotions or whatever, and they don't want to do that. Get into a business that you like, learn it thoroughly, and do it right. The money will come automatically.

■ How to Get Your Cash out of a Property in Good Times and Bad

Many people are afraid of real estate investing because they fear tying up their money in property and then being unable to get their hands on cash if they need it. That's why you must follow the formulas I'm going to show you to be sure that the properties you purchase will generate income for you.

Even when the real estate market is in a down cycle, banks and mortgage companies make real estate loans. When you want to pull your equity out of a property but don't want to, or can't, sell it, take the cash in the form of a refinance, second mortgage, or home improvement loan, and let the rent from the tenants pay it back.

Let's say you bought a duplex a couple of years ago. The seller was elderly and had been neglecting the property for a while, so you were able to buy it below market value with $3,000 cash out of pocket. Today, the property appraises for $90,000; you have a first mortgage balance of $52,000 and are making payments of $600 per month. Your other expenses run about $150 per month. The two units rent for $500 and $600 per month, respectively, which means you've got a positive cash flow of $350 per month. You've already nearly tripled the cash you invested and you have $38,000

A Second Career and a Means to Finance a Mission

Steve Bias loves being a minister, but in caring for his congregation, he was working himself to death and neglecting his family. After reading my book, *Building Wealth,* he decided that a second career as a real estate investor would give him the income he needed to have more control over his life and allow him to spend more time with his family.

His first deal netted $15,000, so he bought another property and then another. "I wanted to prove that this wasn't a fluke," Reverend Bias says. "And after the third house, investing in real estate just got easier and easier." Deciding to invest in additional training, he attended several of my advanced training programs. That's when his real estate business shifted into high gear. Working part-time as a real estate investor gives him more than $60,000 extra a year in personal income, and his net worth is growing every day.

Reverend Bias continues to work part-time in several ministries and is now able to help people in ways he never could before. In addition to providing security for his own family, Reverend Bias is using what he's learned from my training programs to help people who wouldn't qualify for a traditional mortgage become homeowners. He has also become a mentor for the Whitney Education Group; he travels around the country working with our students one-on-one in their own communities and helping them get their real estate businesses started.

equity. You can easily take out a second mortgage of $20,000 (taking the total mortgage amount to 80 percent of the value) that can be serviced by your positive cash flow.

The key is to buy the right properties at the right price, and I'm going to show you how to do that.

■ Math Tips to Speed Your Offers

Investing in real estate is, like most businesses, a numbers game. If you're selling a product, you know that you have to talk to 5, 10, 15, or even 20 people before you get to the one who buys. In real estate, you'll look at a lot of properties that don't fit your parameters in your efforts to find the ones that do. However, as you study and learn and gain experience, you'll discover how to quickly eliminate the properties that have no potential and how to spot the moneymakers right away. It's a skill like any other. Remember the first time you sat down at a computer or typewriter? You were probably lucky to peck out five words a minute. But with training and practice, you learned how to type quickly and accurately. Did you hit the ball the first time you picked up a tennis racket or golf club? Probably not. But again, with training and practice you learned how to play the sport, and your skill level improved. The same principle applies to real estate.

An important part of deciding if a property is right for you is being able to quickly figure whether the property will generate positive cash flow. Here's how to do that fast and with reasonably accurate results.

First, to determine what your mortgage payment will be, use my Kwik Kalc™ formula by simply moving the decimal point on the price two places to the left (or figure 1 percent of the price), and you'll have a good idea of what your monthly mortgage payment will be based on a 30-year loan at 10 percent. If the asking price is $85,000, move the decimal two places to the left, and you see you'll have a monthly payment of $850 at 10 percent for 30 years. If you know you can get a lower rate, subtract the rate you'll get from 10, add a zero, and reduce the payment by that percent. For example, let's say you can get the loan at 7 percent. If the payment at 10 percent would be $850, you take the difference between 10 and 7 (which is 3), add a zero (making it 30) and then reduce the payment by that percent. So you subtract 30 percent from $850 and arrive at a payment of $595 for 30 years at 7 percent on $85,000.

Of course, the final number will vary depending on the interest rate, the length of the loan, and the actual final price, but this calculation will get you close. Then add your monthly cost of taxes, insurance, association fees, utilities, repairs, maintenance, and the like. If the result of adding up the rents is your taking in more money than you'll pay out each month, the deal is worth pursuing. If you'll be paying out more than you'll take in, move on to the next property.

If the property shows a negative cash flow based on the asking price, but you'd still like to make an offer, use my Reverse Kwik Kalc™. Take the amount of deficit monthly cash flow, move the decimal point two places to the right, subtract that amount from the asking price, and you'll have a sales price at which you can make the deal work. Here's how that would look: If with an asking price of $90,000, the property would have a deficit cash flow of $85 per month, you move the decimal two points to the right to get $8,500, and subtract that amount from the asking price to get your offer amount of $81,500. Again, this is based on a 30-year note at 10 percent; if the interest rate is different, adjust it using the technique I explained above.

Russ's Law of Averages

The law of averages says that if you do something often enough, you'll develop a ratio of results. After you finish this book and begin applying the concepts, you might not know what to expect on your first deal, but by the time you've done a few, you'll be able to make some fairly accurate predictions. And the more deals you do, the more accurate your forecasts will be. You'll know what percentage of your offers are going to get accepted and what your average profit will be on each deal. Then you can study that ratio of results and figure out what you need to do to improve it.

■ The Big Three: Cash Flow, Cash Flow, Cash Flow

You've probably heard the old saying that the three most important things in real estate are location, location, location. That's not true. When it comes to investment property, the three most important things—especially for a beginner—are cash flow, cash flow, cash flow. When conventional real estate educators talk about location, they generally mean proximity to shopping, transportation, schools, and other amenities. When I talk about location, I mean a location that will generate cash and profits for you. Here's how to evaluate location as it relates to cash flow and profits:

The most important issue is the income range of the people who live in the area. Your choices are low-income, middle-income, and upper-income properties—and it doesn't matter whether they're single-family homes, duplexes, multiunit apartment buildings, or even commercial real estate. All properties fall into one of those three categories.

The price of real estate in low-income and moderate-income areas is typically lower than in other locations. But what's interesting and particularly meaningful to you is that the rents in lower-income areas are not much different from those in middle-income areas, where the price of the properties is higher. That means you'll pay less for property in low-income and moderate-income areas and profit more.

You may be thinking that you don't want to own property in a neighborhood you're afraid to go into, and that's understandable. But low income doesn't necessarily mean low class or crime-ridden. Throughout history and in every economic system, low-income people exist, and that's not ever going to change. But these people need housing, and that housing ought to be safe, sanitary, and decent. If you look around your own city or town, you'll see plenty of neighborhoods with modest homes that are, for the most part, reasonably well maintained and occupied by decent, hard-working people who just want to pay their bills, raise their families, and enjoy their life. Moderate residential income properties are the most stable investments, and every area has them. To maximize your profit, look for the ones that need cosmetic improvement.

Middle-income properties cost more to acquire, but the rents are not dramatically higher than in low-income neighborhoods, so your positive cash flow will be lower. However, these properties tend to appreciate faster, and that's worth considering. My advice is to start with low-income to moderate-income properties and then balance your portfolio with middle-income properties later on.

Upper-income or prime properties rarely present an opportunity for a beginning investor. The rents are higher, but so is the cost. In my experience, upper-income properties are usually purchased by investors such as doctors, lawyers, and other professionals who want tax shelters for their money or long-term appreciation but don't want to do any of the hands-on work—they don't even want to know what's going on with their property. This is an investment approach I totally disagree with. You never have to lose money on real estate to get a tax break. If you buy right, you'll have positive cash flow and tax benefits at the same time.

Cash flow is simple arithmetic. Figure out what you can expect to get from the property in rent. Then add up what it's going to cost you every month to own the property. That includes the mortgage payments, taxes, insurance, any utilities, association dues, maintenance, and so on. If you would get more in rent than it costs you to own the property, you have positive cash flow, which is good. If your expenses are greater than the cash you'll receive in rent, you have negative cash flow, which is bad. Don't buy a property unless the numbers tell you it will generate positive cash flow. You'll learn more about estimating expenses and reducing costs in later chapters, but for now it's just important that you understand this basic principle.

Another factor that affects cash flow and profitability is *curb appeal*, which is how attractive—or unattractive—the property appears from the street (or curb). Another term for a property lacking curb appeal is *cosmetic distress*. The property may need paint, landscaping, and other minor fix-ups to make it attractive. Consider the property's current and potential curb appeal.

In a strong market, it's difficult to get a really good deal on a tidy property with a well-manicured lawn that has obviously been cared for. But you can likely negotiate to pay less than market value for cosmetically distressed properties in neighborhoods that fit your investment parameters; then you put a little time and money into them to create the necessary curb appeal and the ultimate profits you want.

Conventional buyers (not investors) look for properties with curb appeal—something that has been spiffed up, looks nice, and is clean and shiny. For investors, the worse the curb appeal, the better, because we can buy the property below market and force the value up with cosmetic improvements.

Finally, consider profit, or how much more you can get for the property than you paid for it. This is important whether you're buying to hold for the long term or to flip for a quick resale.

Russ's Rule on Borrowing to Buy Real Estate

A million in debt will be a million in net. Using other people's money to buy appreciating, income-producing assets is always smart. You will be worth tomorrow what you owe today.

■ How to Pull Tax-Free Cash out of a Property without Selling

At some point with every piece of property you own, you'll have equity. Sometimes you'll structure the deal so you have substantial equity at closing. Other times, it will take owning the property for a certain period to gain equity through paying down the mortgage and/or through natural appreciation. One of the best ways to use that equity is to take your cash out of the property without selling it.

Here's how to do it: Find a property that you can buy below market value using the techniques you'll learn in this book and put it under contract. More than likely, the property will be cosmetically distressed, which means it will need some work. Estimate the cost of the work, and if it doesn't exceed 10 percent of the final value of the property, continue with the deal. Buy the property with a no-money-down loan from a hard money lender and use short-term or conventional debt (credit cards or home improvement loans) to do the fix-up. Once the work is done, refinance the property using its new appraised value. You should be able to borrow at least 80 percent of the value (these days, you can find investor loans up to 90 percent), which will let you pay off the hard money lender plus the fix-up debt, leaving you 10 to 20 percent of the value of the property in cash. That money is not taxable as ordinary income because it comes from loan proceeds. Put it in the bank and use it to fund your next deal.

So the deal would look like this: You find a cosmetically distressed house that the seller just wants to be rid of. The house looks much worse than it really is—it needs paint and carpeting, some holes in the interior walls need patching, and some of the appliances need replacing. You figure you can do the repairs for about $8,000, and the house would then appraise at $90,000. You offer $63,000 and get 100 percent financing from a hard money lender. Because you're using a hard money lender, you can close quickly. The seller takes the offer because it solves a huge problem for him.

You charge the repair costs to a credit card, get the work done in a month, and refinance the property. If you finance 80 percent of the new value, you'll borrow $72,000—enough to pay off the hard money lender and your credit card debt (and whatever interest has accrued in that month)—and you're left with a nice property in which you have 20 percent equity. If you finance 85 or 90 percent of the new value, you'll walk away from the closing table with cash.

Remember, you're not likely to find a property in a gated community in topnotch shape that you can buy for below market value. But if you look in moderate-income neighborhoods, you'll find plenty of properties that are essentially sound but need some cosmetic attention—and new ones come on the market every week. You can build a very profitable business using this strategy alone, but don't stop here. Read on.

Russ's Rule on Closing

If you aren't excited about closing, whether you're buying or selling, something is wrong. Step back, take a look at the deal, and figure out what you have to do to make it right.

■ The Basic Truth about Tenants

I have a rule covering tenants that I call my 80-10-10 rule, which means that 80 percent of tenants do what they're supposed to do. They take adequate care of the property; they pay their rent on time; and they don't call you in the middle of the night unless it's a real crisis. Then there are the 10 percent of tenants who are absolutely great. They treat your property as though it's their own; they may even make improvements; they do their own repairs; and the only time you hear from them is when their rent arrives. That leaves 10 percent of tenants who are marginal. They're the ones who are chronically late with their rent; who forget to tell you when something is wrong so you can make a minor repair before it becomes major; who call you at midnight to complain about a leaky faucet; and who manage to do a wide variety of things that annoy the neighbors.

The majority of those marginal tenants are still manageable. The way to deal with those who aren't is simple: evict them.

Consider this: Sam Walton was one of the savviest, most astute businessmen in modern history. When he was running his first retail store, do you think he ever had any shoplifters? Do you think that it's possible, right this minute as you read this, in a Wal-Mart or Sam's store somewhere, that someone is stealing something? I think it's not only possible but probable. Did Sam Walton let that stop him? Did he say, "Hmmm, if I open a store, someone might steal something from me," and because of that decide to not found one of the largest, most successful, most impressive retail chains ever?

Of course not. He recognized that theft (or shrinkage, as they call it in the industry) is a problem for retailers, so he put what safeguards he could in place, factored some losses into his financial forecasts, and built an empire.

Now, I've just told you the truth about tenants. Most pay the rent and quietly go about their own life without bothering you. A few will give you trouble. Should the fact that in the course of owning income-producing property you may have to evict a tenant every now and then stop you from using real estate as a wealth-building vehicle? No.

Some bad tenant stories are bandied about out there, but for every bad tenant you get, you'll have 90 or more good tenants who will help to increase your net worth every month with their rent checks. We'll talk about the specifics of being a landlord in Chapter 11, and when you know my secrets to managing property effectively, your chances of getting a bad tenant will be even less.

Russ's Rule on Change

If you keep on doing the same things, you'll keep on getting the same results. If those results aren't what you want, you have to change what you're doing. For things to be different, you have to do something different.

■ Final Truths

The real estate market is not static; it changes. It's affected by the general economy; it's affected by the political climate; it's affected by a range of local issues. You need to know what to do in any market, and then you will always be in the right place at the right time. I explain certain techniques that will work in almost every market and others that will work under certain conditions. Armed with that knowledge, you'll be able to develop a consistently profitable investment strategy.

As long as you buy real estate with a positive cash flow—that is, as long as the property generates more revenue than it costs you to own it—you'll be able to ride out any economic downturn because you'll never buy anything you're not willing to hold for five to seven years.

Now that you have a solid overview of the business, let's look at specific methods you can use immediately to begin building your portfolio. The first is known as wholesale buying, the subject of Chapter 4.

MILLIONAIRE MENTOR Real Estate Business Highlights

- No-money-down deals are happening every day across the country; don't let anyone tell you they can't be done.

- The six basic ways to do a no-money-down deal are: have the owner do the financing; assume the first mortgage and have the seller carry a second; create a wraparound mortgage; obtain financing from a hard money lender; arrange a lease option; obtain a new first mortgage and have the seller carry a second.

- Good luck usually comes only to those who don't need it, because they understand that what is thought of as luck is actually the positive results that occur when preparation meets opportunity.

■ When deciding what to offer for a piece of real estate, consider the market, the condition of the property, and the cash flow and profit it will generate for you.

■ If you buy properties at the right price, you'll always be able to get your cash out, regardless of the state of the market.

■ The three most important things about a real estate investment are not the old location, location, location but rather cash flow, cash flow, cash flow. Choose locations that will generate cash and profits.

■ Remember the 80-10-10 rule on tenants: 80 percent of tenants will be fine, 10 percent will be great, and 10 percent will be marginal. Of the marginal tenants, most will still be manageable. The way to deal with the few who are not manageable is to evict them.

CHAPTER 4

Wholesale Real Estate

Buying for Quick Profits

When you think of buying wholesale, you probably think first of getting a good deal on retail goods, but you can also buy real estate at wholesale prices. By that, I mean you'll pay substantially below market value and make a fast and equally substantial profit. A little creativity with wholesaling can net you tens of thousands of dollars in a month or less—immediate cash you can use to build lasting wealth.

Properties that fall into the wholesale category are generally in cosmetic distress, often just needing some minor fix-up. Some may require a major amount of work, which you may or may not actually do. You'll learn how to recognize the difference and make money either way.

This type of wholesale real estate generally sells at 40 to 60 percent of its current value. This is because even though you may be able to calculate a reasonable market *value* for the property based on comparable sales and other conditions, the property actually has no market *demand*—meaning no one wants it, not even the owner.

Wholesale properties in this category are typically vacant, abandoned, and frequently boarded up. They lack curb appeal, need repair, and are often located in marginal neighborhoods. The owners don't want to, or for some reason are unable to, take care of the properties, real estate agents don't want to list them, and banks don't want to finance them. All of these elements come together to create a tremendous opportunity for a savvy real estate investor (that's you).

What's most important for you to remember is that finding a wholesale property and finding a *profitable* wholesale property are two different things. Just because you *can* buy a particular piece of real estate at wholesale doesn't necessarily mean you should. Buy only when you know you can make money. I'm going to show you how to find profitable wholesale properties in your own backyard—no matter where you live. The techniques you'll learn in this chapter can be applied anywhere in the country. The only things that will change are the price points, the construction types, and the zip codes.

Words of Wisdom

Getting your name on the deed to a property is not your goal. Your goal is finding deals that will make money.

■ Characteristics of Wholesale Properties

Properties that you can get at wholesale prices have at least one, and sometimes all, of these characteristics: they're in poor condition; the location is marginal (meaning that the neighborhood has declined or that commercial activity has moved close); they have no market demand; or they don't qualify for conventional financing (banks usually won't finance a house that is uninhabitable). Any one of these characteristics creates a motivated seller. More than one makes your job even easier.

The first step in building wealth with run-down wholesale real estate is knowing where to find these properties. Typically, they are in areas where the homes are older (built 30 or more years ago). The neighborhoods have a lot of run-down houses with low-income to moderate-income residents, and rentals abound.

At this point, you may be thinking that you don't want to invest in areas that you're afraid to drive through. Let me make it clear that I'm not suggesting that. But in towns and cities across the country, investors are targeting declining areas and bringing them back to life. Some are being gentrified and turned into upscale communities. Others are working-class neighborhoods that are being cleaned up and turned into safe, attractive places for families to live. The investors who are savvy enough to see these opportunities are finding excellent deals for themselves and other investors, they're helping hard-working folks achieve the dream of home ownership, and they're enhancing the community.

Wholesale real estate comes in all shapes and sizes, but I recommend that you initially focus on single-family homes, duplexes, and small apartment buildings of up to four units. These are the properties that are familiar to most investors; they're financially attainable, management friendly, and easier to sell. If you focus on larger retail, commercial, or industrial properties, your financing opportunities and pool of potential buyers are far more limited. One-unit to four-unit residential properties are excellent wealth-building vehicles, whether you keep them for the long-term cash flow or sell them to a homeowner or another investor for a quick profit.

Truth in Numbers

Of every 30 to 35 wholesale properties that you identify, you'll likely close a profitable deal on at least one. You can locate that many properties in one afternoon, spend another day or two tracking down owners and making offers, and then close the deal and flip it for a quick $4,000 to $10,000—not a bad rate of pay for a few days' work, is it?

■ Finding Wholesale Deals

The two most effective ways of finding wholesale properties are through targeted drive-bys and deal-specific advertising. Driving through neighborhoods is an active way to find deals but requires some effort on your part. Advertising is passive for you; all you have to do is put the ads out there and wait for potential sellers to call. The most effective strategy is a combination of both techniques.

There is no better way to find wholesale deals than driving through neighborhoods looking for houses that are vacant or boarded up. But don't just

Ugly Properties Make Beautiful Profits

After learning how to buy property at wholesale, Rosanna and Michael Reilly bought a boarded-up house with no heating system in a low-income neighborhood for $35,000. It took about three weeks for Michael to install a new heating system and Rosanna to clean and paint the house. The property is now appraised at $95,000 and brings in $1,350 in rent.

The couple's next wholesale deal was an abandoned four-unit building in a very good neighborhood. The building had no kitchens or baths, it had been damaged by a fire, and the owners had stopped the renovation.

Conventional financing wasn't possible, so the Reillys asked the owner to hold a wraparound mortgage (whereby the original financing would stay in place and the new loan would "wrap" around that note) for one year to give them time to complete the renovations and refinance the property. "He agreed and told us about another two-unit property he owned," Rosanna recalls. "He had tenants who weren't paying their rent. We offered to buy that property as well under the condition that he evict the tenants, and he agreed. He also gave us complete possession of the property in the interim, and we were able to put our own tenants in the units before closing."

The Reillys bought the four-unit property for $155,000; it's now worth $450,000 and generates $4,550 in monthly rent. They paid $85,000 for the two-unit property; it's now appraised at $185,000 and brings in $2,800 a month in rent—and the tenants pay for all utilities on both properties. Clearly, ugly real estate can generate some very attractive profits.

drive around randomly; you need a system. Start by choosing two areas that fit the profile described in the previous section (older, low-income to moderate-income residents, lots of rentals). If you've lived all your life in middle-income and upper-income suburbs, this exercise will definitely take you out of your comfort zone—and that's good. Changing your financial circumstances means changing your life and the way you see the world. When you finish this chapter, you'll never look at a boarded-up house the same way you used to. Instead of shuddering and then immediately putting it out of your mind, you'll see an opportunity you won't forget until you've tried to buy it.

Once you've chosen the areas you're going to work, drive through them slowly, street by street. Keep a record of the streets you've covered because you'll do this again; neighborhoods are not stagnant: they change, people come and go, and a house that was occupied on your first trip through may be abandoned the next time you drive by. You want to get to know these neighborhoods so well that when someone mentions an address, you know where it is and can call up a mental picture of the property.

Keep a notepad on the seat next to you and write down the address and a very brief description of every house that is boarded up, vacant, or abandoned. In a matter of hours—just one morning or afternoon of driving—you should find 30 to 50 properties that meet the basic wholesale criteria. Your list might look something like this:

3278 Briarcliff Ave.	Windows boarded up, trash in yard
4190 Briarcliff Ave.	Vacant, yard fairly neat
4356 Briarcliff Ave.	Abandoned, some windows broken, yard overgrown

When you get back to your office, you'll go through the list and begin the fairly simple process of finding the owners and putting together offers, explained in detail in the next section.

While you're looking for houses, you should also be noticing signs of other investors working in the area who are rehabbing and renting houses. Write down their names and phone numbers. These are a great source of potential buyers for the distressed properties you're going to be buying substantially below market value.

You should also make note of the real estate agents working in the area. It's true that most agents avoid these marginal areas, but a few understand the dynamics of these neighborhoods and the benefits of working with investors (some may actually be investors themselves). These agents should be on your Power Team. Give them a call, introduce yourself as a local investor buying in the area, and ask them to alert you to distressed properties they may come across.

Along with driving through neighborhoods, you should also do deal-specific advertising. Run newspaper ads and place signs in the areas you are working to let people know what you do.

Place the ads in the "Real Estate Wanted" section of your local daily paper or in the weekly shoppers—or both, depending on your budget. Sellers of distressed properties usually respond to these ads as a last resort, after they've called (and been rejected by) real estate agents and exhausted other conventional sales methods. This means that by the time they call you, they are both motivated and realistic. It's clear they are motivated because they are taking the initiative to make the call. They're realistic because they've been trying to sell the property and have learned the hard way that no one wants it as it is. With this experience, they know they're not going to get top dollar, so they'll likely be much more receptive to your below-market offer.

Strategically placed signs saying that you buy houses and giving a number to call produces amazing results. You've probably driven by thousands of them and ignored them because you didn't have a distressed property you wanted to get rid of. But, believe me, if you had such a property, you'd be copying down those phone numbers and getting on the phone. The reason you see so many of these signs is that they work.

You can put your signs on utility poles, on stakes in the ground at busy intersections, even on abandoned buildings—such as the houses you're trying to buy. It's a good idea, however, to check local sign ordinances before you start putting your signs out. The signs don't have to be elaborate or fancy, but they must be large enough for people to read them from the street ($18'' \times 24''$ is sufficient) with bold red or black lettering.

Use the same wording on your signs as those in your print ads. This increases your overall name recognition and helps you penetrate the market more thoroughly.

Words of Wisdom
Buy and sell to create cash so you have the money to buy and hold to create wealth.

■ What Should Your Ad Say?

Before you spend money placing ads, think carefully how to write them so you get the biggest bang for your buck. Short and to the point works best. Study the ads other investors are placing. Look at back issues of the publications you'll be advertising in. Seeing the same ad running week after week and month after month is a pretty good sign that the ad is bringing in business. Do something similar, but make it different enough that it sets you apart from the competition. Focus on the issues that are important to the market you're targeting: you pay cash (and it doesn't matter whether you actually have the cash or not, I'll tell you how to get the money later); the condition of the property doesn't matter; and you can make it a quick, easy, and painless process for the seller.

Here are some samples:

Investor pays cash for houses, will look at all, any condition. 888-987-6543

Handyman buys houses, any area or condition. 213-123-4567

I buy houses, cash offer in 90 minutes. Call Mike at 941-567-1234.

Area specialist buys real estate, cash or terms, prices quoted by phone. Call Susan at 847-555-4321.

Smart Thinking
When entering a vacant house, even when the owner is with you, call out "insurance inspector" as you open the door. Don't just walk in; there may be transients inside, and you don't want to surprise them. The phrase insurance inspector *is non-threatening; anyone in the house will*

know right away you're not a cop and they're not getting busted for trespassing.

SUCCESS
STORY

Not All Wholesale Properties Are Distressed

Though we use terms like *boarded-up, vacant,* and *abandoned* to describe many wholesale properties, it's quite common to find wholesale deals on real estate that is not distressed. Two of my students, Diane and Olin T.'s, first investment property is a classic case in point.

Diane was aware of a fourplex that had been listed with a Realtor for $105,000. After learning about wholesaling, she happened to drive by the property and noticed that the For Sale sign was down and a For Rent sign was up. The building was in good condition—not the sort of place that would typically catch the eye of someone looking for wholesale deals. But Diane decided to call the number on the sign and was able to get in touch with the owner. The property hadn't sold, and the owner was still interested in getting rid of it. Diane and Olin's offer of $75,000 was accepted. The property appraised at $111,662 and generates a positive cash flow of $500 per month.

Locating and Contacting the Owners

One of the biggest challenges of buying wholesale properties is finding the property owner. After all, no one is living in these houses, so you can't just knock on the door and ask for the owner. Nor does it make much sense to send a letter to the address because no one is there. It's much easier when the seller calls you, but if you sit back and wait for the owners to come to you, you'll miss out hundreds of thousands of dollars in potential profit that you could have with just a little bit of research. So take your list of addresses of houses that are boarded up, vacant, and abandoned and go looking for the owners.

Your first stop is public records. Most counties have their property records online these days, so it's pretty easy to log on to your county tax assessor's Web site, find the property in question, and see who the owner is. The owner's address should also be listed; it's the address where the tax bills are sent. If your county's records aren't online yet, you can get this information by calling the tax assessor's office. Most will give you owner information on up to three properties per call.

Once you have the address of the owners, you can contact them by mail, or you can take the extra step of looking up their telephone numbers and calling them. Let's discuss how to do it by mail first.

Postcards are more effective than letters. (See the sample postcard in Figure 4.1.) Why? Because people are bombarded with junk mail these days, and often letters from unknown senders go unopened. However, if you choose to send a letter, address the envelope by hand (and actually write it yourself or have someone do it—don't use one of the handwriting fonts available in word processors) and use a first-class stamp, not a postage meter. When you have your envelopes printed, you might also include a phrase such as "Time Sensitive Material Enclosed" or "Immediate Attention Required" on the front, or you can get a rubber stamp to add such a phrase to the outside of your letters.

Postcards are much easier and quicker for recipients to read. Although recipients may not open a letter that looks like a sales pitch, they'll still

---

FIGURE 4.1

■

Sample Postcard

Dear Property Owner:

My name is John Gordon and I am a local real estate investor. My company buys properties in any area or condition.

I noticed your vacant property located at _____ _____ [leave blank so you can fill in the address].

If you are interested in selling, please call me.
John Gordon
888-987-1234

probably scan the message on a postcard. Use a bright color for your card stock to make it more noticeable.

Whether you send a postcard or letter, your message must accomplish four important goals:

1. Tell the owner who you are.
2. Clearly and concisely explain the reason for your contact.
3. Describe the services you offer.
4. Explain how to reach you for immediate assistance.

A more active approach is to call. You have the owner's name and address; it's a simple matter to check your local telephone directory or one of the numerous online directories for a telephone number. When you get the owner on the phone, quickly identify yourself and explain the reason for your call using language similar to what you would write on your postcard or in a letter.

The biggest benefit of calling is that you get an immediate response. If the owner is not interested in selling, he'll say so right away. In that case, make a note in your file and follow up in six months. You've invested very little time to find out this deal won't work right now—although it might be something for the future.

If the owner *is* interested in selling, you'll find that out right away too. Pay attention to his tone of voice and any other verbal cues that will reveal his motivation for selling. Often, owners are very candid about their situation. They might have owned the property as a rental but didn't know how to manage it and just gave up. Or they might have inherited the house and don't know what to do with it. To help you determine exactly what their situation is and to help create a sense of urgency on their part for selling, ask such questions as, "Has the insurance lapsed?" and "Has code enforcement contacted you yet?"

Once you know they're interested in selling, make your offer—right then on the phone. If you have done your homework and you know the neighborhood, you'll be able to easily estimate the as-is and fixed-up value of the property. Your offer should be 50 to 60 percent of the as-is value. Keep in mind that sellers don't know as much about the market as you do—

if they did, they wouldn't be holding on to a junk property and letting it continue to deteriorate.

To calculate the as-is value, know the neighborhood and what houses typically sell for. Figure what the property you're considering would sell for if it were in good condition, then subtract the estimated repair costs to reach the as-is value. Because you're not going to take the time to have contractors do formal estimates until your offer has been accepted, you need to familiarize yourself with the cost of various repairs in your area. Remember that your offer will be subject to a walk-through, so if you underestimate the cost of repairs, you'll have a chance to renegotiate. You can also take a look at the tax records. Many tax collectors list the assessed value (on which taxes are based) as well as the estimated market value (generally 15 to 20 percent higher) as part of the public record.

Remember that the worst thing that can happen is the owner will say "No" when you make an offer. If that happens, he'll have to find another way to deal with his problem property. Ask him to keep your card and call you if anything changes.

If he seems interested but wants to negotiate a higher price, explain again that you are an investor who buys properties like this one all over town for 50 to 60 cents on the dollar to either resell or keep as rentals. Don't be embarrassed about the amount you're offering—this isn't a plush home in a gated country club community but rather a distressed property that can't be financed because no one wants it. You're a businessperson who is only going to do the deal if you can make it profitable.

If he accepts, set up a time to look at the property with the owner. Bring your contract and be prepared to finalize the deal.

If the owner isn't local but accepts your verbal offer, send your contract via an overnight service and don't bother to see the property until the contract is signed.

Did You Know?

Properties that are run-down and vacant are often uninsurable and thus present a problem for the owners—a problem you can solve by taking the property off their hands.

■ Writing the Contract

Once your verbal offer has been accepted, it's time to put things in writing. You can draw up your own contract, buy a standard form at an office supply store, or use the forms available in the software package my company has developed (see the resources section for details). Just keep in mind that your contract doesn't have to be complicated—in fact, the simpler, the better. It should be in your name (or your company name) and/or assigns (allowing you to assign the contract to someone else).

The contract should stipulate that you're making an all-cash offer, that closing will be on or before 30 days, that the purchase is as is, and that your offer is subject to your walk-through inspection within 14 days. Explain that you want time to have the property inspected by a contractor who can give you repair estimates. Don't spend a lot of time looking at a property and figuring out what it needs until your offer has been accepted and you know you're going to buy it. If the owner balks at the 14-day clause (and owners rarely do), stand firm—it's a nonnegotiable issue.

That two-week period also gives you time to show the contract to your title company to find out if it can issue title insurance; and it gives you time to find a buyer. Most important, it gives you time to decide to walk away from the deal, renegotiate, or close the deal with hard money.

Don't clutter your contracts with a bunch of "subject to" clauses; you need only one. Giving yourself a laundry list of ways to back out of the deal brands you as an amateur and makes the seller uncomfortable.

If the property is listed with a real estate agent, earnest money is due on contract acceptance. Don't give earnest money with the offer—it's too much trouble and ties up too much of your cash, because a sizeable percentage of your offers will not be accepted.

If the property isn't listed, put up a small amount of earnest money—typically $10 to $100—when you sign the contract. You need a certain amount of earnest money to make the contract legally binding, but the amount doesn't have to be large. Never give earnest money directly to sellers unless they'll accept a nominal amount, such as $10. If they want more than that, put the money in escrow with the title company so you're assured of getting it back if the deal doesn't close.

Words of Wisdom

It's never the cost of capital that matters when you have a great deal. What matters is that you have access to the money.

■ What You Need to Know about Hard Money Lenders

There will be many times in your real estate career when you'll need the services of hard money lenders. These are investors who provide short-term loans (generally for six months to three years) of 60 to 70 percent of the property's value at above-market rates. Because the loans are based on the value of the property and not the creditworthiness of the borrower, they are generally easier and faster to get than traditional financing.

The best way to find hard money lenders is to call local mortgage brokers. Introduce yourself as a real estate investor and ask if they have any nonconforming investor loans available. (Hard money loans are called "nonconforming" because they don't conform to traditional lending requirements.) If the broker answers that such loans don't exist, thank the broker, hang up, and call another broker.

You can also find hard money lenders by networking in your local real estate club. Many advertise in the classified section of local newspapers as well.

To make a loan, hard money lenders need a copy of the signed contract between you and the seller. They want to check the title work and do an as-is or drive-by appraisal, which will cost $150 to $300. Once the title work is completed, most hard money lenders can close in 12 to 48 hours.

Did You Know?

Many of today's hard money lenders are the wholesale investors of yesterday. They understand what you're doing and know that a good wholesale deal means everybody wins.

■ What to Do with the House Once You Own It

Before you purchase a piece of property, know what you're going to do with it. You have three basic choices: (1) You can fix it up and keep it as a rental for long-term cash flow and appreciation (see Chapters 10 and 11); (2) you can flip it as is to another investor for a quick profit; or (3) you can rehab and sell it. Whatever you plan to do, think what the worst-case scenario is and make sure you can deal with it before you move forward.

There is no shortage of investors out there looking to buy run-down properties, but they either don't know how to find them or they aren't willing to do the work necessary to find them. Many are part-time investors who hold full-time jobs and may have cash to invest and the resources to rehab a property, but they just don't have time to find properties, negotiate with owners, and make deals. Many are landlords looking for properties to fix up and hold; they prefer to spend their time on rehabbing and property management, not on looking for deals. When you provide them with good deals, everybody wins—the original owner of the problem property, you, and the investor you sell to. Once you establish yourself as a deal finder, you'll have investors lining up to take these wholesale properties off your hands. Lester Theiss, one of my students from Missouri, flipped eight wholesale properties in one year for a $122,000 profit—and never took title to any of them.

If you're going to flip the property, you can either assign the contract or you can do a double (or simultaneous) closing.

Assigning the contract means essentially that you sell your rights under the contract to someone else for a fee. That person then takes your original contract and the assignment of contract agreement to a title company to close the deal. When you assign a contract, you never own the property; you just make a profit on it. (See sample assignment of contract in Figure 4.2.)

FIGURE 4.2

■

Assignment of
Contract

FOR VALUE RECEIVED, _____ ("Assignor") [your name/company] assigns and transfers to _____ ("Assignee") [your buyer's name] all rights, title and interest held by the Assignor to the _____ [title of contract executed between you or your company and original seller] regarding certain real property located at _____ ("Contract"). The Contract shall be assigned for the amount of _____ ($ .00) to be paid at the date of closing by Assignee to Assignor ("Assignment Fee"). Upon execution of this Assignment of Contract, Assignee shall pay to Assignor a good faith nonrefundable deposit in the amount of _____ ($ .00) ("Deposit"). The Deposit shall be applied towards payment of the Assignment Fee to be paid at the date of closing by Assignee to Assignor.

Assignee hereby accepts all rights and obligations of the Assignor under the Contract.

This Assignment of Contract shall be binding upon and inure to the benefit of the parties hereto.

Signed this _____ day of _____ , 200___.

Assignor

_____

Print Name:

Assignee

_____

Print Name:

The amount you get for assigning a contract can be anywhere from 15 to 30 percent of the as-is value of the property. Get half in certified funds as nonrefundable earnest money when you execute the assignment agreement; you'll get the remainder plus a refund of your earnest money at closing.

As an alternative to assigning the contract, you may decide to do a double closing, which means you actually buy the property and then sell it in a simultaneous transaction. This lets you use the new buyer's money to pay the original seller. It sounds complicated, but the title company handles all of it for you.

Some title companies won't do double closings, but plenty will. It's really a good deal for them, because they get paid twice on basically the same transaction. If your title company resists doing a double closing, find another one.

■ Assign or Double-Close?

How do you decide whether to assign the contract or do a double closing? It's really your personal choice, but here is one way to approach the decision: If your profit is $7,000 or less, assign the contract. If your profit is more than $7,000, double-close.

Here's my logic: When you assign the contract, the other parties involved know how much you're making on the deal. Few sellers or real estate investors are going to have a problem with your making up to $7,000 for putting the deal together, especially as you tell them from the start that this is how you make your money. But for some reason, some people think it's unreasonable for you to make more than $7,000 on a deal that you might have worked on for only a total of 15 to 20 hours. Of course, you and I know that the value comes not from the hours you work on a specific deal but rather from your knowledge and expertise in finding the property, the sellers, and the buyers and then putting it all together—knowledge that is priceless. Even so, if others knowing how much you're making jeopardizes the deal, don't tell them. If your profit is going to be more than $7,000, do a double closing.

When you're reselling a property you bought for 50 to 60 percent of its value, price it at 80 percent of its value. You'll make money and the buyer will be getting a great deal, too.

Smart Thinking

When you're doing a double closing, ask for a pass-through title insurance policy, instead of using two separate policies for each closing. The seller can pay the premium portion based on the amount for which they're selling, then you pay the difference between that and the premium based on the price your buyer is paying.

SUCCESS STORY

Don't Overlook the Real Estate under Churches

It may not be the first thing that comes to mind when you think about churches, but it's not uncommon for a church to close down, either because it disbands or moves to another facility. Jaret F.'s first deal was a property that included a 2,200-square-foot church and a three-bedroom, two-bath, double-wide mobile home. The church had closed about a year before, and the property was being sold through a closed bid process.

The buildings were distressed, and the property was worth about $50,000 in as-is condition. With the winning bid of $35,000, Jaret put the property under contract with the intention of flipping it for quick cash. In two weeks he received a call from another church, and in another two weeks the property closed for a sale price of $52,500. Jaret walked away from the closing table with $16,627 and without a penny out of pocket or ever taking title to the property.

■ Where's the Money?

Many wholesale properties are owned free and clear by sellers willing to offer financing. You'll also find wholesale real estate that qualifies for city grant money or local investor loan programs designed to encourage redevelopment. Even though these programs can be worthwhile, they often take a long time to process, and you want to do your deals quickly. Find out which of these programs are available in your area and provide that information to your buyers when you flip the property, but don't count on that information as a funding source for yourself.

So where will you find the money for most of your wholesale deals? From the buyer you're going to flip the property to.

FYI

Some states have usury laws capping the amount of interest that can be charged by hard money lenders. Check with the agency that regulates banks in your state to find out the maximum interest that can be legally charged.

■ Advertising for Buyers

Most investors regularly read the newspaper's classified section in hopes of finding motivated sellers. No one is more motivated than you, although your motivation is slightly different from those sellers, but you have property to sell and you're offering a good deal. So put your ad where prospective buyers will see it—typically in the section of the paper focused on the part of town where the house is located. You might also want to place an ad in the "Investment Property" section.

Make these ads simple. Here's a sample that works very well:

Investor Special, 3/1, $42,900 cash OBO, 213-456-1234

■ Finding Buyers

Don't think that you're the only person looking for good deals on wholesale properties—you're not, and that's a good thing. It means you have plenty of people who are interested in the deals you find.

Build a database of prospective buyers. Create a file with their names, contact information, and the types of property they're interested in so you can quickly identify and call them when you come across something that's appropriate. Set up a system that lets you fax "blast" or e-mail the details of a deal as soon as you get it under contract.

A great pool of potential buyers are investors who already own property in the area where your deal is located. It's not uncommon that up to 80 percent of the houses in low-income to moderate-income areas are rentals, and you can find the owners in the tax rolls. Contact them and ask if they're interested in adding to their portfolio. If they say yes, tell them about the deal you have and put them in your database for the future. If they say no, ask if they have anything they'd like to sell.

Finally, contact the investors who have bought from you before. If they did well on the last deal, they'll look forward to working with you again.

MILLIONAIRE MENTOR Wholesale Highlights

- Wholesale real estate generally sells at 40 to 60 percent of its value.

- Wholesale properties are typically vacant, abandoned, and frequently boarded up.

- The two most effective ways to find wholesale properties are targeted drive-bys and deal-specific advertising.

- When you find a wholesale property, contact the owner(s) by mail or phone to see if he is interested in selling.

- Purchase contracts don't have to be complicated; in fact, the simpler you can keep them, the better.

- One-unit to four-unit residential properties are excellent wealth-building vehicles, especially for beginners, in cases where you plan to keep them for the long term or sell them for a quick profit.

- A hard money lender is an investor who provides short-term loans of 60 to 70 percent of the property's value at above-market rates. These loans are based on the value of the property and not the creditworthiness of the borrower.

- ■ Know what you're going to do with a wholesale property before you finalize the purchase. Your choices are to fix it up and keep it as a rental, flip it as-is to another investor, or rehab and sell it.

- ■ Build a database of prospective buyers, so you can contact them quickly when you come across a property that may be of interest to them.

CHAPTER 5

Purchase Options

Controlling Property with or without Ownership, Minimal Cash, and No Credit

It's time to learn how to use your brain, not your bank account, to take control of a property and make money from it without ever actually buying it. Options are a smart and simple way to control property—especially high-priced real estate—with little or no cash. Options can generate lump sum profits, longer-term cash flow, or both—it's all in how you structure the deal. It's not difficult, but it does require planning and attention to detail.

The biggest challenge in using options is that most buyers, sellers, and real estate agents don't understand them. So you have to know them well enough to be able to explain the process and clearly present the pros and cons.

Options can be used in any business where real property, goods, or services are bought and sold. Essentially, an option is a one-way right to purchase property under specified terms. Only the seller is required to perform; the buyer has a choice. Once the option is exercised, the agreement becomes a binding bilateral contract between the buyer and seller. A sample option contract is shown in Figure 5.1. Figure 5.2 contains a list of clauses that can be added to an option agreement.

This chapter focuses on using options in conjunction with leases to invest in real estate. As you learn the techniques, though, you're going to see

FIGURE 5.1

■

Option
Contract

This option contract is made this _____ [date] by and between _____ [SELLER], whose address is _____ and _____ [BUYER], whose address is _____.

The SELLER, for and in consideration of the sum of $_____ in hand paid by the BUYER with other good and valuable consideration, hereby gives to the BUYER the privilege of purchasing, on or before _____ [date] the following described real estate:

_____

[address of property under option]

The terms for said option shall be:
Purchase price: $_____

Terms:

_____
_____
_____

The SELLER agrees to furnish title insurance showing good and marketable title to said real estate in case the privilege of purchase hereby given is exercised upon the terms above written, to convey said real estate to the BUYER by good and sufficient warranty deed, free and clear of all liens and encumbrances.

In case the privilege of purchase hereby given is not exercised and conditions thereof fully performed by the BUYER and written notice of such exercise and performance given to the SELLER on or before _____ [date], said privilege shall thereupon wholly cease, no liability to refund the money paid thereof shall arise, and said title insurance shall be redelivered to the SELLER, and this instrument shall at once be delivered to the SELLER for cancellation. This Contract shall be binding upon and shall inure to the benefit of the heirs, personal representatives, and assigns of all the parties hereto.

In witness whereof, the parties hereto have subscribed their names and affixed their seals the day and year above written.

_____

SELLER

_____

BUYER

I herby certify that on this day, before me, an officer duly authorized by the State of _____, and the County of _____ , to take acknowledgements, personally appeared _____ to me known to be the person described in and who executed the foregoing instrument and _____ acknowledge before me that _____ executed same.

Witness my hand and official seal in the County and State last aforesaid this _____ day of _____, 20 _____.

_____

NOTARY PUBLIC

My commission expires: _____

---

other business applications for options, and your ability to profit from them is limited only by your imagination.

Here's a hypothetical situation that is common in actuality, where a basic lease option in a residential real estate agreement would be the perfect solution. Sam Smith owns a three-bedroom, two-bath home as an investment and is open to either renting or selling the property. If he rents it, he'll have the cash flow and will build equity. If he sells it, he'll have the lump sum profit to reinvest. Rents for similar properties in the area are $900 to $1,000, and Sam could probably sell the house in the current market for $105,000 to $108,000. His mortgage is $92,000.

Bob and Barbara Green like Sam's house and want to buy it, but they don't have enough cash to put down to get the mortgage payments as low as

FIGURE 5.2

■

Option
Clauses

The following is a list of option clauses that can be added to an option agreement.

1. **Option to renew**

   For and in consideration of $_____, the optionee (seller) hereby grants to the optionor (buyer) the right to extend the option to which this document is attached for a period of _____.

2. **Applying rent toward purchase**

   For and in consideration of the mutual promise made by the parties, each to the other, the parties do hereby agree that _____ percent of the total rent payments made by the tenant on the lease attached hereto shall be applied toward reducing the purchase price. Additional terms of the option are contained in the option agreement attached hereto.

3. **First refusal**

   The tenant shall have the right of first refusal to purchase the property at the price and terms of any bona fide written offer made for it. Said right to be exercised by notifying the landlord by registered mail within _____ days of his receiving written notice that such a bona fide offer has been made. Upon submission of a valid contract by seller, optionor has 30 days to exercise the option or this contract shall become null and void.

4. **Prepayment clause**

   The mortgagor shall have the right to prepay this mortgage, in whole or in part, at any time without penalty after _____ year(s).

they want. So Sam offers to rent the house to them under a lease option agreement like this: The Greens will pay a refundable security deposit of $1,000 and a nonrefundable option consideration of $4,000, and will rent the house for two years for $1,100 per month. Of the monthly rent, $330 will be applied to the purchase price of the house if the Greens choose to buy it. At the end of the two-year lease, the Greens have the option to purchase the house for $114,000, using the initial option consideration and the $330 per month, which totals $11,920, as a substantial portion of their down payment.

Lease option buyers enjoy a number of benefits. They can "test drive" the home before purchase; they have a lower up-front cash requirement than they would if they were buying outright; the rent credit builds up a forced savings account for the down payment; although the total monthly payment might be slightly above market rates, the net rent (the amount applied toward rent after the rent credit is subtracted) is generally lower than a comparable straight rental; and the purchase price is locked in. The term of a typical lease option deal is between one and three years, so the tenants have plenty of time to build their down payment credit.

If the Greens decide to exercise their option, they will be able to buy the house with the majority of their down payment created primarily through the rent that they would have had to pay on a place to live anyway. If, for any reason, they decide not to exercise their option—maybe there's an unexpected job transfer in the picture, or they decided they don't like the neighborhood or the house after all—they treat the end of the lease as any rental situation. They can renew the lease or move.

In the meantime, Sam has been collecting above-market rent for his property and building equity by paying down his mortgage with the rent. He has already collected (and probably reinvested) a $4,000 nonrefundable option consideration. If the Greens buy the house, Sam will net more than $10,000 at closing. If they don't, Sam is able to keep their option consideration and the profits from renting the house at above-market rates, and he still has the property to either rent or sell to someone else.

It's a win-win situation for everyone, and it's just one example of how options can make you wealthy.

Smart Thinking

When negotiating lease and option terms, the goal is for everyone to walk away from the deal a winner. However, you'll approach the details differently when you're the landlord than when you're the tenant. Always be fair, but also be smart.

SUCCESS
STORY

Building Wealth Is a Family Affair

Carolyn Rawlings had been a stay-at-home mom for seven years; her husband, Steve, was a utility consultant who had just lost his largest client. They were both ready for a change when they saw my infomercial and decided to invest in education.

They hit the ground running, using what they learned to buy rental properties with no money down. "We wrapped mortgages and used lease options," says Carolyn. "We bought a six-unit hotel and flipped single-family homes with no money down and walked away with cash. In one year's time, we have $2.5 million in property value with more than $400,000 in equity and over $4,000 positive cash flow every month."

More than the financial change, the Rawlings family has enjoyed a major lifestyle change. Real estate investing has become a family business—even the children help out. "Investing in real estate has changed us. We now work together as a family," Carolyn says. "It's possible for anyone to do this. If you believe you can do it, just act on it and it will happen. Write your goals down and go for them!"

■ Use a Lease Option to Buy Your Personal Residence

If you don't already own your own home, you need a plan to buy one as soon as possible, and a lease option may be the best way to do that. Or if you already own a home but are looking to upgrade or downsize, depending on your needs, consider structuring the transaction as a lease option.

Buying under a lease option agreement lets you avoid a substantial down payment, which means you can use that cash to buy income-generating property that in turn offsets any tax savings you may give up by renting rather than buying.

If the property goes down in value before you exercise your option, you can either renegotiate the deal or walk away and find another home to buy or lease option at current market value. If the property goes up in value, you have the lower price locked in with your option.

Obtaining financing for a property you have under lease option is generally easier than a straight purchase loan. Many lenders now view a lease option agreement as a home sale; it's easier to get financing on something you already own than it is to finance something you want to buy. With a lease option, you can often get a refinance loan based on the appraised value of the property and thus might even walk away from the closing table with cash.

■ Traditional Renters versus Lease Option Tenants

There is absolutely nothing wrong with traditional renting. I've made a substantial portion of my own fortune, in fact, as a landlord, and in Chapter 11, I share my secrets for effectively managing property. But there are differences in how you write a lease and manage a property that is lease optioned versus one that is occupied by a tenant with no intention of buying.

For example, it's common for lease option tenants to be responsible for most maintenance and repair expenses—after all, they are going to own this home someday. In fact, for that reason you'll find that lease option tenants generally take better care of the property than do most traditional renters. In a majority of cases, you'll find less management is required with a lease option than with traditional renting. However, some states limit how much a landlord can require a tenant to pay per item for repairs and maintenance; check to make sure your lease complies with the law.

In a traditional lease, a landlord typically charges some sort of graduating late fee. Under a lease option agreement, you can add another penalty: If the rent isn't paid on time, a tenant forfeits the option consideration credit for that month. The combined threat of a late fee and of losing several hundred dollars in option consideration is a strong motivator for paying on time.

Warning

Never use a combined lease option agreement. Always make them two separate contracts. Don't blur the lines between your relationship as buyer and seller and your relationship as landlord and tenant. These are two distinctly different transactions and should be maintained as such.

■ Sandwich Lease Option

With a sandwich lease option, you put yourself in the middle between the property owner and the tenant, and you make money without ever actually owning the property. Here's how it works: You find a motivated owner willing to lease option a house to you for a small consideration or, if possible, no option consideration. Make your lease agreement for a period of two years; make sure it permits subleasing and requires the owner to pay for any necessary repairs within the first 90 days. Then you lease option the property to a tenant. Get a nonrefundable option consideration of 3 to 5 percent and charge slightly above-market rent (certainly more than you're paying the owner). Your tenant should be responsible for repairs and maintenance.

Arrange for your tenant's option to expire three months before yours does. If the tenant exercises the option, then you exercise yours, buy the house, and sell it to the tenant. If the tenant chooses not to exercise the option, you can find another tenant interested in a lease option deal. You may have to extend your own option, but this is usually not a problem; if the owner doesn't want to extend it, then you walk away from the deal with the profit you've made from the tenant.

When you use a sandwich lease option, you don't have to do the fix-up—you can have either the owner or the tenant do it. You make your money from controlling the property, not from owning it. And you don't have to borrow any money to ensure that the deal transpires.

Truth in Numbers

A key to lease option success is the rent credit. If it's too low, the tenant has no incentive to pay above-market rent or to exercise the option to buy. If it's too high, the seller doesn't maximize her profit.

■ Purchase Lease Option

This is the option technique you'll probably use most often. You buy a property and then immediately lease option it to someone else. But don't wait until you own the property to start looking for a tenant; have the tenant ready to move in as soon as you close. Here's how: Make an offer on a property with an escape clause using one of the low or no-money-down payment techniques discussed in Chapter 3. In your offer, give yourself immediate access to the property and acquire the key.

As soon as your offer has been accepted, start looking for a tenant. Place an ad in the paper, call prospective tenants in your database, and let people in your network know you have a good house available. The ad should read something like this:

Rent to own nice 3br, 2ba, 1900 sq. ft., $1200/mo, 30% of rent applies to down payment, 303-555-5555.

Screen the applicants and choose the best tenant. (See Chapter 11 for tips on screening tenants.) You and the tenant should go together to a notary public and have the tenant's signature notarized on both the lease agreement and the option agreement. When the agreements are signed, collect the option money in certified funds and record the option agreement in the public records at your county courthouse. Then you and the tenant will have a typical landlord-tenant relationship according to the terms of the lease until it's time to exercise the option.

Send a notice to the tenant three months before the option expires; don't count on the tenant remembering the expiration date. Find out what the tenant intends to do. If he's going to buy the property, he'll need time to arrange financing and prepare for closing. If he's not going to buy, you'll want a head start on finding another tenant so the house isn't vacant for any length of time.

If the tenant chooses to exercise the option, set up the closing, sell the property, and reinvest the profits. If he doesn't, exercise the option, he moves out at the end of the lease period, you keep the initial and monthly option consideration money, and you find another tenant who wants to rent to own.

■ When the Option Isn't Exercised

It's estimated that 80 percent of options to purchase leased residential property never close. When you own the property, this is good!

What do you do when the tenant doesn't exercise the option? First, talk to the tenant and find out what her plans are. If she wants to stay in the house and delay purchasing the property, renew the lease and the option. Depending on market conditions, you may increase the rent or change some of the terms of the lease. With the new option agreement, you'll collect a new option consideration payment that is nonrefundable (just as the first one was), and you should also adjust the option price (the price you'll sell the house for) to the estimated future market value.

If the tenant has decided not to purchase the property at all and intends to move, you get to keep *all* of the option consideration money she's paid. Remember, your option agreement clearly stated these monies are nonrefundable. Once the tenant has officially given notice according to the terms of the lease, immediately begin the process of finding a new tenant. Inform the current tenant that you will be showing the property, and do so with as much courtesy and consideration as possible. Once you find another tenant, you'll negotiate the lease, collect the option money, and have a landlord-tenant relationship until it comes time to exercise the option.

■ Fixer-Upper Lease Option

One of the most popular ways to make money in real estate is to buy distressed properties, fix them up, and then either sell or rent them. The advantage is that those properties can usually be purchased below market value. The challenge is that you need cash for the down payment, fix-up costs, and interest on the loan until you complete the repairs and can rent or sell the house.

The solution is to lease option the house and let the tenant-buyer do the fix-up. Offer the option with nothing down (no initial option consideration) and half the rent or even no rent for six months to a year until the repairs are complete. Be sure your lease clearly states that the tenant can't move in until the fix-up is done—and periodically go by the house to make sure the tenant isn't living there until you have approved the repairs and the tenant is paying the full rent amount.

When you run your ad for this type of property, make the situation very clear so you don't waste your time screening prospective tenants who don't want to do a lot of work on a house. One ad that works well is this:

El Dumpo! Rent to own, $0 down, u-fix. 601-222-9876.

FYI

The amount of the option consideration is typically 3 to 5 percent of the purchase price and is paid in certified funds.

SUCCESS STORY

Perseverance Pays—and Keeps On Paying

Juan R. already owned two businesses when he decided to begin investing in real estate and became one of my students. His time was limited, but he made the most of it. His first deal was a single-family home he purchased for $23,000 and lease optioned for an initial option consideration of $4,500 and $600 per month rent. His positive cash flow on that unit alone is $330 per month.

Shortly after closing that deal, he found a 16-unit apartment building but had to go to nine different lenders before he found one willing to make the loan. "This just goes to show that when one says no, just move on to the next one," he says. "Don't take it personally; just move on. And don't let other people stand in the way of your dreams."

Juan has since bought a number of other properties, including one 6-unit, two 8-unit, and one 12-unit apartment buildings. Currently, he owns 52 rentals worth more than $1 million that generate a positive cash flow of $6,400 per month. "This is all I have done for now, but I am not finished by a long shot," he says. "There are still plenty of other strategies I have not tried."

■ Quick-Flip Lease Purchase

This is another technique that allows you to profit from a property without ever owning it—or even doing much to manage it. You find the property and get it under a lease purchase contract with low or no money down. Note that I said *lease purchase*, not lease option (see sidebar for an explanation of the difference). You advertise the property, but instead of leasing it to the tenant, you have the tenant assume your contracts. The tenant will pay you a nonrefundable fee for the right to take over the contracts and lease and will ultimately buy the house under the terms you negotiated. Essentially, you get paid for setting up the deal.

The biggest drawback is that you are typically liable if the tenant doesn't pay. You also won't be in control as a landlord. So be sure your original lease purchase contracts clearly state that you are relieved of any obligation upon assignment. Also, make sure all the parties know you are acting as a principal and not as an agent.

■ Lease Option or Lease Purchase: What's the Difference?

If properly executed, the end results of lease option and lease purchase agreements are the same. But there *are* differences you can't afford to overlook.

A lease purchase consists of two separate agreements: a lease agreement and a purchase and sale agreement. Generally, this arrangement favors the lessee, so use this agreement if you are the one leasing the property. The terms should limit the money the seller can keep to the earnest money, which is the same as giving a nonrefundable option consideration. When you are the lessor, you may use this agreement when you want to require the tenant to buy.

A lease option also consists of two agreements: a lease agreement and an option agreement. The tenant has the right to not exercise the option, but if you are the lessor and draft your lease properly, you'll be financially protected through the nonrefundable option consideration and the above-market rent, and you'll still own the property to lease, lease option, or sell to someone else.

Multiunit Lease Option

So far, I've talked about using lease options to purchase single-family homes, but they can also be used to buy multiunit residential and commercial properties. Multiunit properties are generally more expensive than comparable single-family homes and therefore require larger down payments. A lease option lets you take control of the building and build up your down payment before you buy it while profiting from the property's cash flow.

You may also want to lease option a multiunit property when it needs significant repair or has low income as a result of poor management. You can get the repairs done and improve the performance of the property during the lease period, and qualify for better financing when it comes time to close. When it's time to exercise the option, you can assign it to another investor for a fee or buy the property yourself.

FYI

A property is considered residential if it has one to four units; it is considered commercial if it has five or more units.

■ Assigning an Option Contract

The last chapter discussed assigning sales contracts; you can do the same thing with options. Unless there is a provision in the agreement to the contrary, any option can be assigned to someone else.

Plenty of real estate investors would be happy to take over your option contract and pay you well for having found and negotiated the deal. Just be sure all your agreements are signed in your corporate name followed by "and/or assigns" so you can sell the contract.

When you assign a contract, you'll collect a nonrefundable earnest money deposit at the time you sign the assignment agreement and receive the remainder of the fee at closing. Use the same assignment-of-contract form that you would use to assign a wholesale contract; see the sample in Chapter 4.

Truth in Numbers

*To establish the sales price for an option agreement, you have two
choices: study the local market and estimate appreciation based on
historical patterns, or take the current market value and compound it at
5 percent per year.*

■ Making the Numbers Work

One of the attractive issues about a lease option is the ability to charge
above-market rent because you are allowing a percentage of the rent as option consideration. Let's say the market rent on the property is $900. You
charge $1,000 rent but allow 30 percent of the rent to be applied as option
consideration. That means the tenants are actually paying $700 in rent, and
you are setting aside $300 a month for their eventual down payment.
Present the program to your prospective tenants and confidently show them
the benefits they will receive, and you'll encounter few objections or attempts at negotiation.

Of course, the rest of the numbers have to work for you as well. Be sure
the property will generate positive cash flow—the rent has to cover your expenses and allow for a profit. You'll also want to consider your other sources
of profit on the deal. Your up-front profit is the option money less whatever
it cost you to acquire the property and ready it for a tenant. Your closing
profit is what you'll clear when the option is exercised; that number will be
the selling price less the loan balance, the initial option money, the monthly
option consideration, and closing costs. Remember, all the option money is
nonrefundable, and you get to keep it if the option isn't exercised. If the option *is* exercised, you still get to keep it, but it then is applied to the down
payment, which reduces the amount you receive at closing. The option consideration money is still revenue for you; just make sure it's sufficient to
make the deal profitable.

You'll also need to figure out what the property will be worth at the end
of the option period and what your mortgage balance will be. Be sure you're
getting a fair price for the property. Also, do the math to be sure that the

monthly option consideration will leave you with cash after the sale. For example, if you are going to sell the property for $15,000 more than the mortgage balance, you don't want to give the tenant a monthly option consideration of $500 for 36 months.

■ An Option without a Lease

For most residential real estate investors, options and leases go hand in hand. However, there are situations when you may use an option to gain control of property without a lease. For example, options can allow you to take advantage of appreciation in a hot market. If property values are climbing, you may find a seller willing to let you lock in the sales price but delay actually purchasing the property. You may also use options to tie up property and prevent anyone else from buying it while you work on financing or on reselling. Options are also useful when you're developing land.

Of course, the seller is going to expect some sort of nonrefundable option consideration, just as you get when you're granting the option. Use the same option agreement you would use in a lease option deal to finalize the arrangement, and record the option in the public records.

■ Some Final Tips

Always have your leases and option agreements notarized and record the options in the public records at the courthouse. When you have an option on a property, the owner cannot sell it to anyone but you for the duration of the option. By recording the option, you are making that information part of the public record, and anyone who does a title search will see it. If the owner does try to pull a fast one on you, that deal will likely get stopped when the title company does its research for title insurance.

It's also a good idea to escrow the deed (that is, place the executed deed in the custody of a disinterested third party) with a title company or an attorney. This is particularly important if you are doing a sandwich lease, because it means you can close even if the seller isn't around.

MILLIONAIRE MENTOR Purchase Option Highlights

- Options allow you to control property without buying it and with little or no cash.

- Lease option buyers enjoy a number of benefits, including being able to live in a house before they buy it and having a portion of their rent apply to the down payment.

- Lease option sellers can collect above-market rent and a nonrefundable option consideration; they will profit whether the option is exercised or not.

- Lease option tenants generally require less management attention than traditional tenants. They are likely to take better care of the property because they intend to own it one day.

- Make the option agreement a separate document from the lease or purchase agreement; do not combine the two contracts into one document.

- Option contracts can be assigned to other investors for a fee, which allows you to make money simply by finding and organizing the deal.

- Always record your option agreements in the public records at the county courthouse.

CHAPTER 6

Preforeclosures and Foreclosures

Fresh Approaches to Familiar Problems

Every day all over the country, lenders are foreclosing on property because the owners didn't make the payments. *Somebody* is going to make a profit on these properties, and it may as well be you. Not only that, but when you use the techniques I'm going to discuss, you can actually help people at the same time you turn a profit of tens of thousands of dollars in a month or two.

Before going into the process of profiting from foreclosures, let's clear up the most common misperception about them: You can't make money in foreclosures because there's too much competition. That's simply not true. Are other investors out there buying foreclosures? Of course. Will some of them get a deal you wanted? Probably. Will you get deals they wanted? Definitely. Don't worry about competition from other investors; it means the business is strong and will keep you on your toes.

One of the biggest competitors you'll have in foreclosures is not other investors; it's bankruptcy. When people in financial trouble decide to give up and walk away from their problems, you can't help them. But if you can get to them before they reach that point, you may be able to help them salvage their credit, find a place to live, and get their life back in order. And in the process you'll make money—that's what makes this a great business to be in.

When you buy foreclosures using the techniques in this chapter, you typically gain immediate equity in the property, and you'll know how to do this without cash or credit. You'll know how to quickly evaluate deals to determine which ones will work and which ones won't, so you won't waste time chasing unprofitable properties. You'll write your contracts in a way that eliminates the risk for you. And the legal notices of your local newspapers provide you with an abundance of new leads every month.

In this chapter, you learn the three basic ways through which to buy foreclosure properties: preforeclosure, at the foreclosure auction, and after foreclosure. But first, to understand foreclosure, let's take a look at how homes are purchased.

When a couple finds a home they want to buy—whether a house, a condominium, a mobile home, or whatever—they typically have to borrow money to pay for it. The standard procedure is to pay between 5 and 20 percent of the purchase price as the down payment and borrow the remainder from a bank or mortgage company using the property as collateral. At the closing table, the buyers sign a promissory note agreeing to make monthly payments for a certain period, usually 30 years. That promissory note stipulates the various details of the loan, including the interest rate, the number and amount of payments, the due date of the payments, late charges and penalties, and what happens if the borrowers default.

In a perfect world, a buyer makes all the payments on time every month and lives happily ever after. Certainly that's what both the buyer and the lender are hoping for when the loan is made. But life is full of unexpected twists and turns, and borrowers don't always make their payments on time. Sometimes it's for painful reasons out of their control, such as a serious illness, death, or other crisis. Sometimes financial troubles are driven by divorce or job loss. Sometimes it's simply poor financial management. Whatever the reason, when a borrower doesn't pay, the lender takes the actions described in the loan agreement.

It's common for a payment to be considered late after 15 days and for the loan to be in default after 30 days of nonpayment. When a mortgage loan goes into default, the lender begins a series of steps designed to bring the loan current. If those efforts fail, the lender forecloses. The details of the foreclosure process vary by state, but the end result is the same: the borrower is forced out of the home, and the property is sold at auction to recoup the balance of the loan.

■ Different Ways to Foreclose

Every state has provisions for lenders to make loans using real estate as collateral. Though the property secures the loan and the lender is entitled to foreclose if the borrower doesn't pay, the procedures vary. You should know which laws apply in your state by researching foreclosure procedures at a law library or in the legal section of your public library.

The two basic types of foreclosure are *judicial* and *nonjudicial*. In a judicial foreclosure, the lender must go to court for a hearing to obtain approval to foreclose when a borrower is behind on payments. A judge or other third party makes sure due process is followed before a lender can auction or repossess a home. In a nonjudicial foreclosure, the lender may hire an attorney or trustee to handle the foreclosure procedure all the way to auction, and the case doesn't go to court.

You also need to be familiar with the terms *title theory* and *lien theory*. Title theory refers to the modern version of common law mortgage under which the creditor has the legal right to possession (also known as a title interest), even though in fact the debtor remains in possession of the property. Under the lien theory, the lender takes a lien on the property and is not entitled to possession until the foreclosure process has been completed and the premises sold.

■ Finding Foreclosures

One of the easiest and most effective ways to find foreclosures is through the legal notices in your local newspapers. Learn to read the foreclosure notices; they tell you everything you need to know to decide if a property is worth pursuing. A foreclosure notice is just like a news article: it gives you the "who, what, when, where, and why" of the situation. Basically, it tells you who is in foreclosure (the owner of the property), what property is going to be auctioned off (the address and/or legal description), when and where the auction will be held, and why the property is being auctioned (because a lien holder is foreclosing).

■ Small Towns, Big Opportunities

Less than a week after completing training on how to buy foreclosures, Lorne and Angie Saltsman returned to their small town and bought a pre-foreclosure home for $31,000. The home's resale value was $65,000 after $4,000 in fix-up.

Anthony and Joan Peters, who also live in a small town, took a little longer. Within two months of their training, they found a preforeclosure property, reinstated the loan for $6,200, and cleared $29,935.98 on the deal.

The legal notice might not use the word *foreclosure* in the headline. It might say something like "Notice of Sale under Power," "Notice of Trustee's Sale," "Notice of Sheriff's Sale," or "Notice of Commissioner's Sale." If you're having trouble finding the foreclosure notices, call the paper and ask them what section to check. Then study that section so you can learn the language of foreclosure notices in your state.

The notice often includes the property address and zip code, so you can tell fairly quickly if it's in an area you want to work and can also easily contact the owner (assuming the property is currently owner-occupied). If the notice doesn't have an address, you'll have to go to the courthouse to research where the property is. Notices may also include the original loan amount and date. In most cases, you can follow the rule of thumb that the older the loan, the greater the equity in the property. Of course, it's entirely possible that there are junior loans, so never assume the loan being foreclosed is the only loan on the property—something you'll check out as you begin putting the deal together.

In addition to legal notices, subscription services compile and provide the same information. A good way to find the best list provider in your area is to attend a foreclosure auction and check out the other investors; they'll all be holding the subscription list to follow up on the properties they're interested in. You can also check "Realty Related Services" in the classified section of the newspaper or do an Internet search on "foreclosure listing services." My company maintains a list of these services in its office; call 800-741-7877 or use its Web site <www.WhitneyEducationGroup.com>.

You may also want to advertise to get in touch with people who haven't reached the stage of a published legal notice. Try some of the techniques in Chapter 4.

■ What Are You Afraid Of?

Many real estate investors fail to reach their full potential because of fear. Let's address the most common fears of buying foreclosure property and get them out of the way.

Paying too much. If you know the value of the property and the balance of the loans, you'll never pay too much. I recommend that you never pay more than 80 percent of the value of a foreclosure property. For example, if the house is worth $145,000, you would be willing to pay up to $116,000. If the outstanding loans are more than $116,000, don't buy. If they are less than $116,000 and you can work out a deal with the owner, it's usually a safe buy. So figure out what you're willing to pay; if it's less than the loan balance, walk away.

You won't be able to sell or rent the property. If you buy right—that is, if you don't pay too much—you'll almost always be able to sell, even if you have to do it at a discount. If for some reason you can't sell and you need money, you have the option to pull cash out of the property by refinancing or taking out a home equity loan. And if you follow my advice on managing property (see Chapter 11), you'll know how to keep your rental units occupied with good tenants who take care of the property and pay their rent on time.

Liens. Why should you be afraid of the very thing that is creating the opportunity for you? Of course, there may be additional liens on the property beyond the mortgage that is in default and causing the foreclosure. That's why your contracts are always written with the clause "subject to title report." If the title report reveals any liens the owner failed to disclose, and if those liens would prevent you from making the profit you want, you can always back out of the deal.

Bad areas. The way to deal with bad areas is to avoid them. Before you contact an owner, check out the neighborhood. If it's an area you're not comfortable with, move on to the next deal.

Your greatest security is knowledge. When you have a plan and know your options, you will be confident and unafraid—and have all the ammunition you need to become very wealthy.

Words of Wisdom

When you're dealing in foreclosures, you need to know something about the legal issues regarding the process. But it's equally important for you to understand how people get into such serious financial trouble and what their options are. This is not difficult to learn. Your state's department of consumer services will give you information on the consumer credit laws in your state. You should also learn how the bankruptcy process works in your state. Bankruptcy attorneys often offer free seminars to attract clients; if you see one advertised, take advantage of it. Or check with a nonprofit consumer credit counseling agency; it has information that will help you help people facing foreclosure.

■ Stopping a Foreclosure

The first way through which to buy foreclosure properties is known as *preforeclosure;* that refers to the time when the lender has begun the process but you buy the property before the actual foreclosure takes place. It's truly a win-win situation, because you'll make a major profit at the same time you save the sellers from showing a foreclosure on their credit history and you provide them with the cash they need to move and get on with their life.

Here's what a typical preforeclosure deal might look like. A hypothetical couple, Sam and Susan Sunshine, have a house worth $182,000. The principal balance on their first mortgage is $105,000, and they have a second mortgage of $15,000. Sam owned his own business but about a year ago suffered an injury that left him unable to work. He didn't have disability insurance and his business failed. Susan's job doesn't pay enough to support them in their current lifestyle. They've gradually gotten further and further behind on their house payments, and now they're facing foreclosure.

It's going to take $8,000 to bring both mortgages current, and the Sunshines need $5,000 to move into an apartment they can afford. So you offer to assume both loans, bring them current, and give the Sunshines the cash they need. Your total cost to buy the house is $133,000, which means you step into the deal with $49,000 in equity. You could even refinance the house for 80 percent of its value and walk away from closing with $12,600 in cash. You can keep the house and rent it, sell it to another homeowner at market price, or flip it to another investor at a discount. The Sunshines are able to move out, avoid the foreclosure, and get their life back on track.

This example may sound like an exceptional deal, but it's not. Our students do these kinds of deals with these kinds of profits regularly.

Remember that most people know nothing about foreclosure and don't know where to turn when they're facing such a situation. Lenders don't explain borrowers' rights and options; they're just trying to collect their money. Borrowers facing foreclosure are confused and scared, and their self-esteem is below the basement. They need someone who understands the process to help them, and that person is you.

Bright Idea

Pay attention to what other investors are doing. Many owners volunteer information about the other contacts they've received; listen carefully and consider whether you might want to try what they're doing. When you go to a house and find that another investor has left a letter on the door in an unsealed envelope, read it.

■ When the Loan Goes Bad: From the Lender's Perspective

Lenders don't want to foreclose on houses, which is why they do thorough credit checks before they make a loan. They're in the finance business, not the real estate business. At the same time, lenders understand that things happen in life that cause someone to get behind on payments. Borrowers with a cooperative attitude who contact their lenders before the loan is seriously delinquent typically find that the lenders are willing to work with them to find a way to get the account current. However, borrowers who simply don't make their payments and don't communicate with their lenders probably find that the lenders will move through the collection process and into foreclosure according to the terms of the loan.

Typically, lenders use a series of letters and telephone calls that begin after the first payment reaches late status. The first letters are likely to be gentle reminders, but the tone will strengthen if those notices are ignored and payment isn't made.

As much as lenders don't want to foreclose, they have to protect the investment they've made in the loan. That's why most lenders have a policy of refusing to accept partial payments once a loan reaches a certain past due status. A partial payment can reset the foreclosure clock and ultimately cost the lender more than the amount of the payment. But people in financial trouble aren't likely to have two or three payments plus late fees in cash—if they did, they wouldn't be in financial trouble. Another challenge for troubled borrowers is that, if there has been a history of bad checks, the lender may refuse payment by personal check and insist on certified funds.

When the account reaches a certain stage of delinquency, the foreclosure process begins. But at any point right up to the moment the property is auctioned on the courthouse steps, foreclosure can be stopped.

■ Approaching Preforeclosure Sellers

It's important to approach prospective sellers with tact and diplomacy. I recommend a personal visit as soon as possible after you see the legal notice; if the owner isn't home, you can leave a letter. Most would-be investors just mail the letters, but the difference that will make you successful is in going to the door. People facing foreclosure are probably being bombarded with mail by collectors and may not be opening all the letters they get. If you want to use mail, postcards work better because the homeowner doesn't have to open an envelope to see that you are offering a solution to his problem.

You might want to call the homeowner if his number is listed. This can work, but I still prefer a personal visit because it allows you to see the property so you know what you're dealing with. The best time to go to houses that are facing foreclosure is Sunday afternoon. That's when you're most likely to find people at home. Take your business cards, contracts, information release forms, marketing letters, and envelopes. You'll have all the tools you need to either negotiate a deal or leave behind information if the owner isn't home.

Another benefit of a personal visit is that you'll find out right away whether the house is occupied or vacant. A vacant house indicates owners are much more interested in unloading the property as quickly and painlessly as possible. If a house is vacant, immediately begin tracking down the owner. You can find owners by checking telephone listings, checking the tax rolls, or sending a letter to the foreclosure address with "Address Correction Requested" on the envelope so the post office will provide you with their current address.

If a house is occupied, go to the door and ask for the owner by name. If he's not home, leave behind a letter in a sealed envelope. If the owner is at home, introduce yourself and say that you're interested in buying a home in the area and have been told that this house might be for sale. Be prepared for a variety of responses.

You might be asked who told you that, so have an answer ready. A good response is to say that you have a friend in the real estate business who knows the area—but *don't* indicate at that point that you're aware of the pending foreclosure. The owner often admits freely and frankly that the house isn't on the market but is in foreclosure. If he doesn't admit it, you'll have to engage in some conversation to win his trust before he opens up to you.

Once the owner acknowledges the foreclosure to you, tell him you have knowledge and experience in the area and think you can help him. At this point, he'll probably invite you in, and you can go over the numbers to see if you can make a deal work. If he doesn't want to talk—and owners are often not ready to until it gets closer to auction time—leave your letter behind, and tell him to call you if he has any questions or if you can help in any way. See the sample letter in Figure 6.1. Make a note to follow up with mail or phone calls every week or two until the auction date.

When a seller calls you on the basis of either your letter or one of your ads, use an information sheet like the one shown in Figure 6.2 to gather enough preliminary information to determine whether you should pursue the deal. If the numbers don't work, be polite but honest. If the property isn't in an area you want to work, again be polite but honest. If you know of another investor you can refer the seller to, do so.

If the preliminary numbers look good, have the seller call to authorize the foreclosing attorney or trustee to give you information regarding the back payments. Then put together your offer.

If the auction date is imminent, be candid with the seller about how he's going to have to work with you to make the deal happen. For example, let's say he has a nonassumable loan and it's only four days before the auction. In your sales contract, stipulate that you will reinstate the existing loan and maintain it until new financing can be acquired. That gives you the time you need to either refinance the property if you're going to keep it or find a buyer if you're going to sell it. Remember, you only need to refinance the property if you're planning to keep it.

Most preforeclosure deals occur in the last week or so prior to the auction. Until then, sellers are still hoping for a miracle that will allow them to keep their home. Even so, it's a good idea to contact them early and establish a rapport so that they will call you when they realize they have to sell.

Warning

It's usually not a good idea to allow sellers to remain on the premises after closing; you may have trouble getting them to leave. And never give them any cash proceeds from the sale until they have vacated the property.

FIGURE 6.1

■

A Letter
That Works

In the first three months after learning about foreclosures, Bobby Threlkeld had acquired seven properties. He has developed a great letter that gets a response from eight out of ten people he sends it to. It's a letter carefully designed to hit the emotional hot buttons of people in financial distress so that they will take action before it's too late. Here's the text of that letter:

Dear _____:

My name is Bobby Threlkeld. I am an individual who specializes in stopping foreclosure proceedings against homes. There are many individuals who have been told to sell their home through a Realtor, and although this is an alternative, many times the owner will still lose the home.

Foreclosure is a drastically unfair method used by lenders and mortgage companies to completely collect on their outstanding loans. The property is taken away from the owner and sold at a public auction. The proceeds from this sale are used to pay off the mortgage that is in default; this also includes foreclosure costs, attorney fees, and other court costs. The only thing you receive from this procedure is a black mark on your credit, possibly stopping you from ever owning a home again! This is why I spend much of my time and effort helping people avoid the damage caused by foreclosure.

I can offer you the cash to get back on your feet and pay the mortgage up to date in order to save your credit rating.

There are a lot of possibilities that could save you from going into foreclosure. If I can be of service to you in your present situation, please don't hesitate to call. If I can help you over the phone, my advice is free. Please remember:

FORECLOSURE IS NOT THE ONLY
OPTION AVAILABLE TO YOU!

Sincerely,
Bobby Threlkeld

FIGURE 6.2

■

Foreclosure
Property
Telephone
Information
Sheet

Seller's name _____

Day phone _____ Evening phone _____

Property address_____

Details of property:

Age of house _____ Square feet _____

Bedrooms _____ Baths _____ Central Heat/Air _____

Basement _____ Garage _____

Comments _____

Approximate value $_____

Amount of back payments

First loan $_____

Second loan $_____

First   Monthly   Interest
loan balance $_____ payment $_____ rate _____

Second   Monthly   Interest
loan balance $_____ payment $_____ rate _____

Other liens _____

Do all mortgages and liens total 80% or less of value? _____

Appointment to meet with seller_____

■ Going Above and Beyond

Plenty of real estate investors buy houses in preforeclosure—it's really a no-brainer when it comes to setting up good deals. But you're dealing with people who may be spending every waking moment wondering where they're going to live when they lose their house. It's not enough to take the house off their hands; if you want to be a real hero, help them find a place to live.

I don't recommend that you put them in one of your own rental units. No matter how decent they are, people recovering from serious financial trouble have a lot of emotional baggage. Even though it wasn't your fault, they may have times of resenting you for making money when they lost their house, and that could make for a challenging landlord-tenant relationship.

A better approach is to identify apartment complexes with high vacancies that have a variety of unit sizes (one-, two-, and three-bedroom, if possible) and establish a relationship with the leasing manager. Then tell owners you know a place where they can live and that you'll even pay their deposit as part of your offer on their house—if you really want to be helpful, offer to rent a truck and help them move. That, by the way, ensures that they're out of the property when you take control of it.

Smart Thinking

Use a simple contract. Keep it as short as possible but make sure it covers all the bases. Sellers in financial trouble are being hammered on all sides by complicated legal documents. Keep yours simple so you don't scare them out of the deal.

■ Putting Together Your Offer

Work the numbers on a foreclosure just as you would any other real estate deal. Consider what it's going to cost you to acquire the property, what the seller wants and needs, and what you're going to do with the property once you own it. Your goal in a foreclosure property is to buy at 80 percent of the market value or less. If you can't get the property for that, walk away.

When you present your offer, show the seller how it will help her get back on her feet in a short time. If she points out that she has a substantial amount of equity, remind her that if she sells on the open market, she'll likely have to pay a real estate commission of 7 percent and closing costs of 5 to 6 percent as well as go through the hassle of showing the property; and the offers would probably be lower than her asking price. Also, she may not have time to do a traditional retail sale, which typically takes six to eight weeks by the time the offer is negotiated and all the details handled. You're offering an immediate solution that will stop the foreclosure; this is your business, and you have to make a profit on the deal or you can't do it.

■ When the Loan Goes Bad: The Borrower's Perspective

People don't buy houses expecting to default on the loan. But life doesn't always go the way we think it will, and sometimes borrowers are unable to keep up with their payments. The reasons are varied: job loss, divorce, poor financial management, illness, addictions, and other unexpected economic crises. Whatever the cause, when the house payment isn't made, late notices and letters from the lender begin arriving. Late fees are charged, and before the borrower can deal with the situation, another payment is due. There isn't enough money to make two payments, the lender is refusing to accept a partial payment, and the foreclosure process begins.

Once that happens, the borrower has four options: (1) sell the home; (2) borrow the money to catch up on all the payments; (3) file for bankruptcy; or (4) wait out the foreclosure process and move when the house is auctioned.

Most people facing foreclosure resist the idea of selling their home. They're emotionally attached to it and in a state of denial about their financial situation. Chances are that borrowing money is not a workable solution because their credit is already seriously damaged. If they choose bankruptcy, they may be able to keep their home during the process, but they still have to pay the mortgage eventually—and often end up in foreclosure again. All too many people simply wait out the foreclosure process because they don't realize they can do something else.

Doing Your Own Title Search

Certainly, the easiest way to do a title search is to pay a title company, but that takes cash you might not have when you're getting started. But a title search is essential; you must be sure that no one has a claim to the property that you don't know about. Remember: Real estate is the only asset that cannot be moved or hidden, which is why every possible party seeks it out for lien rights (the right to put something against the title for security purposes). You can do the title search yourself, and in most cases you'll discover the same information a title company would. The primary drawback to doing your own title search is that you won't have title insurance when you're finished. A safe approach is to do your own search when you first negotiate the deal to be sure you want to move forward but then have a title company do another search and issue title insurance right before you close so you're protected.

When you conduct a title search, you'll confirm the legal owner(s), so you know you can legally buy the property from the person you're dealing with. You'll also find out what mortgages are on the property; if the real estate taxes are current; if there are any liens for special assessments; if there are any judgments, federal tax liens or other government liens, or mechanic's lien claims; if there are any pending court proceedings that may affect the title (a foreclosure is such a proceeding); any deed restrictions that apply; and whether easements are present. If you find any title issues, go back to the seller to see if they can be cleared up. Some will be fairly easy to handle; others may take so long to resolve that you won't be able to prevent the foreclosure.

Some of the most common title problems are related to marriage and divorce or other life changes. For example, the seller may be a single woman or man, but the title shows two names on the deed and states they are married. Or the seller is the child of a deceased owner who did not leave a will clearly stating what to do with the property. Title problems may also be related to money, such as liens for back taxes or mechanics' liens. To protect your investment, always be sure you have a clear title before you move ahead with buying real estate.

For your preliminary title search to determine whether to move forward with the deal, you need only go back to the date of sale on the legal notices announcing the foreclosure. At that point, a title search was done and title insurance issued; in most cases, your primary concern is knowing what has happened since then. You may find additional liens that could change the terms of your offer, as Chuck and Sherri Hastings did (see sidebar titled "Knock and the Door Will Open"). Before you actually close on a deal, however, you should buy a current title insurance policy, check the records as far back as possible, or do both.

Go to the county public records office, where you'll find that some of the records are computerized and some are not. The staff will explain how to use the files and where specific records are maintained. Start by looking for the seller's name in the grantee's (mortgagee's) index. That refers you to the deed book, where you'll find the title to the property. Then check the grantor (mortgagor) from the date on the title to the present for additional mortgages on the property. Compare the legal description on the deed with the foreclosure notice and be sure they match.

Do a search of all the names that appear on the title. If the name of a deceased person is on the title, check the estate index for the case number and then go to the probate records to find out who the executor is. That individual can sign the necessary documents to complete the sale of the property.

Check the master lien index under the names of everyone who appears on the title. If you find any liens on the property, check the document to confirm that it has been satisfied; generally, this is done by a stamp affixed to the lien. If the lien has not been satisfied, check the date. A statute of limitations covers some types of liens, and they may automatically be canceled after a certain period if they are not refiled by the lien holder. Find out what the statute of limitations is on liens in your state. Something important to remember is that no statute of limitations exists for federal tax liens, so if you see such a lien on a property, be absolutely certain it has been satisfied or walk away from the deal.

You'll also want to take a look at the lot in the plat record books. This will show you if there are any easements you should be concerned about and if the property is on a flood plane. The presence of easements is not necessarily bad, but they could limit your use of the property, so you need to know about them. And if the property is landlocked—that is, it's not adjacent to any public streets—you must be sure you have an access easement so you will always be able to get to the property.

■ HUD Foreclosures

When a property goes all the way through the foreclosure process to auction and is not purchased, the lender repossesses the house and the loan is written off in the case of a conventional loan. If the loan was guaranteed by the Federal Housing Administration (FHA) or the Department of Veterans Affairs (VA), the government pays the lender the amount he lost and takes possession of the property. These homes are usually listed for sale though a real estate agent approved by the Department of Housing and Urban Development (HUD).

These properties are made available to first-time homebuyers for a low, or no, down payment. Sometimes investors can buy these houses, but the government would rather have them owner-occupied. If you don't own a home, HUD foreclosures are a good opportunity for you to pursue for your own residence.

■ Foreclosure Auctions

The second way to buy foreclosure properties is at a foreclosure auction, traditionally held on the courthouse steps (although most courthouses have brought that function indoors). Auctions are advertised in the legal notices of the newspaper, and your county clerk's office can provide you with the information you need to know to attend and buy at the auction. It's a good idea to attend an auction to see what goes on before you go to buy; Chapter 7 tells you more about auctions in general. Foreclosure auctions usually don't attract big crowds; you'll generally see 10 or 20 people watching with maybe only 1 or 2 actually bidding on property. Bobby Threlkeld routinely buys at courthouse auctions and says that's how he gets great deals on properties when the owner didn't have sufficient equity to make a preforeclosure deal work.

In most cases, you'll need cash or certified funds at an auction, although some states allow you to bid with as little as 10 percent at auction and the balance to be paid within 24 hours.

If you want to bid on a property, research it beforehand. Drive by the property. If it's vacant, inspect the house as best you can by walking around and looking in the windows. Compare it with similar properties that have sold in the neighborhood within the past six months. Do a title search; in most states, secondary mortgages are wiped out at the auction, but you still want to be sure you can get a clear title.

When the auction is finished, the typical procedure is for the sheriff to tack a notice on the door of the property telling the residents they must vacate by whatever date state law requires, usually seven days. Do people trash the house during this final period? Sometimes. That's why I recommend bidding only on vacant houses if you're buying at auction.

Bright Idea

When you're showing a house, whether to sell or to rent, have a sign-in sheet near the front door so you can collect the names, addresses, phone numbers, and e-mail addresses of everyone who looks at the property. Build a database with this information, so you can let these people know when you have other properties on the market.

■ After Foreclosure

The third way to buy foreclosure properties is from the lender after foreclosure if the property didn't sell at auction or from the investor who purchased the property at the auction. This can be a lucrative way to buy property, especially in a buyer's market. Lenders are often willing to accept creative offers, such as no money down, no payments for three months (to give you time to clean and fix up the property), under market price, and at low interest rates.

Lenders often turn a property over to a real estate agent within a week or two after the auction. That period is your window of opportunity. A real estate

Knock and the Door Will Open

SUCCESS
STORY

Sherri Hastings wasn't happy when her husband, Chuck, invested in one of my real estate training packages. And because Chuck was working full-time as a finance manager at an automobile dealership, it took him a while to start using his real estate education. But once he learned about foreclosures, he knew that helping people in financial trouble was what he wanted to do.

Chuck's first few deals were moderately profitable—enough that Sherri was willing to help, even though she wasn't totally sold on the idea of a career in real estate. Then Chuck found a foreclosure in the legal notices, and together they knocked on the door and offered their assistance.

The owner agreed to take $5,000 and sign over the property if Chuck and Sherri would take care of the back payments, which totaled $6,200, and assume the mortgage of $65,120. But when Chuck did the title search, he found two small liens. He went back to the owner, who knew about those debts but didn't realize they had been attached to the property, and renegotiated the deal. Instead of $5,000, she agreed to take $2,000, and they closed. Chuck spent about $5,000 on repairs and fix-up and sold the house in 30 days for $149,000. Chuck and Sherri walked out of the closing with a check for $69,806.56—and Sherri is totally on board as a partner in their real estate business now.

agent is going to try to get the highest price possible because the agent's commission is based on the sales price. But if you can make your deal with the lender before the property is listed, the lender makes a quick sale without paying a commission and is more receptive to agreeing on a good price for you.

When putting together your offer, take some pictures of the property's worst problems, such as peeling paint, rotten wood, termite damage, neglected landscaping, broken windows, and the like. Show the lender that it's going to take time and money to repair the house and that the property isn't likely to sell in that condition. As part of your offer package, you might also want to include before-and-after photographs of other properties that you've fixed up to show you have the necessary experience and capability.

Once the property has been turned over to a real estate agent, you can still make an as is offer to purchase. Justify your offer by attaching a letter explaining the logic and reason behind your numbers.

Whether you're going directly to the lender or buying through a real estate agent, the chances of your offer being accepted are much greater if you put together a professional package that answers all of the lender's questions and concerns before they can be asked. Don't be surprised if the lender makes a counteroffer. Take a look at the numbers to see if you can make the deal work. If not, you can either counter the counteroffer or walk away.

Handling the Closing Yourself

If you've used a title company to do the title search, you may opt to have it handle the closing. But if you've done the title search yourself, you can also handle the closing yourself.

If you're assuming the loan, all you need to close is a quitclaim deed or a warranty deed (depending on what's appropriate in your state). It's really that simple. You arrange for the seller to sign the quitclaim, pay the attorney handling the foreclosure the necessary amount to bring the loan current and stop the proceedings, get a receipt, and then head to the courthouse to record your deed. You'll have a more traditional closing when you sell or refinance the property.

Keep in mind that when you close with a quitclaim or warranty deed, you don't have firm assurance that the seller is the home's legal owner and that there are no additional liens on the property other than those the seller has disclosed. That's why you need to conduct a title search.

What to Do with the Property Once You Own It

Once you are the owner of the property, you can flip it to another investor, sell it at market value, or keep it as a rental. In fact, you may be able to assign the contract to another investor before you close, using the techniques explained in Chapter 4. Whatever you do, make it profitable.

MILLIONAIRE MENTOR Foreclosure Highlights

- You can buy foreclosure properties in three basic ways: preforeclosure, at the foreclosure auction, and after the foreclosure.

- One of the easiest and most effective ways to find foreclosures is through the legal notices in your local newspapers. In most cases, the notice will provide enough information to let you get in touch with the owner and discuss possible options. This contact can be made by mail, phone, or in person.

- Buying a property preforeclosure means that even though the lender has begun the foreclosure process, you step in and buy the property before the foreclosure takes place. Most preforeclosure deals take place in the last week or so before the auction.

- You won't always be able to help people in preforeclosure. If they have insufficient equity in the property for you to make a profit, don't do the deal.

- If the owner doesn't stop the foreclosure by selling the property or bringing the mortgage current, the property will be sold at a foreclosure auction at the courthouse. You can get great real estate bargains at foreclosure auctions.

- You can also buy foreclosures from the lender if the property didn't sell at auction or from another investor who may have bought it at the auction but wants to flip it.

- Knowing how to do your own title searches can save you the cost of paying a title company to do the search. Of course, if you do your own title searches, you won't have title insurance. A good approach is to do your own title search early in the transaction to confirm that you want to move forward with the deal. If it looks good, have your title company do another search and issue insurance before you close so you're protected.

CHAPTER 7

Auctions

Fast Buying Means Fast (and Big) Profits

One of the most exciting and potentially profitable ways to buy real estate is at an auction. In large part because of that excitement, however, you can either get a great deal or lose your shirt—and the difference between the two may be only a few seconds.

Most auctions feature a carnival-like atmosphere. When you arrive, you'll likely find vendors selling food and beverages with music blaring. People are milling about, anxiously reviewing their programs. As the auction begins, there's a mad dash for seats and the adrenaline is pumping. This is a competition unlike any other. The potential for profits is almost incalculable, but you have to know what you're doing.

Auctions have been around since ancient Rome. The English and Dutch refined auctions and brought them to the New World; and ever since, they've remained a consistent element in the world of commerce. The strength of the auction process lies in its versatility. It's fast, it's mobile, and it keeps the cost of storing and maintaining an inventory of merchandise—and even real estate—to a minimum. From the buyer's perspective, auctions are an excellent place to pick up bargains. Only someone foolish and inexperienced comes away from an auction paying more than wholesale price.

My fast-track method of building wealth through auctions targets government auctions only. Why? Because government auctions of distressed properties and merchandise are where the best bargains can be found. Retail auctions don't offer many opportunities for the investor looking to buy, but they are an outlet if you have property you need to sell quickly.

Just about anything you can buy through other purchasing channels can be bought at auction—and even some things you can't. In South Africa, surplus wild animals are auctioned off every year. In the United States, government auctions include real estate; property seized because of trade violations, trademark or copyright violations, or other illegal activity; property abandoned at ports of entry or on which duties or taxes were not paid; and government surplus items. This chapter focuses on buying real estate at auction, but the principles apply to buying just about anything. Once you become comfortable with auctions, you'll find them one of the most profitable ways to spend your time.

Words of Wisdom

Attend auctions regularly, whether you intend to buy or not. Attending regularly ensures you don't get dropped from an agency's list of bidders, and each auction is a learning experience.

■ The Auction Process

The key to making big profits at auctions is a systematic approach. Let's take a step-by-step look at the process.

The Announcement

To participate in an auction, you must know when and where it is to take place. You need to know the key places, make sure you receive the announcements, and have a backup source in case you aren't notified. Identify the government agencies that hold auctions in your area and then narrow that list to the ones that fit your requirements—that is, the ones that deal in the type of real estate you want to buy. To get on their bidders list to receive announcements in the mail, send a written request indicating that you are a private investor specializing in auction sales. You should get a written confirmation that your request has been received and processed.

Agencies also announce auctions with public notices, which can be your backup source. These notices are typically in the form of advertisements placed in national publications, such as *USA Today* and the *Wall Street Journal,* as well as in local publications. You have to pay attention if you're going to spot these ads because they could be anywhere in the publication.

The Prospectus

The auction prospectus is an outline of what will happen at the event. It gives the exact date, time, and place of the auction and the prebid conference as well as the times when you can inspect the properties. It also includes the general rules and basic financial requirements. Some prospectuses offer a summary description of each item on the block.

The prospectus does not, however, give you enough information to make a bid or nonbid decision. It probably does allow you to eliminate the items you won't bid on, leaving you with a shorter list of possibilities that you must learn more about before you decide whether to try to buy them and how much you're willing to pay.

Procedural Review

You must understand the procedures that will be used at the auction. There may be a variety of categories, and each may have different bidding procedures. The prospectus should include the terms and conditions of the auction, so take the time to study those details and be sure you understand them.

Keep in mind that the rules could change on auction day. This is common, and anything that is announced on that day takes precedence over anything previously announced. So pay attention. At every auction, you'll watch people head back to the closing table with a happy grin after winning a bid, only to see them back in the room a short time later wearing a glum expression after their bid was set aside and the property posted again because they hadn't understood an auction rule.

Prebid Conference

The prebid conference often gives you the opportunity to meet the broker or salesperson originally assigned to market the property, which is an excellent chance to find out why the property has not sold before. Learn as much as you can about previous offers and why they were rejected.

Another benefit of the prebid conference is the chance to get to know your competition, which gives you an edge when the bidding begins. Listen to the questions others are asking; frequently you need those same questions answered, and they may also give you a clue to your competitor's strategy.

Like attending auctions when you don't intend to buy, going to prebid conferences is a great educational experience. Go to several before you start bidding.

Words of Wisdom

The two most important rules for every auction are research and patience—and they always pay off.

Preview/Inspection/Research

The most important thing I can teach you about buying at auctions is this: Never, never bid on an item you have not inspected and researched. It doesn't matter how good the deal looks on the surface; if you don't do your homework, don't bid.

Consider this possible scenario: Art Auctionbuff makes a bid of $500 on a house he hasn't seen. He recognizes the neighborhood from the address and knows that houses in that area typically sell at $50,000 to $60,000. How could he lose? Here's how: First, the house needed about $13,000 in repairs. If that were all, he still would have gotten a bargain. But had he done his research, he would have uncovered liens for outstanding real estate taxes along with water and sewer charges for the past three years, totaling more than $6,000. If not paid immediately, the county will foreclose on those liens, but Art doesn't have $6,000 in cash. He figured the term *as is* referred only to the physical condition of the building. He doesn't have a bargain but instead owns a major liability—which may be on the auction block again before long.

Inspect and research whatever you buy at auction before you bid. Though I'm talking primarily about buying real estate at auction, this rule applies no matter what you're buying, whether it's real property, cars, jewelry, electronics, or anything else.

Go out to the property and do a basic inspection. Look at the roof. Watch for wall cracks or sloping floors that might indicate a foundation problem. Flush the toilets and make sure all the faucets work. Turn on all the appliances plus each light, and also check the electrical outlets. Check for termites and wood rot. Do an inventory of the cosmetic repairs needed. This is the essential inspection that you would do on any property, whether you're buying it wholesale, retail, or at auction.

Next, do your research, starting with a basic title search. Get the legal description and make sure it matches what is being auctioned. Find out the appraised value, the sales history, zoning, and possible covenants and restrictions. Check for easements—you don't want to wake up one morning to find a crew building an oil-drilling rig or constructing a tower for high tension electrical wires in the frontyard or to see a community driveway in the backyard.

Check with your local tax collector's office to see what types of charges (such as real estate taxes, water, sewer, garbage pickup, school taxes, etc.) might be outstanding. Ask what taxes and charges are levied against the property and who the responsible official is. You may find that some taxes are a separate town levy. After doing the math, you may decide these liabilities are worth assuming, but don't let them be a surprise. Also, touch base with the local official of the Internal Revenue Service. The IRS could have prior claims on the property that will be transferred to the new owner.

If you're not intimately familiar with the area, call the local office of your state Environmental Protection Agency, a good source of information about possible hazards. Find out what comparable properties have sold for in the area recently to determine the true market value of the real estate you're considering. Talk to the neighbors; after all, they've been living around the property for years and probably know everything right and wrong with it.

Wealth Secrets

Every auction should have at least five items that interest you. If not, pass up the event.

Financing

This is an essential part of the auction process; you must have your financing arranged before you bid on any properties. It's this up-front money that allows you to get those fabulous buys. In some cases with government properties, only the earnest money is required prior to purchase. But you'll still need the remainder of the down payment readily available, and you'll have 30 to 60 days to come up with the balance of the purchase price.

FYI

At an auction, the term liquid funds *means cash, money orders, or a certified or cashier's check for the required amount. Have a supply of certified checks or money orders made out to yourself so you can endorse them over to an escrow agent if and when you complete a successful bid. If you don't use them, you can deposit them back into your own bank account. You'll need separate money orders or checks for each property. For example, if the earnest money requirement is $500, then each money order or check must be made in that amount; a money order for $1,000 would allow you to bid on only one property.*

Disposal Plan

No matter how great a deal you get on the buy, your plan for disposing of the property is what makes you money. Before you bid, decide if you're buying the property to keep and rent or to fix up and sell. Run the numbers and make sure the worst-case scenario will still be profitable for you.

The Game Plan

Picture a professional basketball coach who waits until about ten minutes before a game to say to his team, "Go out there; run around the court like crazy; get in the other team's way; and make as many baskets as you can." It's an absurd thought, isn't it? You know coaches spend endless hours preparing their game plans, considering all the factors that could influence their own team and the opposition. Serious auction buyers take the same approach.

To develop your own game plan, first decide what you're going to use the property for. Is it for yourself or an investment? If it's an investment, are you buying to keep or sell? Then develop a profile of the type of property you want. For example, if you want single-family homes, in an auction of hundreds of properties you might quickly exclude all the commercial properties, raw land, condominiums, and multiunit buildings. Do your necessary inspections and research and come up with five properties you're going to bid on.

Next, review all the paperwork to ensure that you can execute the necessary documents to complete the purchase if you should have the winning bid. If you have a question, call the agency ahead of time to get it cleared up. Set your budget and have your financing in place.

Finally, check your personal comfort items. You might want to take an umbrella, an extra sweater, a folding chair, extra writing materials, or even bottled water. Some government auctions go from early in the morning until evening, and they provide little or no conveniences.

If at any point during the auction you have doubts about your game plan, do what the pros do: sit down and abstain. Monitor all bids and track every winning bid. Then use the event as a learning experience when you develop your next game plan.

Finding a Niche at Auctions

Carroll and Melisa Wimett use a variety of strategies in their real estate investing, but one they like the best is buying foreclosure properties at auction. In Chapter 2, I told you about the first two properties they bought at foreclosure auctions that netted more in one summer than Melisa had made teaching all year.

Those deals have become commonplace for the Wimetts. Just a few examples: They bought one house for $66,001 that appraised at $86,500 and now generates $150 a month in positive cash flow. Another was purchased for $90,769 and sold for $118,500. Still another was bought for $73,000 and sold for $115,000. "Our children are always excited when we come home from an auction with a new house," Melisa says.

Auction Day Activities

Registration. Always arrive early at an auction; 45 minutes before "show time" is usually early enough. This gives you plenty of time to register—a process that typically involves merely filling out a card with your name and contact information. Sometimes you may be required to show identification, so have a driver's license or other legal ID with you just in case. You'll be issued a form of bidder's identification that allows you access to the bidding floor and contains a bidder's number that will be used when a bid is consummated. You'll also be required to show that you have in your possession enough liquid funds to use as earnest money for at least one property. If you intend to bid on more than one property, you'll need funds for each successful bid—and those amounts may be different, so read the terms and conditions carefully. Typically, the earnest money required for affordable housing runs around $500, other residential offerings tend to range from $1,000 to $2,000, and commercial properties require anywhere from $5,000 to $50,000 or more.

Catalog review. Once you've registered, take a look at the prospectus to make sure no changes have been made in the properties you're planning to bid on. It's common for properties to be added and deleted right up to the time bidding starts. Review the terms and conditions as though you've never seen them before. Then sit back, take a few deep breaths, and get ready for the show to begin.

Opening announcement. As part of his opening announcement, the chief auctioneer will announce any last-minute substitution of properties that occurred after the catalog went to press. He'll also announce the rules of the auction; he has the last word on this and can change the rules even at the last minute. He'll explain how defaults will be handled when the winning bidder can't perform and what role the backup bidder will have. At some auctions, defaulted items are offered to the backup bidder; at others, they're brought back on the floor. If you are a backup bidder, make sure they take your number as well as the winner's.

Warning

Do not, under any circumstances, overextend yourself at an auction by spending more than you had planned or than you have the resources to pay. Those due dates are real, and extensions or alternative payment arrangements are rare.

The colonel and his cheerleaders. Referring to the auctioneer as "colonel" dates back to the Roman era when the military often held auctions. Today's auctioneers strut across the stage chanting a siren's song designed to lure the unsuspecting into the trap. The voice inflections and the speed at which they speak are calculated to bring a response. Auctioneering is theatrical consumerism at its best—and auctioneers are paid on a percentage basis of what they sell, so their goal is to whip the crowd into a frenzy to get the bids up as high as possible.

The folks running around, waving frantically, and yelling loudly may resemble cheerleaders, but they are the auctioneer's assistants. They are seasoned sales professionals who get into your face, looking to spot your bid and lead you over it. These are not government employees; they work for the auction company, and their job is to get the highest price for their company.

■ How Much Should You Bid and Where Do You Get the Money?

Many rules of thumb address how much to bid, and one is no more correct than another. One of the most popular is the rule of 40-60-80. A limit of 40 percent of market value is wise because it sets a standard for a really good buy. If you are selling to consumers directly (that is, if you plan to put the house on the market and sell to a homeowner rather than an investor), you can buy at up to 60 percent and still make a profit. Consumers buying for themselves should never pay more than 80 percent. Even 70 percent of the total value is high. For merchandise, many use 25 percent of the wholesale price as a rule of thumb.

Where does the money come from? You may have sufficient savings for smaller purchases, or you could put together an investment group of friends and relatives. There are plenty of investors out there who are willing to put up the money for someone who knows what they're doing at auctions.

It's your turn. The moment you've been anticipating is finally here: The property you want is on the block, the bids are coming in, and the starting point you set for yourself has been reached. Make your bid. If necessary, keep bidding until you reach your limit. Then stop.

Once your limit is passed, take yourself out of the bidding for that particular property. You're not leaving the auction; you're just staying within the profit parameters you set for yourself. There will be other properties up for bid, and often previously sold properties will find their way back to the floor. The pros know that the only successful bid is a profitable bid.

You won't win every bid, but there will be a time when your bid is the high one, it's below your self-imposed limit, the hammer falls, and your number is announced as the winner. Don't start the party yet—you're not quite finished.

What did I do? You may experience a moment of panic when your winning bid is announced. That's natural. Just keep in mind that you don't own the property yet. You have to go to the closing area, do the paperwork, and pay your earnest money and whatever other funds are due at the auction (perhaps a down payment or sometimes even the full payment). All of this should be done according to the terms and conditions described in the catalog. Now you can do the one thing the catalog doesn't tell you: Celebrate!

Disposition. But don't celebrate for long. As a real estate investor, now that you own the property, it's time to make money on it. Of course, if you were buying for your own use, you're finished. But if you were buying to rent or resell, it's time to get to work on whatever fix-up needs to be done and begin marketing the property.

Words of Wisdom

Your auction demeanor is important. An auction is a place where patience really pays off. Appear comfortable, almost uninterested. Treat auctions as you would a game of poker, and you'll come out a big winner.

■ How to Bid

A wide range of theories suggest how to bid, and even legitimate experts don't always agree on the most efficient way to proceed. Some experts advise jumping right in to be the first bidder on any item you want because it sends a signal that bidders who are not serious should stay away from this one.

Other experts like to assess the mood of the crowd and scope out their opponents before they start to bid, believing that knowing something about the competition gives them an edge. But there is one exception to this approach: If the auction is slow and one of the first items offered is one you are interested in, go for the first bid. One of the tools an auctioneer has to excite a crowd and get things moving is to let a fast bid go. Then he talks about what a great bargain you just got, enticing the marginal bidders into the fray.

Success Starts with the First Step

When Glenn and Michelle Kuperus bought their first property, it was a rehab they intended to fix up and flip, because they were afraid of tenants. They also had only $3 in cash, an empty checking account, and a maxed-out credit card. But they got an FHA Title I loan, fixed up that property, and moved on to the next one.

In their first year of investing, they bought 4 properties. The following year, they bought 11 properties and walked away from closing at one deal with a check for $26,000. In just two years, they had exceeded their goals, owned income-producing properties worth more than $1.5 million, and were generating enough positive cash flow to quit their jobs. They're not afraid of tenants anymore. Even more important, they say their real estate business has given them more time to spend with each other and their children. And now they have the money to do things they'd only dreamed about before.

Still other experts like to wait until the bid is well established before jumping in. Sometimes, though, this just stiffens the resolve of the other bidders for the short term. If you're looking for a great deal (not just a good deal), your limits will likely be lower than those of most participants.

So if you shouldn't start too early or too late, when *should* you start? No perfect formula or rule set in stone exists. But a general guide is to enter the bidding at the midway point of your bid limit. For example, if you plan to limit your bid to $40,000, you should start participating when the bids reach $20,000.

To bid, stand up or wave your catalog in the air and announce your bid in a loud, clear voice. Keep your hand up and, if necessary, repeat the bid until it is acknowledged.

Now, ignore everyone else, especially the auctioneer's assistants. Concentrate on the auctioneer; listen to the bid increment and don't let him jump it. For example, let's say he is going in increments of $5,000. If the last bid is $25,000 and you bid $30,000, a smart auctioneer sensing a winning bid might suddenly call for $40,000. If you're not careful, and if one of the assistants is trying to distract you, you might think you are not the lead bid and call out $40,000. This is called *bid running* and refers to the way the auctioneer actually makes you bid against yourself. Don't let it happen.

You don't have to bid in the auctioneer's increments. Using the above example, if you were at $25,000, someone else bid $30,000, and the auctioneer called for $40,000, you don't have to jump to that amount. There are numerous bidding signs, but the one most frequently used is the time-out signal like the one used in sports. Stand up, make a T sign with your hands, and, when recognized, announce your bid as $32,000, $35,000, or whatever. If no one bids higher, you'll have the top bid.

■ Correcting a Bad Bid

No bid is final until the gavel is down. If you make a mistake on a bid, immediately jump up and yell "Withdrawn!" as loud as you can.

If your bid is not accurately announced, treat it as a mistake and yell out "Mistake!" Then repeat the bid as you intended it to be. Even in the fast-paced world of auctions, mistakes can be corrected, but you must act in time.

Spotting Illegal Tricks and Tactics

Even though a lot of excitement and pressure permeates an auction, fraud is almost unheard of at major auctions with credible institutions. The auction houses have too much to lose. Even so, you may encounter some questionable actions and must be able to recognize them.

Study the auctioneer and get a handle on his theatrics. Learn the tricks he uses to play up an item. Monitor his cadence so you don't get caught up in its rhythm.

If a high opening bid suddenly vanishes and the action continues lower, always assume that it was not an error but a calculated attempt to force up value. Air bids or phantom bids mean the same thing: The auctioneer has recognized a bid that isn't there to either hype or boost the process. This is a sure sign of a crooked auction. Pay attention early, because once you start bidding, you won't spot it.

Sometimes auctioneers try to assist their friends by accepting their bids before anyone else can bid more. This is known as "fast gavel." Stay alert and assert yourself, and you won't be a victim of this type of auction abuse.

If advance bids are permitted, be wary if it seems that there are a large number of them. Never trust an auctioneer who always seems to start with an advance bid.

Watch for people in the audience who always seem to be in the thick of the process but never there at the end of it. Do they seem to surface only when the bidding gets slow? If so, they are either auction buffoons or shills in the employ of the auction house. Run, don't walk, away from these auctions. There are too many legitimate bargains out there to try to win at a stacked auction.

Don't Catch Auction Fever

Catching auction fever means losing control in the bidding process and bidding far more than you can afford or than the property is worth. This is probably the biggest mistake novices make; they get caught up in the excitement and run the bid up too high. This is why you need to set the price you're willing to pay for a property before the auction and then stick to that number. If someone else wants to pay more, fine. You'll find another property you can make money on at the price you're willing to pay.

To avoid auction fever, it helps to bring someone with you—a person you trust who knows what your game plan and limits are. Pay attention if your friend nudges you and tells you to slow down and back off.

Remember, you don't lose when you don't win the bid. You lose only when you exceed your bid limit and discover later that you have eliminated your profit margin. You win when you get the property at or below the price that makes it profitable for you.

MILLIONAIRE MENTOR Auction Highlights

- Auctions are a great place to pick up bargains on real estate and other merchandise.

- Though auctions may be exciting and chaotic, a systematic approach is necessary. Study the auction announcement and prospectus, attend the prebid conference, and do your research in advance to ensure a profitable experience.

- At the auction, pay close attention to what is going on. Allowing yourself to be distracted by the activity can be very expensive.

- Bids can be corrected if you act in time. If you make a mistake on a bid or if a bid was not accurately announced, immediately yell "Mistake!" and then repeat your bid as you intended it to be.

- Avoid auction fever. Stay in control and never bid more than a property is worth or than you can afford.

CHAPTER 8

Mobile Homes

A Quick Way to Build Cash Flow and Achieve Financial Independence

They're affordable, they're easy to buy, and they can be virtual cash-generating machines. Especially if you're a beginning real estate investor or if you have credit problems and/or no cash, mobile homes are a great way to start and build your business. I call them little boxes that spit out cash.

To make money from mobile homes, the first thing you need to do is get rid of any preconceived notions you may have about "trailer parks." Understand that many people choose to live in mobile homes because of their affordability, but many also enjoy the mobile home lifestyle—just as some people prefer condominiums and others prefer single-family homes. Mobile homes are popular as retirement housing, as seasonal second homes, and as primary homes for young families and individuals in the low-income to middle-income brackets. Though most mobile homes are technically mobile—meaning they have wheels and can be moved—the vast majority of them are installed on a site and never moved.

Let's take a moment to clarify some of the terminology used to describe mobile homes. The terms *mobile home* and *manufactured home* are often used interchangeably; technically, mobile homes are mobile housing units built *before* June 15, 1976, and manufactured homes are mobile housing units built *after* June 15, 1976. The term *modular home* applies to factory-built housing that is designed to be permanently installed; this chapter does not address modular homes.

Mobile homes account for almost 10 percent of the total housing stock in the United States. You'll find them in cities, out in the country, in good neighborhoods, and in distressed areas. They're often close to schools and shopping. And they range in price from a few hundred dollars (for a fixer-upper) to tens of thousands of dollars (for a new, high-end model).

Mobile homes are most commonly found in parks, often called mobile home or manufactured home communities. Typically, a park's owner rents lots on which people place their mobile homes. The parks may feature a variety of amenities, such as a coin laundry, clubhouse, recreation facilities, storage, and so on. The nicer the park, the higher the rent you can charge. Mobile homes on land outside parks are usually in rural areas or other places with relaxed zoning.

Before you begin investing in mobile homes, get to know your local market. First, determine that you actually have a market. You won't find mobile homes in large established metropolitan areas such as New York City, San Francisco, Chicago, or Boston. But you will find them in younger, smaller cities, the suburbs, and rural areas. Once you've identified the mobile home opportunities in your market, visit parks, talk to the managers, even answer some For Rent and For Sale signs just for practice. Visit dealers to see what they have in the way of new homes and trade-ins.

Smart Thinking

Plenty of people would like to invest in mobile homes but can't find the deals. You should use the same techniques you learned in Chapter 4 to flip mobile homes to wholesalers and other investors without ever owning them yourself and make hundreds or even thousands of dollars on each transaction.

Mobile homes are profitable regardless of the economic cycle. They are an excellent way to provide safe, attractive, affordable housing, especially to people in the low-income and moderate-income range, or even senior citizens on a fixed income. *You can keep the mobile homes you buy to rent, or you can sell them to a homeowner or another investor for a quick profit.*

One of the key benefits of renting mobile homes is that the rent you receive is only slightly less than that you'd receive for a similar site-built home. Because your cost to buy the mobile home is a small fraction of the amount you'd pay for that similar site-built unit, your profits are substantially higher.

From a consumer perspective, one of the disadvantages of buying mobile homes is that, much like automobiles, they rarely appreciate in value to any significant degree. However, when you buy them used as an investor, they tend to hold their value over time. So if you've held one for a while and then decide to sell it, you probably won't make a big profit, but you'll likely get your original investment back—which means the money you made from rent while you owned it is pure profit.

■ Evaluating a Mobile Home

To determine whether to buy, and how much to pay for, a particular mobile home, you must first look at its physical condition. Check the floors and ceiling for soundness. Inspect the windows for leaks and airtightness. Be sure the plumbing works. Check all appliances to determine whether they are in good working condition. Take a look at the exterior in general to see if it's solid. Examine the wheels and axles; they'll need to be in good condition if you have to move the home.

To determine the market value of a mobile home, you can hire a mobile home appraiser, but with a little information and practice, you should be able to do this yourself. Study recent sales in the area, keeping in mind all the variables—age, size, manufacturer, accessories, and so forth—until you can comfortably calculate mobile home values.

The National Automobile Dealers Association (NADA) resale book provides a range of market prices for mobile homes, or you can visit <www.nadaguides.com>. Of course, the actual value of the home you're looking at will be affected by its condition, special features, location, and the local market. The year the home was built also has a significant impact on its value. You can use Figure 8.1, the Mobile Home Information Sheet, to help you determine the market value of any particular mobile home.

FIGURE 8.1

■

Mobile Home
Information
Sheet

Seller's name _____

Day phone _____ Evening phone _____

Location of mobile home (address) _____

On leased lot _____ On owned land _____ Attached to land _____

Year _____ Make _____ Model _____

Reason for selling _____

Vacancy date _____ Asking price _____

Is title clear? _____ Lien amount _____

Lien holder _____

Time on market _____

Description of home:

_____ Single-wide _____ Double-wide _____ Bedrooms _____ Baths

Other features _____

Fixtures/Appliances/Accessories included:

_____ refrigerator _____ stove _____ dishwasher _____ washer _____ dryer

_____ carpet _____ vinyl flooring _____ drapes _____ other window coverings

_____ deck _____ storage shed _____ carport _____ garage

_____ awnings _____ wheels _____ axles _____ skirting

Notes _____

Words of Wisdom

Network with mobile home industry professionals, such as park managers, mobile home movers and contractors, and dealers. They'll be a source of referrals, tenants, buyers, sellers, and labor.

Mobile Home Fix-Up

When it comes to fix-up, mobile homes are not the same as site-built homes. The sizes of doors, windows, and fixtures are usually slightly different. In most cases, you'll have to get parts from a mobile home parts supplier rather than your local home and building supply store.

Keep in mind that mobile homes are designed to be moved. That means they are built with lighter materials that can withstand the vibration and stress of being hauled down roads. So when you're doing repairs and renovations, you have to be careful not to affect the structural integrity of the unit.

On newer units—those built in the past 10 to 15 years—the manufacturers should still be able to provide you with the engineering plans, and parts should be readily available. With older units, you may not be able to find the exact part you want, so you'll often have to improvise.

Avoid mobiles that need extensive rehab. For maximum profitability, focus on the ones that need a minimal amount of cosmetic fix-up, such as paint, carpet, and minor repairs.

Bright Idea

A key drawback to mobile home living is the lack of storage space. Make your mobile homes more attractive to renters by adding storage sheds. They're inexpensive to install and the cost can be recouped in a year or less. You can do the same thing with an aluminum carport.

Who Are the Sellers?

Mobile home sellers are much like traditional site-built homesellers—they're all ages, have a variety of family situations, and are motivated for a variety of reasons. They may be selling because they're moving up to a larger mobile home or a site-built home. They may be relocating because of a job. They may have to move for a wide range of personal reasons; or they may have inherited the mobile home and just want to get rid of it. They may be senior citizens who can no longer live independently. They may be investors. Or they may be in financial distress.

Treat mobile home sellers as you would any other seller. Build rapport and ask questions to determine the real reason they are selling and what they need from the deal.

■ Mobile Home Foreclosures

In Chapter 6, you learned about real estate foreclosures, but because mobile homes are technically not real estate, they are not subject to the same foreclosure procedures. That doesn't mean, however, that lenders have no recourse if buyers don't pay. Instead, the process is similar to the one that regulates defaulting on an automobile loan: the lender repossesses the car.

An important difference between a mobile home repossession and a real estate foreclosure is what happens after lenders take back the property. With real estate, lenders foreclose, and the property is sold at auction to the highest bidder. The lenders have the auction proceeds go up to the amount they are owed, and then entities with junior liens are paid with whatever funds might be left over. If a property doesn't sell for enough money to pay off all the mortgages and liens, those debts are wiped out. But with a mobile home, if the lender is unable to sell the home for the full amount due on the loan, the original borrower is responsible for the remainder.

For example, let's say the owner of a traditional site-built home is unable to make his loan payments and the bank forecloses. There is a first mortgage of $75,000 and a second mortgage of $15,000. The house is auctioned on the courthouse steps for $80,000. The first mortgage holder gets $75,000, the second mortgage holder gets $5,000, and the remaining debt of $10,000 is eliminated and the now previous owner walks away owing nothing. By contrast, let's take a situation where an individual defaults on a mobile home loan with a balance of $15,000. The lender repossesses the home and sells it at auction for $12,000. The borrower still owes the lender $3,000, even though he no longer has possession of the mobile home. This is a key reason why people facing repossession of their mobile homes are usually very willing to deal with an investor who wants to help them with their problem. Of

If One Is Good, an Entire Park Is Better

Carroll and Melisa Wimett's first mobile home purchase was a single unit they bought for $6,000 and rented through a lease purchase agreement for a $1,200 initial option and $332 per month. In the meantime, the Wimetts bought a mobile home park. The mobile home tenant didn't exercise the purchase option, and when he moved out, Melisa moved that mobile home into her own park.

Melisa calls their mobile home park "the best, sweetest, and most profitable deal" she and Carroll have done. The property is eight acres with 19 mobile homes, a site-built house, an office, and a laundry building. "It was nasty, old, and falling apart," Melisa says. "There was trash everywhere, and stray dogs and cats. Two of the homes looked like they'd been bombed. The units leaked, the wiring was bad so some of the metal doors shocked you, the carpets were rotten, many of the units didn't have appliances, the mailboxes were rusty, bugs were everywhere, and potholes covered the roads—it was so nasty that we considered just leaving." But they didn't. They took another look at the property through their "investor eyes," imagined the stinking garbage as the smell of money, and made an offer of $479,000. Using seller financing, they structured the deal so they could walk away from closing with $2,400 cash.

The Wimetts fired the park manager, evicted all but two of the tenants, and began the challenging task of getting the property into shape. They removed two homes and replaced them with better models. As the rehabbing on each unit was completed, the unit was rented. All of the mobile homes and buildings on the property were painted to match, giving the park the uniform look of an upscale apartment complex.

At purchase, the property appraised at $480,000 and the rents were $85 weekly. Six months later, it appraised at $685,000 and the rents were $120 to $140 weekly. At full occupancy (and the Wimetts have no problem finding tenants for their attractive, well-managed property), the park generates $7,718 in positive cash flow.

course, finding these folks *before* the home is repossessed can be a challenge, because repossessions don't have the same public notice requirements that real estate foreclosures do. Look for language in the For Sale ads that indicates a financial distress situation, or listen carefully when you talk to sellers for clues.

Finding mobile homes that have already been repossessed is easy. When you visit retail sales centers as part of your market familiarization process, ask who does their financing. Then contact those lenders, tell them you are an investor interested in used mobile homes, and ask for a list of the mobile homes they have repossessed that are for sale. Believe me, they are thrilled to provide you with that information—so thrilled that they'll probably have a messenger hand-carry the list to you.

Typically, these homes are on a storage lot. The good news is that it's easy for you to check out several of them in a short time; the bad news is that you'll have to move whatever homes you buy, so be sure to factor that cost into your calculations when you're making your offer. Another drawback to repossessed mobile homes is their condition. It's likely the owners haven't taken good care of them, especially in the months immediately prior to the repossession. Also, double-wides and triple-wides are separated when they are moved, and the lenders usually don't bother to have them reattached while they are sitting on the storage lot because of the additional cost. The open sides may be covered with nothing more than heavy plastic, which means the unit may have suffered moisture or other weather damage, so inspect them carefully before making your offer.

Insurance Tip

If you're going to own mobile homes and rent them, shop around for your insurance. Rates can vary widely from one company to another, and not all insurers will cover this type of housing product.

■ Mobile Home Financing

Mobile homes are not real estate; they are vehicles and therefore are financed as vehicles or personal property. This is why traditional bank financing is difficult to obtain on mobile homes, and especially used units. When financing is available, you typically pay anywhere from 3 to 5 percent more than you would on a real estate loan. Literally hundreds of thousands of used mobile homes are being resold every year in a market with limited traditional financing options. If you can be creative, you can make a fortune in this area.

Most mobile home sellers understand the financing challenges their buyers face and are willing to provide financing to close the sale. Or you can negotiate a joint venture with the sellers, giving them a chance to share in your profits if they work with you on the acquisition.

You may find mobiles priced low enough that you can take a credit card cash advance to pay for them. Do this only when you're planning a quick flip and you have a buyer lined up. Or use the option techniques you learned in Chapter 5 to control the mobile home until you find a tenant or buyer.

As with site-built homes, you'll find you have plenty of potential money partners who will fund your mobile home deals for a share of the profits.

Depending on the seller's motivation and plans, you may consider a sale-leaseback, in which you buy the mobile home and the seller stays and pays you rent. Approach these arrangements with caution, especially if the seller is financially distressed.

Did You Know?

The average life span of a new manufactured home is 55.8 years.

■ Ownership Documents

The ownership documents for mobile homes are similar to the same type of title you have for your car, truck, or boat.

If you decide to affix the mobile home permanently to a piece of land and have it count as real property rather than as a vehicle, you have to go to your motor vehicle department and apply to have the title eliminated. The state takes the information on the mobile home and combines it with the real estate, the title is removed from the records, and the mobile home becomes real property. Just be absolutely certain you won't ever want to move the home again, because a title is one of the prerequisites for obtaining a hauling permit.

The biggest advantage to eliminating the title to a mobile home is that the process automatically improves the land it's on and enables you to obtain conventional real estate financing at far better rates and terms than you typically get on a mobile home.

■ What You Need to Know about Mobile Home Manufacturers and Dealers

The manufacturing and sales structure for mobile homes is similar to that of automobiles. Each manufacturer has several lines with varying amenities. Some manufacturers focus on higher-end homes, others on economy models. All offer a wide array of option and upgrade packages. Many of the homes look similar but differ in quality and durability, just as the various makes and models of cars do.

A number of ways can be used to determine the year and make of a mobile home. The trade names are found by the front door or at the bottom right-hand corner of the towing side of the home. Red HUD labels are attached to the exterior siding on the rear of the home. Identification serial numbers are stamped into the metal on the front metal cross member or on the tow bar.

Each home has a data plate with information about the home and is recognizable because it includes an outline of the United States. It may be placed on the inside of the master bedroom closet doors, on the wall inside the closet, on the inside of a kitchen cabinet door, or near the electrical box inside the home.

■

SUCCESS STORY

Great Things Can Come in Small Packages

Mobile home parks don't have to be large to be profitable. Two of my students, Su M. and Curt H., found a small four-unit mobile home park they were able to purchase with just $123.34 cash at closing. With all four mobile homes rented, the park generates $500 a month in positive cash flow. And that was just their first investment—Su and Curt have been steadily building their real estate holdings ever since. One of my students says that mobile homes made him upwardly mobile. His first real estate deal was a mobile home he bought for $2,500. Three months later, he sold it for $5,000. He used that cash to buy a house, which he fixed up and sold for a $30,000 profit. He reinvested that money and bought several more houses, then a small apartment building—and then he decided to take a class on real estate.

If he could do that without any training, what can you do with the knowledge I'm sharing with you now?

Typically, mobile home dealers represent one manufacturer. Visit their showrooms and lots to become familiar with what the manufacturer offers. Collect the literature and know what the option packages include. Keep in mind that dealers also take trade-ins, so talk to them about those. If they have used homes for sale, take a look at them; consider their condition and price, and use that information in setting prices for the ones you buy and sell. They probably won't tell you what they paid for any of them, just as car dealers won't tell you what they allowed as a trade-in for a used car on their lot. Many new home dealers simply wholesale their trade-ins to used home dealers—again, just as it's done in the automotive industry. So shop the used dealers, too, to become familiar with the mobile home market in your area.

MILLIONAIRE MENTOR Mobile Home Highlights

- Mobile homes are affordable, easy to buy, and great cash flow generators.

- Mobile homes account for nearly 10 percent of the total housing stock in the United States.

- Mobile homes cost less to buy but generate as much cash flow as low-income and moderate-income rental site-built homes.

- Mobile homes rarely appreciate in value; however, when purchased to use as an investment, they usually hold their value and sell years later for what you paid for them. That means you'll recoup your original investment, and the rent you received is profit.

- Because mobile homes technically are not real estate but vehicles, they are subject to repossession, not foreclosure.

- Mobile home rehabbing is somewhat different from rehabbing a site-built home, because the sizes of doors, windows, and fixtures are different, and the homes are built to withstand being moved. You have to buy parts from a mobile home parts supplier, not a local home and building supply store.

- Traditional financing can be difficult to obtain on mobile homes, especially used ones, but this is an incentive for sellers to provide financing. Also, many used mobile homes are priced low enough that you could charge the purchase price to a credit card if you had to—but do this only when you're going to flip the unit and get rid of that high-interest debt.

■ Mobile homes can be a great starting point for a profitable real estate investing career.

CHAPTER 9

Government Grants and Loans

Resources for Business Owners and Real Estate Investors

Have you thought about who benefits when you achieve financial independence and build wealth? Right now, you're probably mentally listing yourself, your family, close friends, your church, and charities you support. But when you build a successful business, you also have a strong and positive impact on your local community and the overall economy. And that's why it's in the government's best interest for you to become wealthy.

When you think about it, it makes sense. Successful real estate investors increase the value of their holdings and get distressed properties back on the tax rolls to generate income for municipalities. Successful business owners create jobs, and the people who fill those jobs pay taxes and contribute to the overall economy. Clearly, the government has a vested interest in the success of your real estate business, and that's why there are literally thousands of local, state, and national government programs that will help you make money.

Government help in your endeavors to make money is not a new concept. From the earliest days of commerce, governments have helped their citizens embark on a variety of business ventures. As the United States grew from a tiny cluster of colonies on the East Coast and expanded westward, land grants to Americans willing to homestead or farm were plentiful. Local, state, and federal programs that encourage community development and business formation and expansion are abundant. And all you need to do to take advantage of these programs is to ask.

If you're like most people, chances are your interactions with various government agencies have involved paying them money—paying income, property, and other taxes; buying vehicle tags; and applying for driver's and even marriage licenses. You're conditioned to think that if the government is involved, you may as well get out your checkbook and start writing. This chapter helps you reverse that mindset: When the government is involved, you'll get out deposit slips because your bank balance is going to grow.

How much money is available? Literally billions of dollars. Don't let the headlines fool you into thinking there's no government money available for entrepreneurs. Economic and election cycles prompt politicians and pundits to scream and whine about budget cuts and the need to reduce the size of the government. Regardless of where you stand politically, the government is growing and money is available. And you can put that money to good use—improving your community, providing needed housing for deserving people, and securing your own financial future in the process.

■ How the Government Helps

Government assistance is available through a variety of programs. Seven basic types are the following:

1. **Loans.** These funds are lent by a government agency for a specific period with a reasonable expectation of repayment. Government loans may or may not include interest.
2. **Loan guarantees.** Government agencies agree (guarantee) to pay back part or all of a loan issued by a private lender if the borrower defaults.
3. **Interest subsidies.** To help defray the cost of borrowing money, a government agency pays a portion of the interest on a loan.
4. **Grants.** These are funds given by a government agency that do not have to be repaid.

Chiropractors Needed an Adjustment, and They Got It

Jay C. and Brad R. were partners in a successful chiropractic practice, but they wanted more. After deciding to invest in real estate, they bought a HUD foreclosure for $84,000. It was nearly new and in great shape, and in just three weeks they sold it for $101,500 without putting any money or work into the house.

They used the profits from that sale as seed money for their next project: building a duplex to house eight handicapped people for the state. That property is worth $175,000 and is under a ten-year lease to the state—and generates $800 a month in positive cash flow.

In just seven months, they accumulated $345,000 in real estate with a net positive cash flow of $1,050 per month. It won't be long before they make the "adjustment" out of their chiropractic practice and into real estate investing full-time.

5. **Direct payments.** These are funds paid by government agencies to individuals, private companies, and institutions, which may have a specified purpose or be for unrestricted use.

6. **Insurance.** Coverage that ensures payment for losses from specified risks provided under specific government programs. The insurance itself may be actually provided by the government agency or through an insurance company, and premium payments may or may not be required.

7. **Information.** The government provides advice and guidance on various aspects of business, real estate investing, property rehabilitation, and more. The government also collects and disseminates a wide range of statistical information you can use to make investment decisions and develop effective marketing plans.

FYI

Redlining *is a term used to describe the practice of discriminating against customers in a particular geographic area. It originated at a time when banks would draw a red line around certain areas on a map and refuse to make loans to individuals or businesses within those "redlined" areas. Areas that typically would be redlined were predominantly minority occupied, low income, and often high crime. Redlining is illegal, and lenders and other businesses that practice it face substantial penalties.*

◼ Section 8

Section 8 of the Housing and Community Development Act of 1974 is the housing assistance payments program. This program allows very low-income families to choose and lease or purchase safe, decent, affordable privately owned rental housing. The government makes the rent payments directly to the landlord, which means landlords don't have to worry about late rent or other collection problems. As part of the program, families receiving Section 8 assistance also get counseling on how to take care of property and manage their finances—another benefit to you as the landlord.

◼ Community Reinvestment Act (CRA)

One of the most beneficial pieces of legislation for real estate investors is the Community Reinvestment Act (CRA), which is a federal law designed to combat the illegal practice of redlining. Enacted in 1977, the CRA "encourages" federally insured banks and thrifts to meet the credit needs of their entire community, including low-income and moderate-income residents. In other words, all banks offering Federal Deposit Insurance Corporation (FDIC)-insured deposits must comply with CRA regulations, and they are carefully monitored to be sure they do so.

What this means for you and your buyers is that you have access to funding for properties in areas that may not have qualified for financing before passage of the CRA. You can buy distressed properties at wholesale, rehab them, and then sell them to someone who may not be able to qualify for traditional financing.

Many CRA loan products are geared to first-time homebuyers (by definition, those who have not owned their own home in the last three years; displaced spouses also qualify) in low-income to moderate-income brackets. They typically offer market or below-market rates with low down payments from the borrower's own funds. They allow higher debt-to-income ratios and have more lenient credit guidelines than conventional mortgage products. And many banks waive the private mortgage insurance (PMI) that is typically required on low down payment loans. These generous terms mean that borrowers can qualify for more mortgage money than they can with a conventional loan. And the more money your buyer is qualified to borrow, the less likely you are to have to lower your price.

As part of their CRA programs, some banks offer incentives to investors who are looking to create or rehabilitate either rental or ownership housing for low-income to moderate-income residents in your community. Many areas also offer down payment and closing cost assistance, and when you take the time to learn about these programs, you can help your buyers—and that makes selling your houses even easier.

To find out what's available in your area, ask for the vice president of residential lending of all the major banks and then ask that official who the CRA contact is; or ask for the person who handles affordable loan products. This is the person who knows what the bank will and won't do. Ask questions and be sure you completely understand their programs. Make it clear that you'll be referring customers to them. Always remember: The banks *have* to make these loans; the law requires it, and the FDIC is watching them.

FYI

Mortgage brokers don't have access to CRA products, and only a few real estate investors take the time to find out what's available in their areas. This gives you a tremendous advantage in selling your properties.

■ Understanding Income Ranges

How much do people in the low-income and moderate-income ranges actually earn? It depends on where you are. The government establishes the definitions based on an area's median income. Here's how it's figured:

Very low income	Someone who makes 50 percent or less of the median income
Poverty level	30 percent of the median income
Low income	80 percent of the median income
Moderate income	120 percent of the median income

■ What's in It for You?

So now you know how the government helps buyers get into their own homes and how you can benefit from knowing those programs, but what can the government do to help you directly? There are so many programs out there, and new ones are being developed all the time—it would be impossible for you to take advantage of all of them.

HUD, for example, through its Neighborhood Initiatives grants, gives away millions of dollars each year for neighborhood revitalization and affordable housing creation and to improve distressed areas. HUD also acquires properties through foreclosures, abandonment, and estates, which are then sold to investors like you to be rehabbed and resold. This agency is also a great source for first-time homebuyers.

An excellent government program is rehabilitation mortgages. HUD offers a number of programs with various parameters that insure loans to enable borrowers to finance both the purchase (or refinancing) of a house and the cost of its rehabilitation through a single mortgage. With this type of loan, you don't have to get one loan to buy the property and another to do the rehab; you can get a single long-term fixed or adjustable rate loan that covers both the acquisition and rehabilitation of a property.

In Chapter 4, I told you about Rosanna and Michael Reilly and several of their wholesale deals. Their very first deal was a two-unit property that was rented but needed work. Using a 203k loan (a particular type of rehabilitation mortgage), they purchased the property for $105,000 with $2,500 down. The renovations they did enhanced the property sufficiently to allow them to raise the combined rents more than $1,000, and the property is now worth $180,000.

The U.S. Department of Agriculture (USDA) provides loans, loan guarantees, and grants for the construction, acquisition, or rehabilitation of rural multifamily housing for low-income occupants. In some cases, loans and grants are also made for the construction of single-family homes as well.

The General Services Administration (GSA) routinely sells surplus government real estate through a bidding process. Surplus government real estate could include property on or near military bases that have been closed or other real estate the government owns and no longer uses. The agency

Escaping the Rat Race

A student of mine, Teresa I., was on the corporate fast track and looking to invest in real estate as a way to reduce her taxes. She heard me speak and said my story inspired her. She set a goal of replacing her six-figure corporate income with real estate cash flow, and it took her just nine months to do it.

She has amassed more than $4 million in real estate with $1.4 million in equity. She has purchased everything from IRS-seized homes, HUD and VA properties, and for-sale-by-owner properties. She's bought directly from sellers, through brokers, and at auctions. She has rehabbed more than 80 properties, selling some and holding others. Currently, her monthly cash flow exceeds $10,000, and it's growing. Clearly, what started as a tax shelter for Teresa was a path to financial freedom.

also sells surplus personal property, including automobiles. As with other government agencies, GSA programs are constantly changing, so it's a good idea to stay in touch by getting on its mailing list or regularly visiting its Web site (see the resources section for details).

The various federal and state government agencies that guarantee real estate loans are also great sources for buying property under market value. When buyers default on guaranteed loans, the agency involved pays the lender, forecloses on the property, and then sells the property typically at auction or through a bid process. The resources section includes a number of agencies that routinely have properties for sale.

Additional Government Resources

If government grants and loans aren't enough for you, the government is a resource for information and guidance that would cost you a bundle if you had to pay for them.

One of the best sources of information about your local market and business assistance is state, regional, and local economic development agencies. There are nearly 12,000 economic development groups in the United States that charge nothing for their services. They are either public or private, or most often a public-private partnership, and their purpose is to promote economic growth and development in the areas they serve. They accomplish that by encouraging new businesses to locate in their area, and to do that they've gathered all the statistics and information you'll need to effectively invest in the local real estate market.

Economic development agencies can provide you with various market demographic information; details on the real estate market, including costs, availability, zoning, and regulatory issues; and referrals to other resources. For the best overview, start with your state economic development agency, which can guide you to regional and local groups for expanded information.

It's quite common for new real estate investors to resist the idea of turning to the government for help in building their portfolios, but the government may in fact be one of your best sources for properties, funding, and advice—so take advantage of it.

MILLIONAIRE MENTOR Government Grants and Loans Highlights

- When you become wealthy through real estate investing, the government benefits. Not only are you paying more in taxes, but you are increasing the value of your holdings, returning distressed properties to the active tax rolls, creating jobs, and contributing to the overall economy in a positive way.

- Government assistance is available through direct loans, loan guarantees, interest subsidies, grants, direct payments, insurance, and information.

- You have access to virtually countless local, state, and federal programs that help individual homebuyers (to whom you sell or rent) as well as investors.

- Be sure a government grant and loan specialist is on your Power Team so you can take advantage of every opportunity available.

CHAPTER 10

Rehabbing

Quick Fixes for Cosmetically Distressed Properties

It's a rare property that won't need some sort of fix-up before you can either sell it or rent it. Plenty of people use this as an excuse for avoiding investing in real estate, but if you can see the upside, you'll realize that knowing how to fix up property can make you millions on deals others pass up. One of the most basic ways to invest in real estate is by buying cosmetically distressed properties, fixing them up, and then either selling them for an immediate profit or renting them for the long-term cash flow and for building equity. This is how I got started, and it's how countless numbers of investors who are millionaires today got their start.

There's another important reason to know about rehabbing real estate. You should be able to discount the price of any property by the repair estimates—and in many cases by more than the actual cost of repairs, because the amateur eye rarely sees that just $1,000 in paint can add $15,000 to $20,000 in retail value. So whether you're buying to rehab or for a quick flip, you need to know how to estimate repairs. Practice doing estimates every chance you get, even on properties you're not interested in buying. The more you do it, the faster and more accurate you'll be. You'll negotiate better deals when you can honestly show sellers how much things cost.

When I first started, I wasn't at all handy. I didn't know how much materials cost, didn't know how to do repairs, and didn't know how to put together estimates. But I learned. I had contractors give me estimates, and I would meet with subcontractors to pick their brains. I would ask several subcontractors to give me an estimate on the same job so I could see what was different and what was the same about their bids. It didn't take me long to figure out that most estimating is common sense. I realized that I could clean, paint, and do basic fix-up work and save thousands. I could never do plumbing, electrical work, or roofing, so I subcontracted those jobs out and still made huge profits because I understood how to price them. Eventually, I started subcontracting everything out, because my time was better spent negotiating real estate deals that would net $15,000 or $20,000 rather than saving $10 per hour on labor costs.

Whether you're a skilled craftsperson or have ten thumbs, whether you love working with your hands or hate to get dirty, you can apply the techniques described in this chapter for rehabbing properties to significantly increase your profits.

Words of Wisdom

Never fall in love with your investment property. Always remember that this isn't your home, so keep an emotional arm's length—if you don't, you'll end up spending too much on fix-up and won't negotiate the best deals.

■ Why You Shouldn't Overdo It

One of the biggest mistakes inexperienced investors make is treating investment property as they would treat their own. Certainly the repairs should be done with quality and care, but they also need to be done with an impartial attitude. Investment property needn't reflect your own taste and style—in fact, the more neutral you can keep it, the better.

A critical element of rehabbing is knowing which repairs and improvements are necessary and which ones aren't. This is not to suggest that you leave things broken or unsafe—that's not the right way to operate. You want to do the things that will make the property attractive to a buyer or tenant and make it safe and sanitary without spending any more money than you have to. For example, you don't have to wallpaper when paint is sufficient. Colors should be neutral. Fixtures should be functional but simple enough in style to blend with any décor.

When you walk through a house, how do you decide what you have to do to make it a piece of real estate you want to own or can sell? On your first trip through, when you're formulating your initial offer, you'll do "quick and dirty" estimates based on the average costs of similar repairs for necessary work that you can easily see. Once you have the property under contract—and, of course, your contract is written with a "subject to inspection" clause—you'll draw up a detailed list of work that needs to be done, get it priced, and put together a plan of action, including renegotiating the deal if necessary.

This chapter includes some general pricing guidelines for repairs, but you should become familiar with the rates in your particular area. This will come in time as you practice your estimating skills and request bids from general contractors and subcontractors. You might also check with local home improvement and building supply stores; many of those operations have standard pricing information they're willing to share.

Whether you do the work yourself or hire someone is a choice you'll make depending on your own skill level and the complexity of the work as well as your available time and cash resources. The more you can do yourself, the bigger your profit on the property will be. On the other hand, is your time better spent doing labor you can pay someone else $10 to $20 an hour to do or should you be out there looking for more property? The choice is yours to make, based on your own goals and preferences.

Many of my students over the years have chosen to work as teams—spouses, children and parents, siblings, or even unrelated friends—whatever the combination doesn't really matter. One finds the properties and negotiates the deals, while the other handles the rehab. Partnerships like this can be very productive—just ask Pete and Tony Youngs, the brothers who do our foreclosure training and have a real estate investing partnership that has made them millionaires. Be sure all the details of your mutual responsibilities are clearly spelled out in a written partnership agreement. It doesn't matter how close you are or how well you think you know the other person. Business is business; write everything down to avoid any possible misunderstandings down the road.

Most beginning investors find what works best is doing some of the work themselves and hiring handypersons or skilled laborers (such as electricians and plumbers) as necessary.

Dollars and Sense

Never pay skilled labor rates for unskilled work. Always pay a fair and reasonable wage for the work done, but don't pay more than the project warrants.

■ Be Your Own General Contractor

You can hire a general contractor to handle your rehab projects, but why give a contractor such a substantial share of your profits? This is not to say that general contractors aren't worth what you pay them—some are, some aren't. That's not the point. When you pay a general contractor, you're not only paying for the work you have done, you're paying to run their business, do their administrative work, advertise, buy and maintain equipment whether you need it or not, and mark up the cost of doing your work so they can make a profit. If you are your own general contractor, the savings and profits are yours.

Typically, general contractors don't do any of the labor involved in fixing up property. They make estimates, manage projects, supervise subcontractors, hire and fire as necessary, and oversee the jobs to completion. And though they may wear nicer clothes than the workers do, they're on the job just the same.

■ Finding Subcontractors

Where do you find good subcontractors? One way is to check the bulletin board at your local paint store or building supply store, such as Home Depot or Lowe's. You'll probably find a lot of business cards from both general contractors and subcontractors. Don't assume that just because you trust the store that a contractor is reliable and does quality work—check them all out.

Another way to find workers for your rehab projects is to drive through neighborhoods to look for people working on homes. Many will have a sign in the yard promoting their business that says something like "Another quality job by ABC Painting" and a phone number. Even if they don't have a sign, stop and talk to them. You should also talk to the person who hired them for the job and at least two, and preferably four, other references. Most newspapers have a section for handyperson services or home repair services that could also be a good resource for you.

Dollars and Sense

When choosing a subcontractor, first of all, consider quality before price. Certainly price is important and your profits are based in large part on what you pay, but quality results are critical. The lowest price can cost you more in the long run.

■ Hiring a Contractor

Get to know, and be comfortable with, contractors, whether you're hiring a general contractor or subcontractors. You want to develop a long-term, mutually rewarding relationship with them. Here are some tips to find the best contractor for the job:

Get written bids. Before you begin requesting bids, determine the full scope of the work and be sure each contractor is bidding on the same thing. You must be able to make meaningful comparisons and be sure that the contractors understand what you want done. Get every repair bid in writing, no matter how small the job; every detail has to be spelled out or you're risking some unpleasant surprises.

Do a background check. Check both professional and client references. Ask for copies of general liability and workers' compensation insurance certificates, and call the insurance carrier to confirm that the coverage is in force. Keep in mind that the contractor may not be required by law to have insurance; if he's not, make your own decision about how much risk you're willing to take. If your state licenses contractors, ask to see a copy of the license. Check with the licensing agency to see if any complaints are on file. Also check with your local better business bureau and/or another consumer protection and reporting agency to see if the contractor has been the target of complaints.

Ask contractors for five references. One should be by someone who had a problem. Ask that person to describe the problem, how long it took the contractor to correct it, what his attitude was when the complaint was made, and if he charged for fixing it.

Find out what products a contractor uses and where he gets his paint, lumber, and supplies. Call at least one supplier as a reference. Ask if the contractor pays cash or uses credit (although paying cash wouldn't rule out using a particular contractor, charging indicates a greater degree of financial stability) and if the supplier has had, or is aware of, any complaints against the contractor.

Rely on your instincts. How do you feel about the contractor personally? Is this someone you'll be comfortable working with? Does he treat you with courtesy and respect, and use terms you understand? Does he appear to be interested in building a long-term relationship?

Finally, when a contractor has done a good job for you, use him again.

■ Rehabbing without Cash

Be creative when buying things you need for your properties, especially if they're properties you're going to rehab and sell. Here's a technique that will let you do some great things with no cash out of pocket.

Let's say the house needs new carpeting. Go to an independent, mom-and-pop floor-covering business and talk to the owner. Explain that you're a real estate investor and have a property you're rehabbing. Show her what you paid for the house and how much you expect to get for it when you sell it.

Ask if she has any carpet in stock that's been on the shelf for a while. If she does, check it out to make sure the color and texture are acceptable (you don't want some brightly colored, offbeat style of carpet) and then offer to pay full retail price to have the carpet installed. But here's the catch: Instead of paying cash now, you give the carpet store an IOU that says you'll pay the bill when the property sells. Sweeten the deal by offering to pay interest on the amount. Include a provision in the note that allows the carpet store to put a lien on the property if you don't sell and pay the IOU within one year. (If you think it's going to take you more than a year to sell the property, you shouldn't have bought it in the first place.)

This is win-win. You're taking inventory off the carpet store owner's hands that she hasn't been able to sell anyway and getting new carpet for your property.

This technique can work with light fixtures, landscaping, appliances— just about anything you need to rehab a house.

■ Making Contracts Worth More Than the Paper They're Written On

When you write a contract to purchase real estate, you know to be very careful about covering all your bases and leaving nothing to chance. You have to take the same approach when making agreements with contractors and subcontractors who are going to be working on your properties. A poorly written contract for rehab work can cost you your profits and more.

In most cases, the contractor's bid is the foundation of your agreement, so let's start with that. The bid must be complete and detailed, clearly specifying everything that will be done and breaking out materials and labor. There may be times when you'll choose to accept the labor portion of the bid but supply the materials yourself. Be sure the work description includes cleanup and disposal of work-related waste and replaced items (such as old gutters, carpet, fixtures, etc.). Do not accept the phrase "repair or replace" in a contract; find out if it means the contractor is repairing *or* replacing, and be sure his plans are acceptable.

The agreement should include a standard waiver of liability and specify the start and finish dates. Add a penalty clause so that if the work is not finished on time (or within an agreed-on grace period after the designated finish date), a daily fine will be charged until the work is completed. That amount can be deducted from your final payment.

Clearly spell out the payment schedule. This varies depending on the size of the job and the region, but the typical contractor agreement is one-third down and the balance on completion. If you're not planning to keep the property for rental, consider offering 50 percent up front, and 50 percent when the property sells. In any case, never make the final payment until the job is 100 percent complete.

The agreement should stipulate that all changes must be in writing and signed by both parties. Be wary of contractors who resist such detailed paperwork. Although they may do an acceptable job, you won't have much recourse if they don't.

Insisting on a detailed contract doesn't mean you don't trust the people you're dealing with. Rather, it protects both parties because it eliminates the risk of misunderstandings and clearly outlines mutual rights and responsibilities.

Smart Tip

Watch home improvement shows on television. You'll learn a lot about what goes into repairs, and this knowledge will be a tremendous benefit. Keep in mind that most of these shows use high-end materials and tools, so you'll need to consider how to achieve the same end results using less expensive techniques.

■ Getting Started

When you buy a cosmetically distressed property, you don't want to hold it in that poor condition any longer than is absolutely necessary. You have to get moving on the fix-up immediately to be able to sell or rent the property. But before you do anything, take pictures of both the exterior and the interior of the property so you can document the work you're going to do.

When Your Plan Works, Don't Panic!

I am often amused when my students do exactly what I tell them to and are able to find great deals on profitable properties—and then they walk away from the closing table wondering what to do next. What you need to do next is avoid panicking and keep on following my advice. You're on your way to wealth.

That's what happened to my student Max G. Just six weeks after learning how to buy distressed properties, he bought his first fourplex. Two weeks later, he closed on 20 distressed units.

"My thoughts were, 'Okay, Russ, what do I do now?'" he recalls. "There I was, a real estate rookie with 24 distressed units. It was time to roll up my sleeves and go to work for real. Seven months later, I had established a network of contractors and the properties were fully renovated, occupied, and producing nearly $2,000 per month more than the previous owners had been realizing."

Max didn't stop there. He bought more properties, rehabbed them, refinanced them, and rented them. His monthly income and net worth are steadily climbing. He says, "By using what I learned from you, I started from scratch and achieved a very respectable passive income in a very short period of time. I am convinced this is only the beginning of much greater and more successful real estate ventures to come."

As soon as you close on the property (or sooner, if the seller allows), put a For Sale or For Rent sign in the yard. An interested prospect may be willing to take the property as-is or do at least part of the fix-up in exchange for a below-market price. Or a tenant who isn't quite ready to move may be willing to give you a deposit now and wait for the work to be completed. Bobby Threlkeld (a student I first told you about in Chapter 6) says that he routinely puts his rehabs under contract to sell before he finishes the work. His policy is to finish the rehab and get full value for the property, and he maintains it works well for him. My point is that a yard sign is a low-cost marketing tool that can pay off big when you're rehabbing property.

Even if you're not ready to start the work—perhaps because of the un-availability of workers or other factors—put out indicators that you're fixing up the property. A few paint cans on the porch, some old brushes, maybe a bucket or two, and a stepladder are signals to observers that work is under way, which will attract prospective buyers or tenants.

If you're going to sell the property, know your pre-fix-up and after-fix-up price as soon as you put up the sign in case a buyer shows up before you've started the work. Use the repair cost guide in Figure 10.1 to help estimate your after-fix-up price. If you're planning to hold and rent the house, know how much rent you're going to charge and what sorts of concessions you'll be willing to make if the tenant is interested in doing all or part of the fix-up.

When you actually do begin the work, start from the outside in, so people can see it. Most rehabbers start from the inside out, but when the outside looks good, you increase your chances of selling or renting the property faster because more people stop to look at it.

The first thing you must do with a cosmetically distressed property is improve its curb appeal. Begin by pressure washing the exterior of the house, including the house itself, decks, stoop or porches, driveway, and roof. If you hire someone to do this, your cost will be in the $250 to $300 range. If the paint on the house is just a few years old, pressure washing may allow you to avoid repainting. And if the house is going to need paint, you'll want to include pressure washing as part of your prep anyway.

If the house needs painting, then paint it. Choose a light color that is currently popular. Drive through new developments and see what colors the builders are using; try to duplicate the newest theme or trend with colors and paint techniques.

Landscaping is another key element of curb appeal. Keep the grass neatly mowed and the driveways, sidewalks, and curbs sharply edged; trees and shrubs should be neatly trimmed. If any bare spots are in the lawn, put down some grass seed or plugs. If the lot has trees, design landscape islands around small groups of trees, using mulch or pine straw. You don't have to spend a lot of money to make the landscaping look cared for. In fact, the three major areas that cost the least but provide the most value when you're fixing up are painting, carpeting, and landscaping.

Once the outside work is under way, tackle the inside. Your specific plan depends on exactly what needs to be done, but a good strategy is to start by clearing out any trash left behind by the previous occupants; making plumbing or electrical repairs; taking care of such details as fixing holes in the walls and replacing broken windows; painting; and then replacing the carpeting. Use neutral colors and the same color of paint and carpeting throughout.

Pay special attention to the kitchen, master bedroom, and bathrooms—rooms where your prospective buyers or tenants are going to be preparing their meals, sleeping, dressing, and taking care of their personal hygiene. Those rooms should be clean and bright so they don't look as if they'll require a gallon of disinfectant before they can be safely used.

By the way, if a prospective tenant or buyer doesn't like the colors you selected, don't have hurt feelings, and don't argue with the prospect. Instead, point out how easy it is to repaint or recarpet. You can't please everybody.

FIGURE 10.1

Repair Cost
Guide

Use the following costs to do your general estimating. They are based on national averages to do repairs to a typical three-bedroom home and include both parts and labor. Prices can vary widely depending on the location and actual size of the house as well as the cost and quality of the materials used.

Roof—strip and reshingle with conventional shingles	$1.25–$2/sq. ft.
Roof—strip and replace built-up tar and gravel roof	$4–$6/sq. ft.
Reflash chimney	$300–$500
Reflash skylight	$300–$500
Rebuild chimney above roof line	$100–$200/lin. ft.
Resurface asphalt driveway (20'x30')	$400
Replace gutters	$3–$5/lin. ft.
Underpin or add foundations	$300+/lin. ft.
Chemical treatment for termites	$500 and up
Repair minor crack in concrete foundation	$400–$800
Install new circuit breaker panel	$500–$700
Replace conventional receptacle with ground fault circuit receptacle	$60–$90
Insulate open attic to modern standards	$1–$1.50/sq. ft.
Blow insulation into flat roof, cathedral ceiling, or wall cavity	$2–$3.50/sq. ft.
Replace water line to house	$1,500–$3,500
Replace toilet	$300 and up
Replace basin	$200 and up
Replace bathtub, including ceramic tile	$1,500 and up
Replace leaking shower stall pan	$1,000–$1,600
Rebuild tile shower stall	$1,500–$2,500
Replace water heater	$300–$1,000
Carpet	$225–$400 per room
Replace stove	$400–$600
Replace dishwasher	$350–$500
Replace garbage disposal unit	$80–$200
Replace refrigerator	$400 and up

Words of Wisdom

Always take before and after photographs of every job you do. Having a visual record of the quality of your work will help you in countless ways, such as in your dealings with lenders, other investors, or even buyers and sellers.

■ General Rehabbing Tips

One of the things that makes real estate so exciting is that every project is different, and you can expect to learn something new in every deal. Following are some points that will provide you a foundation of knowledge and help prepare you to cope with the surprises.

Open a contractor's account at your local paint store, home improvement store, and building supply center. You'll be eligible for discounts, and in many establishments you'll get faster service by being able to check out at a special contractors-only register.

Don't buy based on price alone, whether you're choosing a contractor or buying materials. The cheapest price may not always offer the best deal. Of course, the highest price doesn't necessarily mean the highest quality. Do a cost-benefit comparison so you can make a good decision. And when you find a product or brand that works, stick with it—it's impossible to assign a dollar value to the peace of mind from knowing what to expect in a rehab situation.

If you must rent equipment to get a job done, try to rent it on a Saturday because many equipment rental businesses allow you to rent through Sundays for free.

Remember that creativity and a nontraditional approach can often mean big savings and bigger profits on a rehab job. Years ago, I was fixing up a house in which the kitchen counters were in decent shape, except for one large burn mark next to the stove, where someone had obviously moved a hot pot off a burner and put it on the unprotected counter. Rather than replace the countertop at a cost of $200 to $300, I found an attractive 12″ × 12″ piece of tile for about $1 and glued it over the burn mark, creating a custom hot pad next to the stove that gave the kitchen a designer look. This is the kind of thinking that starts you quickly on the road to riches.

Any house needing fix-up is going to need cleaning. You don't have to use a lot of fancy, expensive cleaning products. Straight bleach takes care of removing mold and mildew from tile grout. White vinegar applied full strength removes grease from kitchen cabinets (then go over them with Murphy's Oil Soap to bring back their shine). Remember, the goal is to make the house look and smell clean, and that can be accomplished with basic cleaning supplies. If you notice an odor in the house, do your best to find the source and remove it; especially if the house has been vacant, there's an excellent chance the odor is coming from a decomposing wild animal. A product called OdoBan is readily available in most stores that sell household supplies and does a great job at disinfecting and killing odors.

Just about every rehab job is going to include paint, so rely on the following painting tips to make the project easier and more profitable. First, use top-of-the-line paint, which is self-priming and saves you money in both materials and labor in the long run. Before you buy paint, check to see if the old paint is latex or oil. You can paint oil over latex but not latex over oil. One way to tell if the paint is oil or latex is to test it with Goof Off; if the paint melts, it's latex. If you're painting a flaky, chalky surface, add Emulsa Bond (by Flood) to latex paint to make it stick.

To prep the house before painting, mask the surfaces you don't want to paint with the tape available in the paint department of home improvement stores. To cover door hinges and knobs, paint them with contact cement, then peel off the dried cement when you're finished. Don't use plastic drop cloths; paint spills won't dry, and you'll risk stepping in them and tracking paint around the house. Use drop cloths that will absorb spills.

If you hire a painter, tell him to let you know halfway through the job if he's going to have enough paint—that way, you'll have time to buy the additional paint before he runs out and has to stop working.

Dollars and Sense

When rehabbing, consider buying the materials yourself and hiring labor only. That way you can take advantage of any contractor's discounts that might be available from the suppliers and you won't be paying a materials markup to the workers you hire.

■ Low-Cost Enhancements to Fixer-Uppers

You can do a number of low-cost things to a house that will make it sparkle. Some suggestions:

- Install new light switch plates and electrical outlet covers. These are usually made of plastic and get dingy and chipped over time. Put new ones on after you've painted, and the rooms will look totally refreshed.
- Install a new front door. Exterior doors take a beating from the elements. A new door is the first thing a prospective buyer or tenant sees.
- Replace interior doors. Interior doors are hollow and easy to damage but difficult to repair without looking patched. Install new interior doors where needed before you paint.
- Replace doorknobs. These are items that tend to show their age. New ones add an element of freshness to the atmosphere of a house.
- Replace trim where necessary. Check baseboards and other trim for wear and damage that won't be fixed with paint, and replace if needed.
- Install tile in the entryway. Without doubt, tiling entire rooms can be pricey, but the visual impact of tile in a small foyer is far greater than the cost.
- Hang new shower curtains. For just a few dollars each, a fresh shower curtain brightens a bathroom and makes the house feel ready to move into.
- Paint or refurbish kitchen cabinets. Because kitchens are busy rooms, cabinets take a lot of abuse. But in most cases, they don't need to be replaced; a good cleaning or a coat of paint and new door fixtures makes the kitchen look new.
- Add an attractive mailbox. Many rehabbers overlook this technique for contributing to the curb appeal of the property.

When the Job Is Finished

When you've finished your work, take photographs of the property for your files. Use these before-and-after photos to demonstrate your knowledge and skill to investors you may be considering partnering with, to lenders, and to sellers. Then move on to the next project. When you focus your rehab efforts in a defined area, you'll drive overall neighborhood improvement and push up all property values. This means bigger profits on the properties you buy to sell and greater appreciation on the properties you buy to keep. You'll be helping the community and increasing your net worth—all while doing something you enjoy.

MILLIONAIRE MENTOR Rehabbing Highlights

- The price of properties that need repairs can be discounted by the cost of the repairs or often more, creating a tremendous profit opportunity for the savvy investor.

- Don't become emotionally involved with your investment property. Do quality repairs and renovations, but remain detached and spend no more than you have to.

- Operate as your own general contractor on your rehab projects, and hire subcontractors to do the actual work.

- Screen subcontractors carefully and completely. Get written bids, do background checks, contact references, and pay attention to your instincts.

- Your contracts with workers should clearly spell out the work to be done, break down materials and labor, include a waiver of liability, specify the payment schedule, and stipulate that all changes must be in writing and signed by both parties.

- You don't have to finish your rehab work before you sell the property. If you get a good offer, take it.

- Practice making estimates until it becomes second nature to you.

- Take before-and-after photographs of every property you rehab for your files. These pictures enhance your credibility with lenders, other investors, and even sellers.

CHAPTER 11

Property Management

Profit from Managing for
Yourself and Others

The advice to buy a house and rent it out sounds so simple—and it is, but there are things you need to know about managing real estate if you're going to own it. And once you understand how to manage property, you might also make property management a profit center of your business and do it for other real estate investors.

Good property management begins with buying good buildings. That's why I've spent so much time discussing how to invest well. If you use the techniques you've learned so far, you'll have good buildings, whether they're single-family homes, duplexes, or multiunit buildings.

Of course, you know you can make plenty of money buying and selling property without hanging on to it, such as buying a distressed property, fixing it up, and immediately selling it. You can even make money without ever actually buying a property but just putting it under contract and selling that contract (as explained in Chapter 4) or using options (see Chapter 5). The only real drawback to these techniques is that as profitable as they are, the money stops coming in when you stop using them.

Let me show you what I mean. Let's say you find a cosmetically distressed house that you buy for $70,000. After $7,000 and three weeks of fix-up, the property is now worth $100,000. You want to get rid of it fast, so you fire-sale it for $94,000; you find a buyer in two weeks, and it takes another three weeks to close. Your profit on the deal is $17,000, and it took you about two months to do it.

But let's say that instead of selling that house, you decided to keep it and rent it out. You refinance to roll your fix-up costs into a first mortgage of $77,000, and your payments are $770. Your other expenses are $100 per month (which covers maintenance, administrative costs, vacancy allowance, etc.), and you rent the property for $1,000 a month. Because you put the For Rent sign in the yard as soon as you started the fix-up, you found your tenant before the house was ready; the tenant moved in and began paying rent just one month after you bought the property. That tenant stays for two years at the same rent and then moves. When you rent the house to the next tenant, you increase the rent to $1,100. When that lease comes up for renewal after a year, you note that rents in the neighborhood have gone up, so you raise the rent to $1,150 but allow the tenant to sign a two-year lease, which he honors.

It's now five years later, and you've netted $12,600 in positive cash flow from the rent alone. In the meantime, the rent has been paying down your mortgage, and the property has been naturally appreciating. Using the national average of 5 percent per year of appreciation, the property is now worth $127,600, and your mortgage balance is down to $70,000. If you sold the house for $125,000, your profit would be $55,000. Or you could refinance the property, pull your equity out tax deferred, and let future tenants continue to pay your mortgage with their rent. And these numbers don't consider the tax advantages you'll get from owning real estate.

Now, let's say you did one deal exactly like this every two months the first year. If you fixed up and sold each property, your total income from real estate would be $102,000. Sound good? Of course. But you haven't gained any appreciating assets, and if you stop doing deals, the money stops.

Instead, suppose you fixed up and kept those six properties. At the end of the year, you'd be taking in $9,360 per month in positive cash flow— that's $112,320 annually; and that money will keep coming in even if you never buy another property. You'd own $630,000 worth of real estate with a net worth of about $168,000 from those holdings alone.

This is why I advise that you buy and sell (or flip) for cash but buy and hold to build wealth. The property you own is always working for you, no matter what you're doing. Ron Watke, a student of mine from Michigan, puts it this way: "I like to hold property. I don't like selling and paying the capital gains tax consequences. As the old saying goes, 'Don't cut down the apple tree when it's still bearing fruit and you can pick the apples.'" Instead, he pulls his cash out of properties on a tax-deferred basis by refinancing them.

Of course, to build wealth by owning real estate, it's not enough to simply have your name on the deed—you have to manage the property effectively.

Warning

Keep your relationship with your tenants strictly professional. It's OK to be friendly and pleasant, and it's certainly OK to be concerned about their welfare, but maintaining a business relationship is essential. Getting personally involved with your tenants can interfere with your ability to make sound business decisions and will cost you money and possibly goodwill.

■ Should You Manage Your Property Yourself?

Once you've decided to invest in rental property, the next question becomes whether you should hire a property management company or manage it yourself. This is a question much like whether you should do the rehab work yourself or hire subcontractors, and the right answer is whatever you decide to do as long as it's profitable.

If your investment property is not in the local area—many of my students have income-producing property in several states and even some foreign countries—it's a good idea to hire a local firm to do the management. Of course, most people begin investing in real estate by buying property nearby. But whether you manage your own property or not, you have to understand the process. And once you know how to manage property, you can turn that function into a profit center. Property managers typically get 10 percent of the rent for their fee, although that can vary by location, type of property, and other terms; that fee is always negotiable. Whatever amount or percent you settle on, insist on multiunit discounts as you acquire more property.

Managing property certainly has its headaches—no business or job doesn't. But it can also be immensely rewarding, both financially and emotionally. You can make a lot of money and have the satisfaction of knowing that you're providing people with safe, clean places to live.

Wealth Secrets

Profit from other people's mistakes. Look for poorly managed rental property and either try to buy it or offer to take over the management for a fee. Often these properties are owned by people who just aren't cut out to be property managers and who might see your offer as a win-win solution to their problems.

■ How Much Rent Should You Charge?

Set your rents in line with the local market. Do a survey of similar rental units in the area to find out the going rate, and set your rent levels accordingly. This doesn't have to be a complicated, scientific process—just read the classified ads and make a few phone calls. Be sure to find out what the rents include; the more extras you offer, the more you can charge.

SUCCESS
STORY

Turning to Real Estate Let Him Turn In His Badge

Jay and Kasey London were living paycheck to paycheck on Jay's police officer's salary. After attending my training, they realized that real estate could be their ticket to financial freedom and wealth. In an 18-month span, they acquired $850,500 worth of rental properties with equity of more than $570,500.

Each rental unit generates no less than $250 in positive cash flow every month, and the Londons' total monthly positive cash flow from their real estate is $5,475. With that income, Jay was able to resign from the police department and devote himself full-time to their real estate business.

Typically, tenants renting single-family houses pay charges for water, sewers, garbage pickup (unless it's included in the taxes), electricity, and gas. The landlord pays insurance on the property (but not on the contents) and taxes.

In a multiunit building, it's easiest if you have separate meters for utilities. When you have shared utilities, you can do one of two things: set your rents high enough to consider the approximate cost of the utilities or prorate the shared utilities and bill tenants each month. If you choose to prorate shared utilities and services (common electrical, water, sewer, garbage, etc.), then base your calculations on the number of people, not the number of units.

Smart Thinking

When a tenant pays by check, make a copy for your files before you deposit the check; you may need the bank information for future collection efforts.

■ Tenants Are Everywhere

How can you find new tenants? With just a little effort, you'll have so many prospective tenants you'll be able to pick and choose the folks you want to rent to. Here are some techniques for locating prospective tenants:

- *Newspaper ads.* Running newspaper ads is often your most expensive option, especially if you use a large circulation daily newspaper, but you'll get a large amount of exposure. You should also consider smaller community papers, shoppers, and newsletters that target the area where your property is located. When placing newspaper ads, you want to get your point across in as few words as possible. Be sure to include all the important facts: number of bedrooms and baths, location, price, key amenities, and a phone number. You'll attract prospective tenants with a few descriptive words, such as "dramatic," "historic," "luxurious," "sparkling," "traditional," and "magnificent."
- *Signs.* Place yard signs at the property for rent as well as at nearby busy intersections. Keep the sign simple and include only the basics. For example: "For Rent: duplex, 2/2, $650, 704-555-1234." Be sure the phone number is easy to read and includes the area code.
- *Internet.* The Internet offers ways to find tenants that are limited only by your imagination. Entrepreneurs across the country are developing Web sites where landlords can post available rentals; you can find the ones in your area by checking your local Yellow Pages or doing a Web search. You can also develop your Web site to list your properties.
- *Schools.* Most colleges, universities, and adult technical and vocational schools have housing offices. If your property is near a school, call to find out if you can make the information available to students who may be looking for housing.

- *Churches.* Many churches have bulletin boards where you can post property for rent notices. These boards are also likely to include a "Help Wanted" section, which could be a great resource if you're looking for maintenance and rehab workers for your properties.
- *Local housing authority.* If you're interested in low-income tenants who are receiving government subsidies, such as Section 8 funding, register your property with the local housing authority, which is listed in the government section of your telephone directory.
- *YMCA/YWCA and similar agencies.* If the Y in your area offers housing (some do, some don't), or if there are other agencies that provide temporary housing or offer counseling and assistance in moving from shelters to permanent housing, let them know what you have available.
- *Real estate agents.* Most real estate agents are more interested in sales than rentals, but they can still be a source of tenant referrals. Let the agents who work your area know that you have rental property, and offer a referral fee.
- *Financial community.* Members of the financial community, including mortgage brokers, lawyers, and accountants, can be great resources for tenants. As with real estate agents, let them know you have rental property and offer a referral fee.
- *Posting notices.* Look for places where you can post notices about your rental units. Besides schools and churches, you'll often see community bulletin boards in restaurants, public coin laundries, grocery stores, gyms, and other facilities where you can promote your rentals. Add your phone number at the bottom of the notice in tear-off strips so people can take your contact information without taking down your notice.
- *Fliers.* Put together a one-page flier describing your property and be creative in distributing it.
- *Existing tenants.* If your existing tenants are happy with their home and your management style, they'll be glad to refer their friends when you have a vacancy. You can encourage this by offering a referral fee.
- *Your own files.* If someone responds to one of your ads or notices but the property has already been rented, don't just say "sorry" and hang up. Get the caller's name, contact information, and type of property they're looking for; keep it on file for when you have a vacancy.

These ideas are just a starting point. With a little creativity, you'll have more tenants than you have units. And the same applies to prospective buyers when you have properties for sale. Take a lesson from one of my students who got a good deal on a block of distressed properties in a neighborhood that was struggling to revitalize itself. Instead of trying to tackle a huge rehab job himself, he went to a nearby church and found buyers in the congregation who were happy to buy the houses at less than market value (but for more than my student paid, of course) and do the fix-up themselves.

FYI

What's the difference between a rental agreement and a lease? The biggest difference is the period of occupancy. Typically, rental agreements are for a short term, usually 30 days or less, and automatically renew themselves. Leases are for longer terms, usually 6 months or a year and don't automatically renew at expiration.

■ Screening Tenants

Each prospective tenant should complete an application. (See Figure 11.1 for a sample application.) Any reluctance to do this is a red flag; the prospect may have something to hide. Tell prospective tenants you are going to do a credit and criminal background check. If they have a problem, this should stop them from applying. Also, prospective tenants should pay an application fee of $20 to $35, which will cover your cost of doing a credit and background check.

Always ask prospective tenants how long they've been where they are now and why they are moving. If they've been where they are a very short time, that's a sign they may not stay in your property much longer. If they're moving because they need more room or to be closer to work or school, that's fine. But if they're moving because they're being evicted, you probably don't want to rent to them.

Ask to see a legal photo ID, preferably a driver's license or government-issued identification card. Make a copy for your records, and be sure the information on the ID matches the person presenting it as well as the information on the application and credit report.

If possible, take a look at where prospective tenants are currently living so you can see how they take care of the property. Offer to meet them there to complete the paperwork. When checking their references, call one or two previous landlords besides the current one. Current landlords might be inclined to say nice things just to get rid of a bad tenant. Also, be sure you really are talking to former landlords and not phony references. Verify the address of the property and the length of time a tenant lived there; and make sure these items match the information provided on the application. If you're calling a property management company, verify the listing in the telephone directory. If a former landlord claims to be an investor who owns and manages properties in his own name, do a quick check of the public records to be sure he really owns the property where the prospective tenant lived.

Your evaluation should include an analysis of a prospective tenant's debt-to-income ratio. The rent should be no more than 35 percent of her total monthly income; and her other obligations and expenses should not exceed 65 percent of her income.

Smart Thinking

Always have current emergency contact information on file for every tenant. In most cases, the contact is the nearest relative not living on the premises. Explain that you must know how to contact someone in case the tenant becomes ill or otherwise incapacitated, or if there is an emergency such as a fire or other natural disaster and you are unable to reach the tenant.

Showing the Property

When showing a unit to a prospective tenant, use a bit of salesmanship. Open curtains or blinds so the rooms are bright and cheery. Walk through each room with the prospect, pointing out features and suggesting how they might be used. Use words to help your prospects visualize living in the house or apartment. Say such things as, "The floor plan is very open, and

FIGURE 11.1

■

Application
for Rental

Applying for Unit # _____ Address _____ Rent $_____

Name _____ SSN _____

Spouse _____ SSN _____

Present address _____ How long _____

Employer _____ How long _____

Position _____ Supervisor _____ Phone _____

Address _____ Salary _____

Other income (source and amount) _____

Spouse's employer _____ How long _____

Position _____ Supervisor _____ Phone _____

Address _____ Salary _____

Other income (source and amount) _____

Current landlord _____

Address _____ Phone _____

Previous landlord _____

Address _____ Phone _____

Previous landlord _____

Address _____ Phone _____

List children who will be occupying property:

Name _____ Age _____

Name _____ Age _____

Name _____ Age _____

Name _____ Age _____

List anyone else who will be occupying property:

Name _____ Relationship _____ Age _____

Name _____ Relationship _____ Age _____

Name _____ Relationship _____ Age _____

Bank _____ Checking/Savings Acct # _____

Bank _____ Checking/Savings Acct # _____

Nearest relative not living with you

Name _____ Relationship _____

Address _____ Phone _____

References

Name _____ Address _____ Phone _____

Name _____ Address _____ Phone _____

I/We, the undersigned, acknowledge that all information given above is true and complete, and authorize [insert your company name] to verify any or all of the above statements.

_____   _____

(Signature)   (Date)

_____   _____

(Signature)   (Date) it's great for entertaining but still quite cozy"; "The kitchen is extremely efficient; you can make everything from a quick snack to a gourmet dinner here"; and "The bedrooms are arranged so you have plenty of privacy but you can still keep an eye on the kids."

This is also a good time to ask questions and learn about the prospects so you can decide whether you want them as tenants. When you point out a feature, give them an opportunity to react so you can gauge their interest in the property. Encourage them to talk about their hobbies and interests—this also gives you insight into what type of tenant they will be.

You may find yourself showing property that isn't quite ready to rent—it may not be clean or painted or need repairs, or the previous tenant has given notice but not yet moved. In these situations, tell the prospective tenants what you're doing and help them visualize how good the place will look when you're finished. In fact, you might even offer to let them choose paint or carpet colors if they sign the lease before you do the work.

During the time the property is on the market, available either for rent or for sale, be sure to maintain it. Make sure the lawn is mowed and that any outside trash and debris are promptly removed; and keep the interior clean and free of excessive dust, litter that may have been left behind by prospects, dead bugs, and the like.

◼ When You Buy a Rented Building

When you buy a building with tenants, the existing tenants should receive a takeover letter as soon as you close. In that letter, introduce yourself, provide the tenants with your company name, address, and telephone number, and let them know that your goal is to provide a well-managed and maintained property they will be proud to call home. Include a tenant information sheet and ask them to fill it out and return it to you. The sheet should have a space for the tenants to provide you with the names of all occupants (adults and children), the address of their unit, their day and evening phone numbers, their employer, how long they've lived in the unit, the amount of their security deposit, what fixtures they've added, a list of pets, emergency contact information, and any tenant concerns. Be sure that all tenants have a current signed lease; if they don't have one when you purchase the building, make getting a lease signed a top priority.

Don't merely show up on the property with a cocky attitude as though you've done them a favor by buying the property. Explain that you are a responsible, concerned landlord and that you care about the housing needs of your residents. If you intend to raise rents, give the existing tenants ample notice and be prepared to justify the increase. When tenants understand the logic behind higher rents—such as market conditions, property improvements, rising costs, and the like—they are more likely to accept them and stay.

Smart Thinking

If you write your own rental documents (lease or rental agreement, any addendums, application, property rules, etc.), have an attorney check them to make sure they are enforceable, that they don't violate any fair housing or other antidiscrimination laws, and that they are otherwise legal under all applicable local, state, and federal housing regulations.

■ Lease Details

The most important thing you need to know about leases is that you must have one for every tenant—no exceptions. Whether the tenant is under an open-ended month-to-month rental agreement or a fixed-term lease, have a written contract on file that covers every occupant of every property.

When leases are prepared by an attorney, they often have language that tenants find difficult to understand. Of course, if tenants sign a lease, you can legally enforce it whether they understood it or not, but a better way to operate is to have your leases written in common, easily understandable language. That way, your tenants know what's expected of them and what they should expect of you. This is especially important with low-income housing, because often those tenants' reading skills are on a fairly low level. I have found that low-income and moderate-income tenants follow the rules and honor their obligations so long as they understand what they are supposed to do.

Your lease or rental agreement should comply with all relevant laws, including rent control ordinances, health and safety codes, antidiscrimination laws, and other state laws. Each lease should include the following:

- *Names of all tenants.* Every adult who lives in the unit should be named on the lease and sign as a responsible party. Children should also be listed.
- *Occupancy limits.* Clearly state that occupancy is limited to those listed in the lease agreement. This allows you to evict a tenant who lets a friend or relative move in or who sublets the unit without your consent.
- *Tenancy terms.* What is the length of the tenancy—month-to-month or a longer fixed term? State it in the lease.
- *Deposits and fees.* State the amount of the security deposit, how it may be used and not used, when and how you will return the deposit, and any nonrefundable fees, such as those for cleaning or lock changing.
- *Repairs and maintenance.* Clearly define your and the tenant's responsibilities for repairs and maintenance. Include restrictions on tenant alterations.
- *Legal right of access.* State how much notice you provide before entering for repairs and maintenance.
- *Restrictions on illegal activity.* Explicitly prohibit such illegal activity as drug dealing and such disruptive behavior as excessive noise.
- *Other rules and restrictions.* Detail other important rules and restrictions, such as limits on pets, use of common areas, parking issues, and so on.

In addition to the lease, each tenant should sign a Move-In Condition Inspection form. This can be a simple, one-page checklist that indicates the condition of the unit and eliminates any dispute over possible damage when the tenant moves out.

■ Don't Discriminate

It's your property and you can rent to whomever you want, right? Wrong. Federal law prohibits housing discrimination on the basis of race, religion, ethnic background or national origin, sex, age, having children (except in certain designated senior housing), or a mental or physical disability. Some state and local laws prohibit discrimination on the basis of sexual orientation or marital status.

■ Keeping Good Tenants

Tenants are your customers, and you need to treat them well or they'll start looking for another place to live. All of your residents deserve to be treated with respect. Learn your tenants' names and call them by name when you're talking with them. Respond to their requests promptly, and if for any reason a requested repair cannot be made within 24 hours, let them know why and when they can expect service. Remember your tenants' birthdays with a card or a small gift.

You punish bad tenants with such actions as charges for late payments, repair fees, and eviction. Using the same logic, you should reward good tenants. The rewards can range from simple—perhaps just a verbal thanks—to the more tangible, such as prizes or gifts for rent payments made on time over a certain period, much like the perfect attendance awards you used to get in school.

Offer referral fees to tenants who recommend one of your properties to someone they know. To encourage quality referrals, make the fee contingent on the prospect's fulfilling the terms of a lease for six months. For example, you can offer your tenants a $100 bonus in the form of a rent discount if they refer a tenant who meets your requirements and rents from you for six months. Of course, if the tenant making the referral moves before then, the offer is void.

Diane and Olin T., who I first told you about in Chapter 4, tell me that they don't have to advertise for tenants; all their tenants come to them through referrals. "We are very proud of the relationship we have built with our tenants, and they apparently have a great deal of respect for us," Diane says. "We very rarely have tenants pay their rent late, and they take very good care of the properties. We have focused on purchasing properties in an area of town where most landlords neglect their properties and maintain a low regard for their tenants. Because of our different style of management, we have managed to get better tenants even though we charge higher rents."

Wealth Secrets

When adding rental properties to your portfolio, keep them as geographically close together as possible. This will help build your reputation as a good landlord in the area and save you time and money in management and maintenance.

Back to School

If you own property near a college or university, you may find an opportunity in targeting the student market. If on-campus housing is limited (and it almost always is), off-campus student housing is at a premium.

On the plus side, college students typically don't require much in the way of luxury. They're generally happy with houses or apartments that have large open spaces where they can live with three or four other students. The drawback is that students have an often-deserved reputation for loud parties and damaging property. But that's a manageable issue; you can rent to students quite profitably and without any additional management headaches if you get started right.

Before you rent to students, make sure there are no zoning regulations or deed restrictions that would limit the number of unrelated adults occupying a single dwelling. Many communities have such restrictions to maintain the integrity of single-family neighborhoods. Also, be sure you have adequate parking. Consider this: You may rent a four-bedroom house to four students, each of whom has a car. The students are model tenants in every way, but the house has only a one-car garage and space in the driveway for one more car, so two cars are parked on the grass, which could justifiably annoy the neighbors. A similar situation could arise with small multiunit buildings.

Whether you are renting houses or apartments, each occupant of a unit should have his or her own lease, complete with security deposit. This protects you and the other tenants if one person should decide to move out during the term of the lease. The occupants have to be responsible for their own utilities.

Make the term of the lease one year. Many students take the summer off, which means your unit could be vacant during that period. A one-year lease protects you against the potential of lost revenue when students are not in town.

Establish rules and enforce them. Make it clear that excessive noise, illegal activities, or property damage are causes for termination of the lease and eviction. (The eviction process is discussed in detail later in this chapter.)

■

SUCCESS
STORY

A Very Special Way to Fly

Carlos and Melissa Budet were working people who decided to change their life by attending our training and investing in real estate. Over the course of two years, they purchased 14 wholesale properties, half of which they sold to generate cash and half they kept to build wealth.

The Budets found an interesting niche market: two boarding houses for pilots. Melissa says there's never a problem collecting rent; she stops in on the first and all the checks are tacked to the bulletin board in the kitchen. And they have a waiting list of about 25 pilots who will become tenants as soon as there is room.

Warning

Be sure your rental units and common areas meet all local code requirements for safety and security. Your local building code enforcement office will be happy to provide you with the information you need to get, and stay, in compliance. Install the proper number of smoke detectors; be sure hallways are well lit; and provide adequate lighting for parking areas. Install peepholes and chain or deadbolt locks, and when tenants move, change the locks.

■ How to Make Your Properties More Profitable

Having income-producing property is good. It becomes great when that property is producing the maximum amount of income possible. Here are some ways to make sure your properties are reaching their full profit potential.

Raise the rent. This is a basic concept, so it amazes me how many land-lords are reluctant to raise the rent. Your rents should always be in line with the market. Of course, it's easy to raise the rent for a new tenant, but you must also consider rent increases when leases come up for renewal. Give tenants 60 days' notice of rent increases and justify the new amount. Put the notice in writing; an oral notice of increase won't hold up in court. Explain that the increase is in line with the market or that you have enhanced the property or whatever. Will some tenants move? Probably, and when they do, you'll replace them with tenants paying a higher rate. Most tenants, however, understand that prices go up on everything and their rent is no exception.

Reduce your tax assessment. You don't have to accept the value the tax assessor's office places on your property. Challenge the assessment; in many cases, you'll lower your tax bill. All you need to do is write a letter offering a logical reason for reducing the assessed value. For example, one of my students had a single-family home with a drainage problem that had been caused by nearby development. Because she couldn't sell the property without disclosing the problem, she rented out the house. When her tax bill arrived showing a property value increase, she wrote to the tax assessor, explaining that in the current buyer's market, the drainage problem made the property virtually unsellable. The tax assessor dropped the assessed value by $10,000. The reduction in value reduced her taxes but didn't reduce the amount of rent she was collecting. This is an especially important technique to use on properties you've just purchased, because you can use the fact that the property has been mismanaged and is rundown when making your claim for a lower assessment. Also, many jurisdictions limit the amount assessments can increase each year, so getting the value knocked down before you fix the property up can save you on taxes for years to come.

Add laundry and vending machines. If you own a multiunit property, consider installing a coin-operated laundry along with vending machines dispensing detergent, soft drinks, and snacks.

Provide storage. If there is room on the property, install aluminum storage sheds and rent them to tenants for an extra monthly fee.

Charge for extras. If units have washer-dryer hookups, offer to provide those appliances for a monthly fee, such as $25 to $30. You can even charge a nominal fee for such extras as ceiling fans or bathroom grab bars.

Do maintenance as needed. Delayed maintenance can be expensive. Pay attention to small things that need repair before they turn into major problems. Remember that proper maintenance can extend the life of mechanical items such as air conditioners and appliances. Also, look for subtle money wasters, such as dripping faucets or leaky toilets, that can drive up your water bill.

Smart Thinking

If you're handy, you may do a lot of the maintenance and repairs yourself—especially in the beginning when you have a small number of units. There will come a time, however, when you have to hire people

*to do maintenance work and repairs; just don't wait too long to
assemble a maintenance team because it will cost you more in the long
run if you aren't operating as efficiently and cost-effectively as possible.*

■ Insuring Rental Property

Adequate insurance is an important part of protecting your real estate
investments. Chapter 16 discusses asset protection in greater detail, but you
need property coverage to repair and replace the buildings in the event of
theft, fire, natural disasters, and the like, and liability to protect yourself in
case someone is injured on the premises. You are *not* responsible for insuring your tenants' contents; be sure your lease makes this point very clear.

Many insurance companies and agents are happy to assist you with developing a risk management strategy. They will send someone to inspect
your property and make safety and security suggestions, which, when im-
plemented, can lower your premiums.

In Chapter 2, I discussed having an independent insurance agent on
your Power Team, and I want to stress again how valuable this is. A good insurance agent has an abundance of information and advice for you, and you
don't have to pay for it.

Warning

*Do not accept partial rent once the eviction process begins. This could
give the tenant grounds to claim that you have agreed to a repayment
plan or have called off the eviction.*

■ Dealing with Problem Tenants

In Chapter 3, I explained my basic rule about tenants—80 percent are
fine, 10 percent are great, and 10 percent have the potential to be problems. What is a problem tenant? It's someone who is frequently late with the
rent or regularly writes bad checks. It's someone who plays music or the tel-

evision so loud the building vibrates and all the neighbors complain. It's someone who paints the walls bright colors in violation of the terms of the lease, leaves trash in the hallways, knocks holes in the walls, parks junk cars in the driveway, changes the locks without telling you, gets a pet after you've said no animals—you know what I mean.

In many cases, you can turn bad tenants around to your way of thinking so they take care of the property and pay their rent on time. Sometimes all it takes is a few conversations. Remind tenants that they received a copy of the rules when they signed the lease. Be respectful but firm and, if possible, offer an alternative to the offending behavior. Make your initial approach to the situation such that problem tenants can change their behavior without losing face. If the tenants refuse to change, they must go.

The most common tenant problem you'll have is *late rent payments*. Don't let this scare you—90 percent or more of your tenants pay their rent on time, and most of the ones who pay late still pay in time to avoid legal proceedings. But you need a plan for how you'll deal with the few who don't pay.

Give tenants from the first to the third day of the month to pay their rent, and then start adding late fees as described in your lease. On the fourth day, deliver a notice to pay or quit the premises. If the rent is not paid by the eighth day of the month, go to the county and file an eviction notice. Don't accept any excuses for nonpayment of rent. Regardless of what they tell you, start the eviction process—you can always stop it when they pay. Consistency is the most critical aspect of property management. Tenants need to know that you will enforce the rules. Not only that, if you enforce the rules for one tenant but fail to do so for another, you could be charged with discrimination.

When You Can't Fix a Problem Tenant: Eviction

When the rent hasn't been paid or a tenant is willfully violating the lease terms and ignoring your notices to correct the situation, you must get the tenant out. You can either hire an attorney to handle the eviction or do it yourself.

If you decide to hire an attorney, be sure she is experienced in handling evictions. Ask how many she does each month, how long the average eviction takes from beginning to end, and how fast you can have the tenants in court. A competent eviction attorney expects these questions and has immediate answers to them.

There's no reason why you can't handle the eviction yourself. In most states, this is a fairly simple legal proceeding, and the courts are accustomed to landlords filing evictions without attorneys.

Though specifics of eviction procedures vary by state, the overall process is similar. The first step is a termination notice. The most common termination notice is a Pay Rent or Quit, which gives the tenant a few days (usually three to five) to pay the rent or move out. A Cure or Quit notice is given when the tenant is in violation of the terms of the lease, such as a no pets clause. The notice offers the tenant a specified amount of time to correct the violation. If the tenant fails to "cure" the violation, he must move or face eviction. An Unconditional Quit notice is an order for the tenant to vacate the premises without the opportunity to correct any lease violations or pay late rent. In most states, unconditional quit notices are allowed only after repeated violations of a significant lease clause, repeated late rent payments, serious property damage, or serious illegal activity on the premises, such as drug dealing.

If the tenant does not correct the situation or move by your notice date, go to court and file an eviction lawsuit; and have the tenant served according to state law. Once you receive the final judgment (which is usually a fairly quick process), you turn it over to a local law enforcement officer, who gives the tenant notice that he must leave within a certain amount of time (typically a few days) or he will be physically removed.

You may be tempted to bypass normal legal procedures to get rid of a problem tenant—but don't! Such shortcuts as intimidation, threats, changing locks, turning off utilities, and attempts to physically remove a tenant without a final eviction judgment are illegal in most states and leave you open to a lawsuit and civil penalties.

You need to understand the eviction process, but if you screen your tenants properly and treat them fairly, you probably won't have to use it very often. Lester Theiss says in almost five years of landlording, he's had only one eviction—and he's not unusual.

Smart Tip

When you refund all or part of a security deposit, get proof that you did so. For in-person refunds, have the former tenant sign a receipt for the check. If you mail it, send the check by certified mail and keep the certificate on file. Should the post office return a security deposit refund as undeliverable, verify that you sent it to the forwarding address the tenant provided, then keep the unopened envelope on file as proof in case the tenant claims it was never sent.

■ Managing Cash Flow and Recordkeeping

You may be having fun with your real estate business, but this isn't a hobby. You're dealing with valuable assets and people's homes, so managing your cash flow and maintaining good records is essential.

Follow basic accounting procedures in tracking income and expenses. Use good business practices when buying goods and services for your properties.

Set up a file on each rental unit and tenant. The file should include a copy of the lease, move-in inspection, maintenance records, copies of correspondence, and notes of any conversations.

The Advantage of Software

If you are serious about managing your rental properties efficiently, you should invest in property management software. A number of products are on the market, so you should investigate them carefully. When it comes to software, price is definitely *not* a good indicator of features and quality.

The software you choose should be relatively easy for you to set up, understand and use, and allow you to grow. Try a demo version before investing in a full working copy of the program. Typical property management packages offer features that include basic accounting functions; reminders to help you track late rents, lease expirations, maintenance, and repairs; tenant files, such as personal information, incident reports, and correspondence; property details; vendor files; important contacts; and forms.

FIGURE 11.2

■

Sample
APOD

Annual Property Operating Data (APOD) Statement

John and Hilda Sample Investor
5432 MyProperty Street, My Town, FL 00000

Single Family
Purchase Price: 45,000.00
Market Value: 50,000.00

Financing

Loan Type:	New Loan	New Loan	New Loan
Loan Priority:	1st Mortgage	2nd Mortgage	3rd Mortgage
Principal:	$40,000.00	$0.00	$0.00
Interest Rate:	6.500%	0.000%	0.000%
Term (months):	360	0	0
Pymts/Year:	12	12	12
Payment:	$252.83	$0.00	$0.00
Annual Debt Service:	$3,033.96	$0.00	$0.00

Expenses

Accounting/Legal:	$1.00
Advertising:	$8.00
Reserves:	$0.00
Association Fees:	$0.00
Electricity:	$0.00
Insurance:	$45.00
Lawn Care:	$55.00
Management Fees:	$0.00
Payroll:	$0.00
Pest Control:	$15.00
Property/RE Taxes:	$75.00
Repairs:	$50.00
Secretarial:	$0.00
Security:	$0.00
Services:	$0.00
Supplies:	$0.00
Trash Removal:	$20.00
Utilities:	$0.00
Water/Sewer:	$0.00
Miscellaneous:	$0.00
Monthly Expenses:	$269.00

Income

Monthly Rental Income:	$650.00
Other Operating Income:	$0.00
Interest Income:	$0.00
Gross Monthly Income:	$650.00
Vacancy Allowance:	$32.50
Operating Income:	$617.50

Annual Operating Income:	$7,410.00
(-) Annual Operating Expenses:	$3,228.00
(-) Annual Debt Service:	$3,033.96
(=) Cash Flow Before Taxes:	$1,148.04

Check out the software publisher; be sure the company is established with a track record you can research. Ask for user references and give them a call; find out how good the publisher has been with such issues as repairing glitches, issuing upgrades, and providing technical assistance. Finally, before you buy, test the publisher's tech support by calling its support hot line. How fast does someone answer? If you have to leave a message, is your call returned promptly? What is the charge for tech support? This service should be free for at least the first few months you own the product, but after that a moderate charge is fair.

If you already own rental property, making a software decision will be a little easier because you'll have a practical understanding of what you want the software to do. But even if you're still looking for your first investment property, you should know enough by now to be able to evaluate a property management software package.

MILLIONAIRE MENTOR Property Management Highlights

- Buying property to hold and rent out is one of the best ways to create wealth, because it generates ongoing cash flow as well as building your net worth through appreciation.

- When you own rental property, you can either manage it yourself or hire someone to do it for you.

- If you decide to manage your property yourself, remember that the skills involved in doing that are the same skills you can use to start a property management business, managing properties for other investors for a fee.

- Property management fees are always negotiable.

- Set your rents in line with the local market.

- Methods for locating prospective tenants include using newspaper ads, signs, and the Internet; contacting schools, churches, the local housing authority, agencies such as the YMCA and YWCA, real estate agents, and members of the financial community; posting notices and fliers; and relying on your existing tenants and your own database.

- Screen your tenants thoroughly and carefully. Each tenant should complete an application and provide photo identification. Any reluctance to do this is a sign that the tenant could be a problem.

- When you buy a building that is already rented, immediately send a takeover letter to the existing tenants introducing yourself and telling them how to contact you. Make sure the information the seller has on file about the tenants is current and complete to your standards.

- Be sure the leases cover every occupant of every unit.

- Develop tenant retention programs that reward good tenants and provide them with an incentive to stay with you and refer people to you.

- Take steps to ensure that your property is as profitable as possible. Don't be afraid to raise the rents if market conditions support a higher amount. Look for ways to add revenue streams, such as coin laundries and vending machines. Consider challenging your tax assessment to reduce your taxes. Do maintenance as needed.

- Be firm and consistent when dealing with tenants. Keep your relationship strictly professional.

- If you screen tenants properly and treat them fairly, you won't have to deal with evictions very often, but be prepared to take that action if it becomes necessary.

- Keep complete and accurate records on your rental properties.

CHAPTER 12

Commercial Real Estate

Different Zoning, New Opportunities

After you've established a track record in residential real estate, you may want to consider making the move to the commercial side of the business. This chapter offers a taste of what that's all about and shows you how to develop a strategy for beginning to invest in commercial properties.

I can't tell you how many times one of my students has left a training program on residential real estate investing and literally bought a property on the way home. Even though that's certainly possible with commercial real estate as well, it's not nearly so common in that area. Most people find that it takes a little longer to learn the market and the business, find the properties, and put the deals together. Now, it's still real estate, and if you can do residential deals, you can do commercial deals. I don't want you to fear commercial real estate, but you have to respect it. You'll be doing yourself a tremendous disservice if you jump into this side of the business without a solid understanding of how it works. That's why we've established prerequisites for our Commercial Real Estate Advanced Training; you must have a minimum amount of previous education and real estate experience before you can take this course. With that as a foundation, you'll quickly learn what you need to know to make smart and profitable commercial real estate investments.

■ The Difference between Residential and Commercial Real Estate

A commercial property is simply a property that is zoned commercial. It doesn't have to be a towering highrise or a sprawling mall; it could be a small office building or retail strip center, and it may not cost much more than houses in good neighborhoods. In fact, many commercial properties were once residential. You see those buildings in cities and towns across the country—homes that were converted to business use as commercial activity expanded into neighborhoods and properties were rezoned.

Of course, that simple issue of *zoning* creates a number of important differences. In general, commercial real estate buyers, sellers, and brokers are more sophisticated than their residential counterparts. They're usually dealing with higher dollar figures, and it's quite common to have a number of investors involved in a single deal. Commercial leases are more complex than residential ones. Property owners and tenants are often dealing with government regulatory issues that don't affect residential real estate.

It's not totally different, however. Many of the same basic principles of residential real estate investing can be applied to commercial properties, such as buying at wholesale, buying distressed properties and rehabbing them, or picking up a great deal on a property facing foreclosure. But whereas the fundamentals may be similar, the process in the real world can be more complex.

Did You Know?

Strip centers are called that because they are built on a strip of commercial land between a road and land zoned for another use, typically residential—not because they are built in a strip layout, although many of them are.

■ Types of Commercial Properties

Under the broad umbrella of commercial real estate are four property types: retail, industrial, offices, and multifamily residential. You should be familiar with all four types, but I recommend that you choose one of the four to specialize in. Don't try to do them all, especially at first. Select a specialty and take the time to learn it thoroughly before you actually begin investing.

Retail property. Retail property includes shopping centers, malls, free-standing buildings (occupied by a single tenant), and commercial strips. To successfully own and manage retail property, you have to understand such concepts as *tenant mix and placement, trade area,* and *percentage leases.* Tenant mix (the types of establishments in the center) and placement (where the establishments are in relation to each other and to elements on the property) are issues you learn by doing. Putting together the right combination of tenants isn't a science; it's more intuition and common sense. You also have to think about the needs of your tenants' customers. Will they want storefront parking, curbside drop-off and pickup, or even benches outside the store? If you take the time to understand the basics of how your tenants operate and what they need to do to keep their customers happy, you'll be in a better position to provide a property that contributes to their success.

Industrial property. Industrial properties can range from bulk ware-houses, office-warehouse and office-service combinations, multitenant build-ings, freestanding buildings, research and development facilities, large manufacturing plants, and industrial parks. I recommend that you stay away from large manufacturing facilities in the beginning because the pool of prospective tenants is naturally small. On the other hand, you could do well with single-tenant and multitenant combination buildings. One of the positive features about industrial property is that the tenants tend to be stable and there for the long term; once they're in and settled, they'll be with you for years.

Offices. Offices accommodate businesses that don't need manufactur-ing, warehouse, or other industrial facilities. Office buildings tend to cluster in downtown areas and modern office parks. Categories you'll need to be familiar with are highrise (exactly how high depends on the area); midrise and lowrise (again, varies by area); and garden (one and two stories, heavily land-scaped buildings). Office buildings are also classified as A (new or less than 4 years old in great locations and easily accessible with the latest and great-est amenities); B (8 to 10 years old with dated amenities); and C (15 or more years old). B and C buildings are less desirable because of their age, location, or construction factors. Class A buildings command the highest rent and cost the most to maintain; class B buildings rent for an average of $4 to $5 per square foot less but also cost less to maintain; class C buildings generally rent for $2 per square foot less than class B buildings, but the operating costs are just a few cents lower. Office building ratings are very subjective. A class A building in one submarket might rank lower if it were located in a distinctly different submarket just a few miles away that contains higher-end products. Overall, office buildings in recent years have shown steady income growth, with expenses not increasing as fast as income.

Multifamily residential. In general, residential investment property with five or more units falls in the commercial category. This includes small sixplex, eightplex, and larger buildings; town house apartments; garden apartments; highrise residential buildings; and sprawling multibuilding apartment complexes. Before investing in multifamily residential buildings, study your market and look at the trends and projections. Is the area growing or declining? Are households getting larger or smaller? Why? Will the units you're considering accommodate the market, or are they too large or too small?

Your own background and interests will have a major influence on what type of commercial property you choose. Many of my students have already owned businesses, so they have experience as commercial tenants and naturally gravitate toward the type of property with which they are familiar. If you're not sure where to start, I would recommend a small apartment building, a small office building, or a building with retail on the ground floor and some apartments above. From both purchase process and management perspectives, these types of buildings are not substantially different from single-family or one-unit to four-unit residential properties. Get a few of those under your belt, and you'll be ready for bigger deals.

Warning

Avoid commercial buildings that are specially designed for an uncommon specific use. The universe of tenants or prospective buyers for such buildings may be very small. The larger your potential market for a property, the more likely it is to be profitable. Don't confuse this advice with appealing to niche markets, such as certain types of retailers, restaurants, or manufacturers. Niche markets can be very lucrative; but oddball buildings without much flexibility can be difficult to rent or resell.

■ Shopping Center Categories

The Mall of America is a shopping center. So is the simple building at the edge of a neighborhood that houses a convenience store, a dry cleaner, and a coin laundry. The following size ranges will help you define the term *shopping center* for investment purposes:

Superregional	1,000,000+ square feet
Regional	300,000 to 1,000,000 square feet
Community	100,000 to 300,000 square feet
Neighborhood	30,000 to 100,000 square feet
Strip	10,000 to 20,000 square feet

■ Shopping for Commercial Real Estate

It's a good idea to invest time shopping for buildings long before you are actually ready to buy. The sellers and brokers are a tremendous source of knowledge and education about the local market, the process of investing in commercial real estate, and even managing commercial property. And as you're well aware, knowing your market is critical in any real estate deal but especially with commercial property.

When the ad for a property says "business also available," forget the business and focus on the property *only*. If the property alone doesn't work, don't buy it. But if it does work, and you also get the business and that's profitable, too, great—you got a bonus.

Don't just look at what's currently on the market. Study the recent sales of properties in your price range or that you might have been interested in. Who sold? Who bought? How much? Visit the property and take a look at the tenant directory. Watch what the new owner does in the way of improvements and management changes.

One of the early pieces of information you'll get on a property is the seller's pro forma, which includes the financial statements and other documentation of the property's performance. Your initial review of these documents tells you whether you want to pursue the deal further; if you do, verify everything on the pro forma and don't accept anything without checking it out. You also want to be careful when calculating your property tax estimates. Don't assume that you'll pay the same amount the seller has paid; when the property sells, it could be reassessed at a substantially higher value and your taxes increase accordingly.

You also need to make sure that the leases are accurate—that is, the square feet the tenants are paying for is what they're really getting. Don't just review the lease abstracts—read the leases! The abstract is a brief summary of the business terms of the lease, and it's what the property manager uses to manage the building. When you own the property, you'll create your own abstracts to streamline the management process. But when you're buying, don't rely on someone else's abstract; read the entire lease. If it's a large property with many tenants, or if the leases are complicated, or if you just want some extra reassurance that you understand the terms, have a real estate attorney review all the leases and related documents and go over them with you.

Beyond the property itself, take a look at the neighborhood. What's nearby, and does it work for you or against you? Check with the local planning and zoning board to see if any changes are in the works. What's the growth potential for the area?

When you have researched every aspect of the property—and what I've offered here is *not* a comprehensive list—then it's time to put together an offer.

Wealth Secrets

When you're buying investment property, especially multiunit residential and commercial buildings, ignore the "it could be getting more rent" line. Buy based on the income the property is generating now; don't pay a seller for what hasn't been done.

■ Determining the Value of Commercial Property

An important component in determining the value of residential property is the "comps"—that is, what people have been willing to pay for comparable properties in the area recently. With commercial property, comps are considered but typically don't carry as much weight because it's hard to find commercial comps. Commercial real estate doesn't turn over with the same rhythm and pattern that residential properties do. And though you might find recent commercial sales, finding truly comparable properties may be a challenge. Think about the makeup of commercial areas where

SUCCESS
STORY

■ If They Don't Answer the First Time, Ask Again

The asking price on the eight-unit apartment complex was $195,000. The owner was an investor who was selling off his properties so he could retire. When Lester Theiss, a student you first met in Chapter 4, began the negotiations, he asked, "What will you take for an all cash offer?" He had to ask three times before the seller finally answered.

"He said, 'How does $170,000 sound?' I said, 'I'll take it,'" Lester recalls. Because the building appraised at $195,000, the purchase price was less than 90 percent of the value, so Lester was able to finance the full $170,000—a no-money-down deal. "The banker was impressed that I knew how to talk to him, and that I had put together a complete presentation on the property," he says. Four years later, the building is worth $215,000 and is generating $2,200 in positive cash flow each month.

you live. You can drive down the street and within three blocks pass a large strip center anchored by a chain grocery store; a freestanding building housing a restaurant; a child care center; a car wash; a small strip center with a convenience store; a gas station; a two-story office building; a veterinary hospital; a single-story office building with warehouse space and loading docks; a large apartment complex; and a medical complex. Those are all commercial properties, but they aren't comparable. Certainly a good appraiser will do his best to find comparable properties or note other properties that have sold recently, even though they might not be comparable, but comps are usually going to be a small part of a commercial appraisal.

The bigger factor on which the value of commercial property is based is its *net income*. This means you can increase the value of a building by increasing the income it generates and/or reducing the expenses. So if you buy a distressed building that is vacant or only partially rented, you can force some rapid appreciation by fixing it up and getting it fully leased. Then—and this technique should sound familiar!—you can either pull your equity out by refinancing the property or selling it at the new value for a substantial profit.

The capitalization rate, or "cap rate," is a ratio used to estimate the value of income-producing properties. The cap rate is the *net operating income* (NOI) divided by the sales price, or value, expressed as a percentage. This calculation does not include the mortgage but is done as though you paid cash for the property. The cap rate is essentially the rate at which you'll earn money. Commercial real estate brokers, appraisers, and lenders can tell you what the cap rate for a given area is. That means you can take a property's NOI, divide it by the cap rate, and come up with an estimated value.

Let's say you're considering a small multiunit office-warehouse building. The asking price is $1.5 million. The property's NOI is $188,000. The cap rate would be 12.5. If the cap rate for the area is 12.5 or lower, the property is reasonably priced. If it's higher, the price is probably too high.

You can also use the cap rate to determine what you're willing to pay for a property. Decide the rate at which you want to earn money—12 percent, 15 percent, whatever. Let's say the property's NOI is $95,000, and you want to earn 13 percent. Divide the NOI by .13 (a cap rate of 13), which is $730,769—the market value of the property.

Of course, the cap rate is only a starting point when it comes to setting a price for commercial property. You also need to consider possible inflation, risk, and other opportunities in the marketplace. If the property is leased, consider how much revenue is being generated, the quality of the tenant(s), and the length of the lease(s). If one tenant is occupying 65 percent of the property but the lease is expiring in ten months and the tenant is planning to move, the value of the property is reduced. On the other hand, if that same tenant is sound and in the first year of a five-year lease, the value is increased.

Let's talk for a minute about calculating operating income, which is typically done on an annual basis. Your gross operating income is the total potential rental income (the market rent times the number of units or square feet) plus other income. To calculate the net operating income, subtract the vacancies, credit losses, and operating expenses. Operating expenses typically include such items as advertising, insurance, maintenance, property taxes, property management, repairs, supplies, and utilities. They do not include depreciation, interest, and amortization (the mortgage payment).

As you examine a property's NOI, consider that the current owner may not be managing the property as efficiently as you can. Or she may be spending too much or too little on various operating expenses. Look for signs of deferred maintenance—is the NOI great because the building is well managed, or does it just look good because the owner isn't spending money on upkeep? You should also consider the potential for additional sources of income. For example, would tenants be willing to pay more for exterior signs? Could you rent space on the roof to communication companies for their satellite dishes or antennas?

Another common ratio to use when estimating the value of income-producing property is the *gross rent multiplier* (GRM), a useful tool when you have current and detailed financial information about similar properties in the area. You can use the GRM of similar properties to estimate the value of these properties. The GRM is calculated by dividing the sales price by the yearly potential gross income. Use the GRM as an initial screening tool to decide if a property is worth pursuing.

Be wary of people who use the PFA method of calculating real estate value. It's a common technique in commercial real estate, but it shouldn't be trusted. By the way, PFA stands for "plucked from the air."

■ In the Zone

The distinction between a commercial and resident property is the zoning—that is, what the local governing body (city, town, county, etc.) says the property can be used for. As communities grow and change, zoning of given properties changes. Sometimes the government initiates the change; other times, the property owner requests it.

A smart investment strategy is to buy residential properties adjacent to commercial areas and then either wait for them to be rezoned or initiate the rezoning yourself. Once rezoning occurs, your equity increases dramatically, because commercial properties are almost always more valuable than residential properties.

You're probably familiar with a number of areas in your own community that are in transition from residential to commercial. Maybe a street has been widened, and heavy traffic has made it unsuitable for residential living, so the single-family homes are being converted to offices. Maybe the business needs of a once small downtown area are spilling into adjacent neighborhoods, again driving the conversion of houses to business use. Whatever the reason, these changes spell opportunity. You can buy a house at the residential price and rent it to cover the cost of the mortgage and create some positive cash flow while you wait for the rezoning to take place. When it does, you can either replace your residential tenant with a higher-paying business tenant or sell the property at its higher commercial value.

To find out what properties are likely to be rezoned in the next few years, contact the city planner. Explain that you are a real estate investor and would like to review the comprehensive land use plan for a particular area. The city planner can also tell you the procedures for applying for rezoning a property when you'd like to expedite the process. Another resource for finding properties that are likely to be rezoned is the local planning or transportation department. Find out what road projects are scheduled and evaluate the impact on the neighborhoods. Then decide how you can buy now, profit now, and profit even more later from zoning changes.

Truth in Numbers

If you have a consistent occupancy rate of 100 percent, you may not be charging enough for rent.

Commercial Leases and Rent Structures

In sharp contrast with the simple documents you use to rent residential property, commercial leases are lengthy, complex contracts. A key element of a commercial lease is the way the rent is structured, and the lease is typically referred to in terms of the rent structure. The primary types of leases are the following:

- *Flat lease.* This is the oldest and simplest type of lease. It sets a single price for a definite period and is now used less and less frequently.
- *Step lease.* Under a step lease, the rent increases on an annual basis in an effort to cover the landlord's expected increases in expenses. The challenge of step leases is that they are based on estimates rather than actual costs, so there's no way for either party to be sure in advance that the proposed increases are fair and equitable.
- *Net lease.* Using the same concept as the step lease, the net lease increases the rent to cover increased expenses but does so at the time they occur. Tenants may resist net leases because they are unpredictable.
- *Cost-of-living lease.* Rather than tying rent increases to specific expenses, this type of lease bases increases on inflation. It appeals to tenants because even as their rent increases, so does the price of their products and/or services.
- *Percentage lease.* This lease allows the landlord to benefit from a tenant's success and is very common for retail space. The rent is based on either an agreed-on minimum or a percentage of the tenant's gross revenue, whichever is higher. Percentages generally range from 3 to 12 percent, and the tenant is required to periodically furnish proof of gross sales, usually in the form of sales tax reports.
- *Ground lease.* This is a long-term lease of land that allows a tenant to make improvements, such as a building or parking lot, at his own expense.

Commercial leases tend to be for a much longer term than residential leases, which is why they commonly include escalator clauses that provide for rent increases. It's customary—and also a good idea—to require six months' notice to renew or terminate a commercial lease. Set up your leases so they don't expire in the same year; ideally, you should limit your potential turnover to 20 percent in any one year.

Among the multitude of points a commercial lease must address are the issues involved in making the space appropriate for the needs of the tenant, a process referred to as the "build-out," which could involve substantial renovations. You have to decide what you're willing to allow and who is going to pay for it.

When a tenant wants lease terms that aren't to your advantage, don't agree. Commercial leases usually involve a fair amount of negotiation, and saying no to some requests won't automatically kill a deal, especially if you offer a palatable alternative. You can always blame some of your own requirements on your lender, saying something such as, "My bank won't let me do that," or "My bank insists that I do this." Most commercial tenants are going to have the lease reviewed by their attorney before signing it, and they may use that in their negotiations, saying such things as, "My attorney says this needs to be in the lease." Be aware of these negotiating techniques and be reasonable in the give-and-take process, but don't agree on lease terms that are not profitable . . . period.

FYI

Most commercial leases have a rules clause that allows you to change or create rules. This gives you the option of making adjustments in such areas as smoking policies, parking rules, security, and so on without affecting the terms of your leases.

■ Commercial Building Management

In many ways, commercial tenants are a lot like residential tenants: some are great, a few are real trouble, and most of them just pay their rent on time and you'll rarely hear from them. Commercial tenants tend to stay put longer than residential tenants—after all, moving a business is a lot more complicated than moving a household. If you manage your commercial properties well, you should be able to attract and retain solid long-term tenants.

Apart from the courses we offer, one of the best sources for information about owning and managing commercial real estate is the Building Owners and Managers Association (BOMA). Most metropolitan areas have local chapters, and contact information for the national organization is in the resource section at the back of this book. BOMA has a guide for understanding the Americans with Disabilities Act (ADA), which will help you be sure your buildings comply with federal accessibility requirements. The association also has information to help you understand your risks and obligations regarding potential environmental issues, including sick building syndrome, asbestos, and hazardous materials. You might find these and other regulatory and management issues intimidating, but that's only if you don't understand them. Take the time to educate yourself, and you'll handle whatever occurs with efficiency, accuracy, and confidence.

Positive communication is one of the most critical parts of successful building management. You need to be a hands-on manager, or hire someone who is. Talk to your tenants regularly. This lets them know you care, which increases tenant loyalty. It also gives you an opportunity to see how they're doing and provides an early warning of possible problems. When tenants complain about something, respond immediately. If it's something that can't be corrected right away, let them know and then keep them advised as you work on the problem.

Walk through every commercial property once a week. Make sure all the lights are working, check the restrooms and make sure all the plumbing is functioning properly with no leaks, and in general look for those small items that can be fixed before they turn into major problems. Keep in mind that unlike residential real estate, most commercial properties are public places, and you want to be sure your buildings are both attractive and safe for tenants, their customers, and anyone else who happens to visit. Regular inspections not only help with maintenance but they also make you visible to your tenants and help you build a reputation as a good landlord.

Of course, just as you want to be a good landlord, you want to choose good tenants. Thoroughly screen your commercial tenants. Ask to see their business plan, including financial statements, marketing plans, and long-term forecasts. If a tenant is a small company, it's best if the owner plans to be on the premises. Know who the corporate officers are and, if you can, get those officers to personally guarantee the lease. Ask for and check references. Check the better business bureau and consumer protection agencies for a record of complaints; you don't want a local television station filming the outside of your building as part of an exposé of a tenant who has ripped off a bunch of people. Check tenants' credit ratings and find out why they're moving. A good tenant interested in long-term occupancy won't object to this process.

Anything Can Happen—and Usually Does!

One of the great things about real estate is that it's always interesting, usually challenging, and often even easier than you thought it would be. My students Lorne and Angie Saltsman are a perfect example. They've used my techniques to buy several income-producing properties with owner financing and no money down.

One of the differences between commercial and residential real estate is that people tend not to flip commercial properties the way they do residential. Sure, it happens, it's just not as common as it is with

houses. But Lorne and Angie found a commercial building, bought it, and flipped it less than two hours later for a $12,010 profit. Angie estimates they worked on the deal for about eight hours total. It was their first commercial property flip, and I'm betting it won't be their last.

■ Some Final Thoughts on the Subject

When it comes to investing in commercial properties—or any kind of real estate, for that matter—it's not about pride of ownership; it's about income. You don't have to own landmarks or architectural marvels; you need to own buildings that generate positive cash flow and will appreciate in value.

I urge you to play it safe. Commercial real estate is a dangerous place for pioneers. Don't venture into the unknown; buy and build where there is a history. Let the risk takers clear the path; then you follow along and build a fortune.

Without a doubt, commercial real estate can be extremely lucrative, and I would never discourage anyone from venturing into it. But don't jump into the proverbial deep end of the pool if you don't know how to swim. Start with residential properties, learn the business, develop your management skills, educate yourself, and then, after you're comfortable and confident, take the next step.

MILLIONAIRE MENTOR Commercial Real Estate Highlights

- The basic principles of investing in real estate apply to both residential and commercial property, but certain aspects of commercial real estate are more complex and require additional education.

- Zoning is the issue that determines if a property is commercial.

- The four types of commercial properties are retail, industrial, offices, and multifamily residential.

- Take your time when shopping for commercial real estate and let the sellers and brokers educate you about the market and the property management process.

- The biggest factor on which the value of commercial property is based is its net income.

- Residential properties that are in line to be rezoned commercial offer a tremendous opportunity for savvy investors.

CHAPTER 13

Real Estate Notes

Secrets of the Discount Buy

Something I hear often: "Russ, I know you can make a lot of money in real estate, but I'm not a hands-on kind of person. I don't want to rehab or be a landlord or do the other things you have to do when you're buying, selling, and renting houses." The good news: You can make a fortune in real estate without ever owning the first piece of property by buying and selling notes, or "paper."

Real estate notes, also known as mortgage notes or deeds of trust, are contracts with a promise to pay that are secured by real property. What are known as privately held notes are notes created when a real estate transaction takes place, and the seller agrees to finance the deal. These notes can be discounted and then bought and sold at tremendous profits.

Real estate notes represent a $400 billion industry and a virtually unlimited opportunity for creating wealth. Mortgage notes are generally produced by banks or mortgage companies and secured by the federal government. To get cash to create new loans, lenders bundle their existing loans into packages and sell them at a discount on what is called the *secondary mortgage market.*

When it comes to privately held notes, the process is very similar but on a much smaller scale. An individual acts as a lender in a real estate transaction. The seller and buyer agree on a down payment amount, the duration of the note, and the interest rate. When the transaction is closed, the seller becomes the note holder and receives payments, usually on a monthly basis, from the buyer. If at some point in the future and for whatever reason—for example, the note holder either wants or needs cash—the note holder sells the note at a discount to an investor for a lump sum, and the investor begins collecting the payments. Why is the note discounted? Because of the time value of money—the value of money in the future is worth less than the value of money today.

You can make money in paper two ways: (1) by actually buying the notes at a discount and collecting the payments or (2) by brokering the notes to a funding source (and I'll tell you how to find and use funding sources later on in this chapter) for a commission. This business works as a stand-alone operation or in conjunction with any of the real estate investing techniques in this book.

Truth in Numbers

Note brokers earn a percentage of the principal balance of the note. The average is 6 to 7 percent; the low is 3 percent and the high 10 percent.

■ Why and How Private Notes Are Created

In previous chapters, I've made several references to situations where sellers are willing to finance all or part of the price of the real estate. They do this for two primary reasons: to make the deal happen and/or because they enjoy the cash flow.

When interest rates began climbing during the late 1970s, private paper became abundant because people couldn't afford traditional loans. Then during the savings and loan crisis of the 1980s, institutional loans were hard to get. Again, sellers had to hold notes to close their deals. These were individuals who didn't particularly want to be lenders, so they were willing to sell their notes to investors at a discount (i.e., less than the principal amount) to get their cash.

As the economy goes through its natural cycles, there are times when seller financing is more popular than other times. And as the awareness of seller financing increases, so does the amount of notes created each year. But even though this financing technique is becoming more and more common, most individual note holders have no idea how to find an investor to buy their note—and that's where you come in. You serve as an educator, explaining that they can sell their note and get the cash now, and then you serve as a facilitator, making the sale happen either as a broker or investor.

As a real estate investor, there may be times when you hold a note on a property you sell. You may opt to hang on to the note for the long-term cash flow, or you can sell it for immediate cash. That's what Lester Theiss did—Lester is one of my students I first mentioned in Chapter 4. He's an ordinary guy who has enjoyed extraordinary success in real estate. He agreed to hold a note as part of a creative financing package on a property he sold. He let the note age for six months; then he sold it and used the cash to buy more property.

■ The Rest of the Story

Plenty of note holders like collecting the payments and profiting from the interest on the loan, but plenty more find holding paper a burden they'd love to shed. A note holder may want to sell the note for any one of a number of reasons. He may need the cash or may just be tired of collecting monthly payments. If the note holder has died, the heirs may prefer to have a lump sum of cash rather than payments made to the estate over a long period. Whatever the reason, you can help.

Once you have identified a potential note seller, you must gather preliminary information about the seller, payer, and property secured by the note, which you submit to a funding source. The funding source reviews the information and tells you what they're willing to pay for the note. From that amount, you deduct what you want to make on the deal and present an offer to the note holder. If the offer is accepted, a formal application is submitted to the funding source.

The funding source researches the note (a process known as due diligence) to determine that the facts are indeed as the note holder has presented them and evaluates the risks associated with the note. If everything checks out, the offer is formalized and arrangements are made for closing. That process is similar to a real estate closing in that the necessary documents are executed and recorded, and the associated payments are distributed. The note holder receives a lump sum payment for the sale of the note, the broker collects his fee, and the funding source now owns the note and may keep it to receive monthly cash flow or resell it at a profit.

Smart Thinking

When a seller provides all or part of the financing in a real estate deal, he has greater control of the transaction. He can set his own interest rate and often will get a higher price for the property. Another benefit is that because of the easier qualifying and minimal amount of paperwork, owner financing attracts more buyers.

■ What Motivates Note Sellers?

People are motivated to sell their notes for a variety of reasons, including:

- Debt
- Job loss
- Education expenses
- Divorce settlement
- Medical expenses
- Retirement
- To reinvest funds
- Vacation
- A variety of other reasons

■ Getting into the Business

Whether you want to broker or buy, the first step in getting started in the note business is to research your market. The goal of your research is to create a list of note holders who may be interested in selling their notes either now or in the future. The industry is rich with resources to find these prospects. Your three primary research areas are discussed in the following paragraphs.

Public records. Public records contain a wealth of real estate transaction information that provides direct, up-to-date details about prospective clients. These records, usually located at the county courthouse or land records office, provide one of the best sources for finding excellent business leads. In Chapter 6, you learned how to search public records for information on foreclosures. The process is very similar when you're looking for note holders. Use the same search techniques to find properties that are mortgaged but not facing foreclosure. If the note holder is a bank or mortgage company, pass it by. (You'll be able to tell by the name; e.g., First National Bank or General Mortgage Corp.) If the note holder is an individual or even two people (e.g., John A. Brown or Sam and Mary Smith), you have a prospect.

Your own referral network. Develop your own network of people who deal with real estate notes on a daily basis. They know who might need your services and can provide you with a steady flow of leads. Build a relationship with them and make it worth their while to work with you. Your network should include real estate brokers and agents; mortgage brokers; other note buyers; attorneys; financial management experts; accountants; title companies and escrow agents; bankers; builders and contractors; insurance agents; real estate appraisers; and rental property owners.

Property sellers. Identify properties that are for sale by the owner. When you contact sellers, explain how offering financing can make it easier for them to sell their property. Tell them about your service so they understand they don't have to hold the note for a long period. In fact, they can create a note and sell it to the funding source at the same time they close on the sale of their home.

FYI

Mortgages don't have to be recorded to be legal, but they do have to be recorded to become public information.

■ Searching Public Records

Before you head to the courthouse, consider these tips for performing a public records search:

- Decide how much time and effort you are willing to commit to your search. Manage this set-aside time carefully to maximize your efforts.
- Hire a research assistant to help you. You can either pay an hourly rate or offer a commission for leads that develop into sales.
- Learn the procedures for how real estate records are recorded and filed in the county in which you are conducting business. In most cases, you'll find the county employees very helpful and willing to teach you what you have to know.
- Search four to five years back. This technique helps you find established mortgages with a payment history, which are preferred by many investors.
- Concentrate some of your efforts on rural areas or counties. This is a good way to develop leads with little competition.

■ A Simple Process

Once you've located a list of privately held notes, the next step is to contact the owners. One of the most effective ways to do this is by telephone. Keep in mind that you are not the only note broker/buyer out there, so it's important that your presentation be polished and professional. Practice on a friend before you make the calls. And remember to *listen*—what you have to say is certainly important, but equally important is what the note holder tells you. What the holder says reveals his motivation for selling and any doubts he has about the process. This information is essential to consummating the deal.

The following sample telephone script shows you what to say to a note holder when you make your initial contact by telephone:

You: May I speak to Susan Adams, please? Ms. Adams, my name is Bob Mitchell, and my company buys private mortgages. I'm calling to ask if you'd be interested in selling the mortgage you currently hold.

Adams: I don't know. What are you talking about?

You: I'm talking about a way for you to get cash for the note you're currently receiving payments on. You can have a lump sum now instead of waiting years to collect your money. Could you use the cash today?

Adams: Of course. How does this work?

You: It depends on the specifics of your real estate note, but in general, we will pay you the amount due on the note less a discount, in return for the right to collect the payments you are now receiving. You can have the cash now to do whatever you want—pay bills, take a vacation, buy a new car, whatever. How does that sound?

Adams: It sounds good. What do I have to do?

You: I need to get some information from you about your note, and then I'll be able to tell you exactly how much cash I can pay you for the note. Do you have a few minutes to answer some questions?

Adams: Yes.

(Use the mortgage worksheet in Figure 13.1 as a guide to ask questions about the note. Fill out the worksheet completely. In addition to getting the specifics on the note, try to find out what the note holder might do with the cash.)

You: Okay, Ms. Adams, I have the information I need. When is the best time for me to call you back with the quote?

Adams: In the morning after nine o'clock is good.

You: I'll call you as soon as I have some numbers for you. Is there anyone else I need to go over the quote with, or are you the one who will make the decision to sell?

Adams: It's my decision.

You: Okay. I'll get a quote and call you in the morning after nine.

If the holder is interested in selling, you have to find out three key pieces of information before you can begin negotiating a deal:

1. Does the prospect still own the note?
2. Is the prospect the only person who can make decisions about the note, or are there other mortgagees? If others are involved, find out who they are and how to reach them.
3. Does the prospect have, or have access to, all the documents you may need to close the deal? This includes the original note, the mortgage or deed of trust, payment history, property insurance, and title insurance.

The next step is to complete a mortgage worksheet, which is a form that identifies the seller and details about the property, the conditions of sale, and terms of the note. This is what the funding source uses to establish the integrity of the note and decide whether to pursue the transaction. Mortgage worksheets are typically supplied by the funding sources and their format may vary, but the information required is essentially the same (see Figure 13.1).

After you fax the worksheet to the funding source, you'll receive an initial quote for the note. From that quote, subtract the amount of money you want to make on the deal and make an offer to the note holder. If the offer is accepted, you'll need to complete an application package for the funding source. This is more detailed than the mortgage worksheet and provides sufficient information so the necessary due diligence can be conducted.

When a funding source examines a potential transaction, he will assess the financial value behind the note and the degree of risk involved in buying the note. The financial value includes the principal amount of the mortgage, the discounts and yields that can be applied in the transaction, the number of payments applied under the term of the loan, and the present

FIGURE 13.1

■

Sample
Mortgage
Worksheet

Date: _____ File #: _____

1. Your Information
   Your Name: _____
   Member ID#: _____

2. Note Seller Information
   Note Seller's Name: _____
   Mailing Address: _____
   Home Phone: _____ Office: _____

   Mortgagor(s) Name: _____ (Payor)
   Mortgagor(s) SIN#: _____ (Payor)

3. Note Seller Motivation
   Has note seller expressed an interest in selling?   Yes   No   (1) _____
   Does the note seller have possession of the
   original note?   Yes   No

4. Property Type: (Check one)
   Single family _____   2-4 Family _____   Condominium _____   (2) _____
   Row House _____   Land _____   Mobile home _____
   House/Office mixed use _____   Other _____

5. Property Information
   Address: _____   (3) _____
   City: _____ State: _____ Zip: _____
   Occupancy: (Circle one)   Owner   Tenant   Vacant   (4) _____
   Last Sales Price/Market Value: $ _____   (5) _____
   Sale Date: _____   (6) _____

6. Mortgage Information
   Original amount of subject mortgage: $ _____
   Interest rate: _____ %   Term: _____ (months)
   Monthly Payments: $ _____
   Lien Position: First _____ Second _____ Third _____   (7) _____
       If subject was a second mortgage, what was the balance of the
       first mortgage at the time of the sale? $ _____

First Payment was due on: (original first payment) $ _____
Loan Balance: $ _____   (8) _____
Balloon feature in note?   Yes   No
If yes, balloon due on: _____

7. Loan-to-Value Ratio
   Total balance of all mortgages divided by the market value: _____   (9) _____
                                                   Total Points   (10) _____

For Investor's Use Only:

Net to note seller: $ _____ Date: _____
Fee to Broker/Finder: $ _____ Date: _____

value of the note. The level of risk is decided by evaluating the loan-to-value ratio; investment-to-value ratio; type of property securing the note; credit-worthiness of the note payer; and the appraised value of the property that secures the note.

Once the funding source has completed the due diligence process, he will issue a commitment to purchase the note. This solidifies the deal and puts everything in writing, setting the stage for the closing, where you receive your payment.

Wealth Secrets

Always be sure the decision maker is going to be present when you make your offer and negotiate the final terms of the deal. Remember, many note holders will be sophisticated negotiators and may know how to use the "I need to check with my partner/spouse/attorney/ whoever" technique as well as you do.

■ Making Offers

Before you make an offer on a note, you should find out how much cash the note seller needs up front. This is not difficult to do; when people are interested in selling their notes, they are usually very candid about how much money they need and why they need it. With this information, you'll be in a better position to structure the deal advantageously so the seller can get the money he needs and you can get the commission you want. The information also lets you know if the seller must sell all of the note or only part of it.

Gather the information about the note, obtain the quote from the funding source, calculate your profit, and then take the number back to the seller. When you are ready to make an offer, it's a good idea to have options so the seller can choose one rather than give you a yes or no on a single deal. For example, if the note holder needs only half of the face value of the note in cash, offer the choice of selling all or part of the note. If that's not practical, try to build some negotiating room into your offer.

FYI

Purchasing a note is not an all-or-nothing transaction. Note holders don't have to sell the entire note; they can sell a portion of the payment stream.

■ What's in It for You?

How much profit should you make on a deal? That's entirely up to you. Note brokers earn as little as 3 percent and as much as 10 percent of the face value of the note on each transaction. You might want to create a fee structure for yourself as your guide for structuring your deals. For example, you might decide that you want to make at least $3,000 on deals of $100,000 or less and between $6,000 and $10,000 on deals between $100,000 and $200,000. Knowing your limits before you start helps tremendously in both structuring the deal and in negotiating.

When you put your deals together, always remember that every time a note is sold, it's discounted so someone can make a profit. Here's a hypothetical scenario based on a situation that is very common. Widow Mary Brown decided to remarry and move into her new husband's home. Her mortgage had been paid off years ago. When she sold her house for $100,000, she received a $25,000 down payment in cash and agreed to hold a note for $75,000 at 10 percent secured by a first mortgage. The payments are $659 a month. Three years later, after receiving a total of $23,724 in monthly payments, Mary wants the cash. The principal balance of the loan is now $73,580. A take-out buyer—that is, a person or company who buys paper—offered $65,486. You as the broker offer Mary $60,786. Mary is still netting well over the current value of the original note, the take-out buyer is getting a seasoned note at a good interest rate, and you get a commission of $4,700 for putting the deal together.

Here's another hypothetical example to show you how the process works. When George Smith sold his house, he received part of the down payment in cash and took back a second mortgage of $12,000 at 8 percent for ten years. A year later, George is tired of collecting monthly payments of

$146. You find a take-out buyer willing to pay $10,060 (90 percent of the principal balance of the loan), and you offer $9,334, which means a $726 commission for you. Or because you recently flipped a few houses and have the cash, you buy the note yourself for $9,334 and receive payments totaling $15,768 over the remaining nine years—a profit of $6,434.

Obviously, the bigger the mortgage, the bigger the profit for you and the note buyer. Of course, there's more competition for those large notes, too. A good strategy is to start with smaller notes, build your confidence and reputation, and then move up to the larger notes.

FYI

Most notes are paid off in 3 to 5 years, even though the contracts are for up to 30 years.

■ A Review of the Paperwork, or Why Many Trees Give Up Their Lives for You

Don't be alarmed at the amount of paper required to close a paper deal. Even though no property changes hands with a note sale, it's important that all of the required documents are complete and accurate to protect all parties to the transaction. Before you make your first offer, you have to be familiar with these documents:

- *The original note.* A note is a negotiable asset that can be bought and sold.
- *The mortgage, or deed of trust.* This document shows you the amount of the mortgage, position of the mortgage, the interest rate, whether the rate is fixed or adjustable, the term of the mortgage, if the mortgage is assumable, and if taxes and insurance are included in the monthly payment.
- *The closing statement.* This shows you the costs involved in the original purchase and sale of the property.
- *Payment history.* This documents how the mortgagor has paid on the note and can be in the form of a certification or copies of canceled checks.

■ *Estoppel letter.* This is the letter you send to the mortgagor to ensure that the conditions of the original note have been followed and that no payments of which you are unaware have been made.

The funding source will issue the closing instructions, which will thoroughly detail the documents necessary to complete the transaction.

Smart Thinking

Note buyers can be a good source for property to buy. If they have to foreclose on a note but don't want to own real estate, they may be happy to have you take the property off their hands.

■ Funding Sources

Locating funding sources is one of the easiest parts of the paper business. The consultants at Whitney Education Group maintain a current list of funding sources we know and can confidently recommend. In addition, many individuals and companies are looking for the opportunity to invest their money in real estate notes. Just a small amount of research and networking will help you locate an ample number of potential funding sources. You'll meet people who deal in paper and who are either a funding source or can refer you to a source at your local real estate investors organization. Or get on the Internet and do a search for "mortgage note funding sources" —you'll find more than you can ever work with. Note buyers are always on the lookout for sharp brokers, and most have already assembled a new broker package that they're happy to send you.

Once you find them, establish a solid relationship with your funding sources. Learn how they prefer to operate so you can submit the type of deals you know they want in the format that works best for them.

Don't work with any funding source that takes more than a few hours to get a quote. A motivated note seller doesn't want to wait days or a week to find out how much he can get for his note. This industry is built on speed.

The faster a funding source gives you a quote, the faster it—and you—can make money.

MILLIONAIRE MENTOR Real Estate Notes Highlights

- Real estate notes allow you to invest in real estate without owning property or can supplement your real estate investments to keep your portfolio diversified.

- Notes (also known as "paper") allow you to make money in two primary ways: by actually buying at a discount and collecting the payments or by brokering the notes to a funding source. Brokers typically make between 3 and 10 percent of the face value of the note as their commission.

- One of the most common ways privately held notes are created is a seller agreeing to finance all or part of the deal when a real estate transaction takes place. These notes can be discounted and then bought and sold at tremendous profits.

- People sell their notes for a variety of reasons. In many cases, they need the cash for various reasons, or they might just be tired of collecting payments.

- The most common way to find privately held notes is by searching the public records at the courthouse.

- The documentation required to close on a note sale is similar to what's required to close on a real estate sale. The funding source should handle most of this and guide you through what you have to do.

CHAPTER 14

Tax Certificates

High Yield, Low Risk, No Sweat

If the paper business appeals to you, consider *tax lien certificates* as well as mortgage notes. Tax lien certificates are one of the most predictable, certain, and secure real estate–related investments available. You buy them from the government, you get paid by the government, and the local tax collector does all the work.

You won't hear about tax lien certificates from financial advisors or brokers because they don't earn commissions on this incredibly lucrative investment, so they have no incentive to share information about this investment with their clients. It's also likely that many brokers don't even know about tax liens, so don't expect them to be particularly enthusiastic when you decide to make this investment part of your portfolio. But the tax lien certificate market is more than $10 billion and growing—and that kind of money is worth your attention.

Tax lien investors travel around the country attending sales and auctions, and their travel costs are tax deductible as business expenses. If they happen to play a little golf in Arizona, ski in Colorado, go to the beach in Florida, or enjoy some fine cuisine in Louisiana while they're buying tax lien certificates—well, it's still a business trip. Sound attractive? I hope so. And being able to travel to fun places on business is just a minor benefit.

When you invest in tax lien certificates, you can earn anywhere from 12 percent to 24 percent interest the first year and as much as 24 percent to 50 percent in the second year, depending on individual state law, the bidding system, and the period of redemption (all of which I'm going to explain). Those rates are part of state statutes—they are totally legal and can be changed only by the state legislature. This means it doesn't matter what's happening in the market with interest rates; your tax certificate rate is fixed by law and guaranteed. You can buy tax liens for as little as $100 or less and possibly double your money in two years, and your investment is protected by the property tax code.

Wealth Secrets

There is no restriction on the number of tax lien certificates you can buy. You are limited only by how much cash you have to invest.

◼ What's Bad for Property Owners but Great for You?

In most situations, tax liens are not good news for real estate investors; they can cloud titles and reduce profits. But tax liens *are* good when you want to buy tax lien certificates, because you are not buying property but rather the rights of the taxing authority. Here's how it works.

For whatever reason, a property owner doesn't pay his taxes. At a certain point dictated by law after the taxes become delinquent, the county (or governing taxing unit) places a lien on the property. Then the county sells the tax lien certificate to an investor for the amount of tax owed plus penalties and interest due at the time the certificate is sold. Eventually, the property owner pays the amount paid for the certificate plus additional interest to the county. The tax collector notifies the investor, who returns the certificate and collects those funds. If the taxes aren't paid within the time set by the taxing jurisdiction (typically one to three years but sometimes longer), the owner of the certificate gets the property.

It really is that simple. You could buy a tax lien certificate for $2,500 at 17 percent interest and after a year enjoy a profit of $425; or if the property owner takes two years to pay, you'll net $850. And your investment is secured by the real estate and protected by the laws of the state.

Governments sell tax lien certificates because they need the cash to fund services—a classic example of the time value of money in action. The governments could let the interest continue to accrue and eventually collect more money, but they need the cash to meet payroll and other operating expenses now, not two years from now. So they're willing to take a little less than the amount they could ultimately get, and investors are willing to pay less now to get a substantial return on their money later.

When you buy a tax lien certificate, you're paying the delinquent taxes on a property and buying the rights to collect those taxes plus additional interest from the property owner. You aren't foreclosing. You aren't forcing anyone out of their home. In fact, it's very rare for property owners to forfeit their real estate for the taxes; rather, the fact that losing their property is a possibility gives them the incentive to pay off the tax lien. If a property owner wants to sell, most buyers are going to insist that the tax lien be taken care of before they'll do the deal, so you'll get your money then. In the unlikely event that the buyer overlooks the tax lien, you're protected because it stays attached to the property until paid. Remember, a tax lien is superior to all other liens on the property, including the first mortgage.

What's important to keep in mind is that you buy the certificate from the tax collector's office (or treasurer or whatever the particular government entity is called), not from the property owner. The property owner pays the taxes to the tax collector, not to you. In most cases, you'll never deal directly with the property owner. Even in the unlikely event that the owner doesn't pay the taxes and you have to foreclose, an attorney or possibly even a government employee will handle it for you under the laws of the state.

Did You Know?

Tax lien sales are included in the public record. You can find out who your competition for this type of investment is by checking the public records to see who bought certificates last year.

■ Why Don't They Pay Their Taxes?

The dollar amount of tax liens ranges from very modest to substantial, and they're attached to properties of all types and descriptions. You might wonder how people can afford to own property and not pay the taxes. The reasons are many.

It's possible that the owner died and the taxes didn't get paid while the estate was being settled. Or the heirs may have overlooked the taxes, especially if they live in another state or they're hoping to sell the property without having to put any cash into it.

Sometimes people just get into temporary financial difficulties and are unable to pay their taxes on time. People have also been known to deliberately delay paying taxes because they have their cash invested elsewhere and want to wait until the last possible minute before pulling the money out of the investment vehicle to pay bills with it.

■ Getting In on the Opportunity

Tax lien certificates are usually sold at a public auction, and the details of the bidding process vary by state. There are approximately 3,300 counties in the United States, each of which has its own rules. Though state statutes govern how tax liens are sold, local governments interpret these statutes, which means local rules, even in neighboring counties, almost always differ slightly from each other.

Your first step is to decide what type of tax lien certificate you want to buy: liens on raw or improved land or on commercial, residential, waterfront, upscale, or moderately priced property, and so on. This decision is important for two primary reasons. First, the type of property is related to the chance that the taxes will ultimately be paid. For example, taxes on an owner-occupied house are more likely to be paid than taxes on an odd-sized strip of raw land. Second, because there is always the possibility that the owner won't pay the taxes, be sure the property is one you want to own.

Once you know what you're looking for, contact the county tax collector's office to find out when the next sale or auction is, what the required payment methods are, and what you need to do to register as a bidder. This information is published in local newspapers, but you should also be able to get it over the phone or on the county's Web site. Be sure you're getting the information on the tax lien certificate auction—you don't want to end up at the police department's unclaimed property auction by mistake.

You'll also want to find out how to get a copy of the delinquent property list; again, this is typically published in local papers and may also be available online. The final thing you want to ask for in your initial call is the tax collector's Rules of the Sale document, which tells you the sale procedures of that particular agency.

In many counties, you can actually speak to the tax collector directly about how tax sales are conducted. Whether you speak to the tax collector or someone else in the office, it's a good idea to confirm that the information provided matches that in the state statutes. Statutory information should be available in the public library, or you can contact your state's general information number to find out who to call.

Study the delinquent property list and select the properties you might be interested in. The list will rarely give you enough information to make a sound decision about bidding on any particular lien, but it should give you enough data so you can eliminate the listings you definitely don't want.

Research the liens that appear promising. Check online or at the county records office for a better description of the property and to determine if it's owner occupied or an investment property. (Remember, the general rule is that if the tax statements are being sent to the property address, it's likely owner occupied.) Find out if any liens may be superior to the lien you're considering purchasing. In most cases, a property tax lien is superior to all other liens, but you want to be sure no other state, or possibly federal, liens are on the property.

Get out a map and figure out where the property is, and then do a drive-by inspection to get an idea of the neighborhood and the general condition of the house. Is it occupied? Is it being maintained, or is it run-down? What's the area like? Does this look like a property the owner would want to keep, or does it look abandoned? And if you ended up with the property, would it be something you could make money on?

If the property looks like something you'd want to own, mark the lien as one worth bidding on.

FYI

Tax sales can be as brief as a few hours or as long as five days—it all depends on the procedures of the particular county, the number of certificates offered for sale, and the speed of the bidding.

■ Choosing the Right Certificates

Imagine that you bought a tax lien certificate for $5,000. The property the lien is attached to is a 4,000-square-foot home in an exclusive gated community with an appraised value of $650,000. After two years—the length of time the law allows the property owners to pay—you haven't received your money, so you foreclose. You now own a $650,000 house you paid $5,000 for.

Is this scenario possible? Absolutely. A good friend of mine bought a tax certificate for $15,000. When it wasn't redeemed, he became the owner of an eight-unit apartment building worth more than $200,000.

Does this sort of thing happen often? No.

What's more likely is that at some point during that two-year period, the property owner will pay the taxes plus interest, and you will have earned somewhere between 12 and 24 percent on your money.

Between 95 and 97 percent of the property owners whose tax liens are sold pay their delinquent taxes plus the interest and penalties in 24 months or less. But even though chances are slim that you'll eventually get to own the property, it's a good idea to buy certificates only on properties you're willing to own so you don't get stuck with something you don't want.

Improved property is better than raw land because resale is quicker and easier. Also, most improved property has a mortgage on it, and lenders rarely let properties go to a tax sale, which means you have greater assurance of getting your cash.

Unless you are extremely experienced with tax liens and familiar with commercial real estate (see Chapter 12), stick with certificates on residential property. Commercial property tax lien certificates are definitely high-yield, but they carry a corresponding risk. Always consider: What will you do with the property if you become the owner? Do you really want an empty warehouse in an industrial park or a run-down office building in your portfolio? If you know what to do with those types of properties, go for it. But if you don't, pass on those certificates.

Owner-occupied residential properties are the least risky, because these owners are the most likely to pay their taxes—and if they don't, it's fairly easy to sell or rent the house after you foreclose on it. Certificates on properties that are being maintained are more likely to be redeemed. Neglected, distressed properties are at a greater risk of not being redeemed—but you know what to do with that type of property, so if you do have to foreclose, it's like winning the lottery.

A Florida man (*not* one of my students!) took a very creative approach to buying tax liens and deeds. He bought lakes and adjacent submerged property at tax deed sales and then put up fences blocking the water view for the people who thought their houses were on lakefront property. He offered to sell the submerged land to the individual homeowners for more than 300 times what he paid for it. The investor insisted he was just taking advantage of a legal opportunity created when people don't pay their taxes. I tend to agree with the attorney for one of the nearby homeowners, who said that this is capitalism at its worst. This guy may make money, and he may do it legally, but in my opinion what he's doing isn't moral or ethical.

This story provides two very important lessons. First, most investment techniques can be used both positively and negatively. Always invest so that everyone wins and nobody loses. Second, when you buy real estate, be sure you know what you're buying and where your property boundaries are so something like the Florida example above doesn't happen to you.

Wealth Secrets

If a property owner doesn't pay next year's taxes, you, as the previous year's certificate holder, can buy the certificate for the subsequent year. You aren't required to do this, but it's a worthwhile investment. If you don't buy that certificate, it goes up for auction.

■ What Are the Risks?

There is absolutely no such thing as a totally risk-free investment. Tax lien certificates come about as close as anything, but they still carry risks. For example, it's possible you could end up owning a property with an environmental problem. That's rare in general and even less likely if you stick to residential properties.

Another potential risk is that a property owner could file for bankruptcy. You'll still be paid because bankruptcy doesn't wipe out tax liens, but there could be a delay.

Something that some people consider a risk is that you may not get as much money as you'd hoped, depending on when the property owners pay the taxes. If they pay the delinquent taxes shortly after you buy the certificate, your profit will be much lower than if they wait a year or more. You'll get the same percentage rate, but your yield will be lower.

The biggest risks in tax lien certificates are a result of not understanding the process and consequently making mistakes when you buy or failing to properly notify interested parties if you intend to foreclose. For example, each state has rules governing when you must pay your bid, but if you miss that deadline, you could lose your entire deposit. If you allow a property owner to talk you into accepting a payment plan, your lien could be disqualified.

Avoid the risks by learning the rules and procedures. These are written into state law and are provided by the county to interested bidders.

Warning

Avoid buying tax lien certificates for houses in neighborhoods that were built on redeveloped industrial land. Although chances are that the property is not contaminated, there is still a greater risk of an environmental problem than there is with properties that have never had an industrial use.

■ At the Auction

If only a few certificates are up for sale but the room is filled with bidders, treat the auction as a learning experience and do your buying elsewhere. But if the room is nearly empty and hundreds or even thousands of certificates are available, you've got the opportunity to make some serious money, so take advantage of it.

For most people, the biggest challenge of investing in tax lien certificates is understanding the bidding systems, which aren't like those of a general merchandise auction, where you bid a dollar amount on a particular item. In some states, you bid in a certificate auction the amount that is owed the government plus a surplus to acquire the certificate. In other states, your bid reduces the interest rate, and the bidder who is willing to accept the least return gets the certificate. In still other states, the highest bidder gets the certificate.

The bidding is intimidating only if you don't understand it. But it all boils down to simple arithmetic—you just need to understand how to do the calculations necessary to make a profitable bid in each state, and state laws can tell you that. Keep in mind that some states allow more than one bidding system, so the techniques may vary by county within a state.

At the auction, resist the urge to ask other bidders for advice and information—they may know less than you do but don't want to admit it. Get facts from reliable sources, such as the state statutes, the printed material furnished by the taxing agency, and individuals recognized as experts who provide certified training programs.

The end of the auction is not necessarily the end of the opportunity. If not all the certificates are sold at the auction, states have procedures in place to sell the remaining ones through other means. Many tax lien investors choose to avoid the auctions, which can be very competitive, and buy afterward through an over-the-counter, mail order, or subsequent sale process. Of course, there is no guarantee there will be certificates remaining, and any surplus may not be worth buying. Ask each tax office what is done with leftover certificates and if any certificates can be bought other than at auction.

Truth in Numbers

Of all tax lien certificates sold in the United States, an estimated 95 to 97 percent are redeemed by the property owner without going to foreclosure.

■ How Payday Comes

When you hold a tax lien certificate, you get your money in one of four ways. The first is by the property owner's paying the back taxes plus any accrued interest. The second is by the owner's selling the house; in the process you receive the money due on the tax certificate. Third, if the mortgage is in arrears and the lender forecloses, you're first in line to be paid when the property is sold or auctioned—*before* the lender. Finally, if state law allows, you may sell the certificate. Typically, this happens after the redemption period has expired and another investor pays the taxes and interest in order to gain ownership of the property.

If you don't get your money in one of those four ways, you'll get the property. But remember that you buy tax lien certificates to generate cash returns, not to get property. If your goal is to acquire property, use the other strategies I've already explained.

Smart Thinking

Your strategy should include buying multiple liens because there is no way to predict when they will pay. The more certificates you own, the more spread out your cash flow will be.

■ A Secret You Can't Keep

When you're approaching the end of a redemption period, you may be tempted to start making plans for what you're going to do with the property and hoping that the owner doesn't realize how close the foreclosure is. But you can't keep quiet and just pounce on the property when the final deadline passes.

■ Tax Lien States

Not all states sell tax lien certificates. Many just wait until the taxes become sufficiently delinquent and then sell the property at a tax auction. This is known as a tax deed sale, and you can pick up some great deals in real estate at these auctions.

The following states sell tax lien certificates:

Alabama	Louisiana	North Dakota
Arizona	Maryland	Oklahoma
Colorado	Massachusetts	Rhode Island
Florida	Michigan	South Carolina
Georgia	Mississippi	South Dakota
Illinois	Missouri	Texas
Indiana	Nebraska	West Virginia
Iowa	New Hampshire	Wyoming
Kentucky	New York	

Before you can foreclose, you must give proper notice to all parties with a legal interest in the property, including all lien holders, mortgagees, heirs, creditors, and owners. The notice serves as a last chance for the interested parties to redeem the tax lien certificate before you take the property. Each county has its own rules about how and when notice must be given, and if you fail to follow those rules, you risk losing your entire investment.

In some counties, the tax collector's office (or appropriate government agency) issues the notices for you, but it's your responsibility to make sure they do it at the proper time.

Tax lien certificates are a great investment regardless of the current economic cycle. When the economy is strong, there will still be people who don't pay their taxes. When the economy is weak, there will be even more people who don't pay their taxes. And when the economy dips into a recession, the tax lien certificate market thrives.

Is it any wonder that wealthy people have been buying tax lien certificates for decades? And isn't it time for you to get your share?

MILLIONAIRE MENTOR Tax Lien Certificates Highlights

- Tax lien certificates are one of the most predictable, certain, and secure real estate–related investments. They can earn from 12 to 24 percent the first year and up to 24 to 50 percent the second year.

- When a government agency sells a tax lien certificate, it is selling the right to collect the delinquent taxes plus interest and penalties. It does this because it needs the cash to operate.

- If property owners redeem certificates, you profit by the interest and penalties they must pay. If certificates aren't redeemed after a certain period stipulated by state law, you get the property.

- Between 95 and 97 percent tax lien certificates sold by government agencies are redeemed in 24 months or less.

- Tax lien certificates are usually sold at a public auction.

- Check out the property covered by a certificate before you bid on it to make sure it is something you would want to own.

CHAPTER 15

Credit

A Powerful Wealth-Building Weapon

Regardless of the current status of your credit, you can still build a successful real estate business. However, you have to understand how credit works and how to establish and maintain a strong credit rating. If you have good credit and are careful to preserve it, things will be much easier for you. And if you've damaged your credit rating along the way, you must start working on repairing and rebuilding it right now.

The technical definition of credit is the privilege of delayed payment extended to a buyer or borrower by a seller or lender who believes that the debt will be repaid. When we use the term *credit* in conversation, we usually mean someone's credit rating—which, of course, has a significant bearing on one's ability to get credit. But there's more to the issue of credit and wealth building than that.

Consumers' (and poor persons') approach to credit is to use it for immediate gratification. They buy depreciating assets such as cars, electronic gadgets, furniture, clothes, and jewelry on credit and are often still making payments on items long after they've outlived their usefulness.

Investors' (and wealthy persons') approach to credit is to use it to make money. They buy appreciating assets such as real estate and profit from the positive cash flow while they own it, and then profit again from the appreciation when the property is sold.

Credit is a very powerful wealth-building tool. Rich people use it to get richer. And that's what you need to do.

■ Use Credit the Way the Wealthy Do

I know many millionaires and some billionaires. One thing we all have in common is that we all have millions of dollars in debt. It was the wise use of debt that helped us build our fortunes, and it's the continued wise use of debt that will allow us to become even wealthier. You can use the same principles and techniques we do—and I'm going to tell you how.

Credit is not a complicated concept; use it—that is, other people's money—to make money. In the beginning stages of your investment career, never buy anything on credit that's going to go down in value. Always use credit to buy appreciating assets; use as little of your own cash as possible.

Let's say you've got $25,000 in a savings account and have decided to invest it in real estate. First, congratulations—a wise decision. But you can invest it smart, or you can invest it smarter.

To invest smart, you find a distressed property that you could buy for $100,000. Fixed up, it would be worth $150,000. So you take your $25,000, put $10,000 down and finance $90,000, and then use your remaining cash to do the $15,000 in repairs. It takes you two months to do the fix-up, then another two months to sell the property for $145,000 (two weeks to find a buyer happy to get the property for less than market value and six weeks to close the deal). Your profit at closing is $30,000. That's smart.

But you can do it smarter. Buy that same property using only $2,000 down and financing $98,000. Then take out a short-term home improvement loan to pay for the repairs. Four months later, when the property sells for $145,000, you've made the same $30,000 profit (less a small amount of interest) and only tied up $2,000 of your cash. And while this deal is in progress, you've still got $23,000 in cash to use for other deals.

That's just one example of how you can use credit to build your own fortune. Here's another: Instead of selling this property, keep it for long-term cash flow. Rent it out; the rent revenue should be sufficient to pay for the mortgage, maintenance, and other expenses as well as generate some positive cash flow. Your mortgage payment should hold steady (assuming you bought on a fixed-rate mortgage, and I sure hope you did!), your rent will increase every year with inflation, and the property value will appreciate. At any point, you can pull your equity out of the property by refinancing or taking out a home equity loan. If that property appreciates at 5 percent per year (the national average), it will be worth more than $190,000 in five years. So you put $2,000 of your own money down, borrowed $113,000 ($98,000 for the first mortgage and $15,000 for the improvements), and in five years you could sell the property for a $77,000 profit; and that doesn't include the positive cash flow you collected every month while you owned it.

What's really great about this example is that everybody wins: The bank made money on its loans, your tenants had a nice home to live in, and you made a nice contribution to your own personal fortune. And you could take your remaining $23,000 in cash and do the same thing with 11 or 12 more properties.

Remember, lenders want to lend money. That's how they make money. And if you borrow right—as I'm going to teach you—you'll make money too.

◼ If the Cash Stops Flowing

If for any reason you are unable to pay your bills on time, communicate with your creditors. Let them know what's going on (whether it's a job loss, illness, divorce, tough time in your business, whatever) and ask for suggestions on how to deal with the situation. They may temporarily reduce your payments, allow you to skip a few payments and tack them on at the end of the loan or pay them off later, drop late fees and other charges, or even rewrite the loan. Communicating with creditors may also delay formal collection steps such as repossession, foreclosure, or litigation; failing to let them know what's happening and that you're concerned and trying will likely accelerate formal collection steps. I have seen creditors do all kinds of creative things to help customers avoid defaulting on a debt—but only when the customers were up front about their problems and asked for help. So never hide from your creditors. It might seem like the easy way in the short term, but it's not the best approach for the long run.

■ How Lenders Think

One of the most important elements in making credit work for you is understanding how lenders think. When I say lenders, I'm not talking about the credit card companies and other merchants that bombard you with preapproved offers. Typically, those companies make their decisions primarily on the information in your credit report by using a credit scoring system (more about that in the next section), and you rarely get the opportunity to say or do anything to influence the decision.

When you're dealing directly with banks, mortgage companies, and mortgage brokers for real estate loans, your credit history is only part of what they consider. Whether they do it systematically or subconsciously, many loan officers use what is commonly referred to as the six Cs of credit when they make lending decisions. This is why you need financial people on your Power Team and why you need to put together complete and polished loan application packages.

Though the numbers are important, the first thing a lender considers is you, the borrower. Will you honor your obligations? Do you have the character, the integrity, the sense of responsibility to be trusted to repay the loan? Demonstrate this by being totally professional in all of your dealings with the lending institution. Dress appropriately; would you lend $200,000 to someone wearing stained shorts and a ripped T-shirt? Borrowing is a business transaction, so wear business clothing. Depending on what's customary in your area, a suit for men or a dress for women may not be necessary, but "nice casual" should be the very minimum. Develop a demeanor that is confident but not cocky, respectful but not fawning, courteous but not subservient.

A well-prepared loan package includes financial information that shows your capacity to repay as well as your net worth (capital). It shows the collateral, which is the property you want to buy. Include more than a simple legal description and appraisal; explain how you plan to improve the property and how you expect the value to increase. The Whitney Education Financial Statement Software will automate this entire process for you and give you everything you need to satisfy the banker's needs. You'll also want to address conditions—for example, if the area where the property is located is undergoing a number of renovations, point that out. If you have any negatives on your credit history, be prepared to explain them.

The idea is to sell yourself and your project to the loan officer. Make her believe in it as much as you do. In fact, what you really want is for the loan officer to believe in *you*, in your ability to manage money, handle credit responsibly, and make a profit for yourself and the lending institution.

■ The Six Cs of Credit

1. **Character:** integrity, trustworthiness, reliability
2. **Capacity:** ability to pay off the debt based on earnings and other obligations
3. **Collateral:** security for the loan
4. **Conditions:** any economic or regulatory influence that could be a factor
5. **Credit:** credit history
6. **Capital:** net worth determined by a financial statement

■ A Winning Loan Application Package

Before you approach a lender, be prepared to demonstrate why making the loan is a smart decision. Your loan application package needs to be sharp and letter-perfect. Put it together in a neatly organized folder so the loan officer can easily find all the information. Include the following documents:

- *Cover letter.* This is essentially a résumé in paragraph form, introducing yourself, giving information about your background, and establishing your character.
- *Financial statement.* This statement lists your assets and liabilities to show your net worth.

- *Copies of your credit report.* If you have a recent credit report (and you should), include copies with a brief explanation of any negative entries.
- *Copies of your federal income tax return for the past two years.* Include the entire return, not just the front page.
- *Statement about the project.* Describe the property and what you intend to do with it. Include worst-case scenario details to show that you've thought it through completely.
- *Rent roll statement.* Project future monthly and yearly rents and expenses in addition to showing current ones.
- *Accepted offer.* Include a copy of the offer the seller has accepted.
- *Contractors' estimates.* If you are going to rehab the property, show how much the work is expected to cost.
- *Legal description and any other information about the property.* Show the lender that you have done your homework and completely researched the project.
- *Photos of the property.* Take some snapshots with a good 35mm camera or a high-quality digital camera.
- *Details on other properties you own or have rehabbed or managed.* Include before-and-after photos, financial information, and other details that show you have experience doing what you propose.

Words of Wisdom

When you want to borrow money, tell the banker what you want to accomplish and then ask which loan vehicle will work best for you. I have seen cases where someone latches on to a particular technique, thinking that's the only way to accomplish a goal and consequently missing out on other opportunities. Often, lenders call the same loan product by a different name, or they have a way to lend you the money you want by using a different strategy. The key is to make sure the banker you're dealing with has the experience, knowledge, and desire to help you.

■ Do You Know the Score?

It's extremely important for any investor or businessperson to understand *credit scoring*, which is a system creditors use to decide who gets credit, how much they get, and sometimes even at what interest rate. Essentially, credit scoring reduces your entire credit history to a single number.

Using a statistical program, creditors compare information about you and your credit experiences with the credit performances of customers with similar profiles. The scoring system awards points for each factor that helps predict who is most likely to repay a debt. The total number of points is your credit score, which helps predict how creditworthy you are.

Credit scoring systems allow creditors to evaluate millions of applicants consistently and impartially on a variety of characteristics. The models are complex and often vary among creditors and for different types of credit. In general, they evaluate the following information in your credit report:

- *Payment history.* Do you pay your bills on time or have you paid bills late, had accounts referred to collections, or filed for bankruptcy?
- *Outstanding debt.* The amount of debt you have and how that number compares to your credit limits is considered. Total debt close to or at your available credit probably has a negative impact on your score.
- *Length of your credit history.* The models consider how long you have been using credit.
- *Recent credit applications.* The inquiries listed on your credit report are considered. A lot of inquiries may indicate that you've been trying to obtain too much new credit too quickly.
- *How many and what types of accounts you have.* Generally, established credit accounts are good, but too many may reduce your overall score. Some models also consider the type of account; for example, a home mortgage is good, but a loan from a finance company may reduce your score.

Beyond the information in your credit file, credit models may also consider such information as your job or occupation, your length of employment, and whether you own your home. Credit scoring systems may not use race, sex, marital status, national origin, or religion as factors.

■ The Three Major Credit Reporting Agencies

	To Order Credit Reports	To Report Fraud
Equifax	800-685-1111	800-525-6285
Experian	888-EXPERIAN	888-EXPERIAN
TransUnion	800-916-8800	800-680-7289

FICO Scores

Perhaps the best-known credit scoring system is FICO, so named because it uses software developed by Fair, Isaac and Company (FICO). The three major credit reporting agencies use this system when providing scores to lenders, although each calls it a different name. At Equifax, the score is known as Beacon; at TransUnion, it's Empirica®; and at Experian, it's the Experian/Fair, Isaac Risk Score.

FICO scores range from 300 to 850. The higher the score, the lower the predicted credit risk for lenders. However, even though lenders tend to give FICO scores heavy weight when making credit decisions, they also have their own individual strategies for using FICO information for other purposes. For example, many mortgage lenders offer better interest rates to customers with higher FICO scores. Many people aren't aware of this strategy, but it can save you a substantial amount of money over the life of a loan. That means that even though you have a good credit rating and a FICO score of maybe 650 or 675, it's worthwhile to bring that score up to the 700s or higher.

Keep in mind that your files with different credit reporting agencies may contain different information. Because FICO scores are calculated on the information contained in your credit report, they may vary depending on which agency issued the report. That's why it's critical that you check your credit report with all three major agencies at least once a year to be sure it's accurate.

You can get your FICO score by going to <www.myfico.com>. To improve your score, pay your bills on time; maintain low balances on credit cards and other revolving credit accounts; and apply for and open new credit only as needed. Remember that as the data in your file at the credit reporting agencies change, so will your FICO score.

Wealth Secrets

One of the cardinal rules of credit: Use credit only to buy assets that will appreciate, such as real estate; never use credit to buy depreciating assets, such as cars, furniture, vacations, and electronics.

Credit Categories

Lenders often grade their borrowers as A, B, C, or D. Some lenders accept only A borrowers, whereas others specialize in C and D customers. In addition to knowing your own grade for managing your personal and business credit, understanding the system helps you help your buyers when you are selling property.

A grade of *A* means you have perfect credit or maybe just one very small blemish and a FICO score of 640 or higher.

A *B* grade means you have a few minor glitches, maybe up to three 30-day delinquencies, and a FICO score of 580 to 640.

Those earning a *C* grade pay about half of their bills on time and have a FICO score of 500 to 580.

People earning a *D* just aren't paying attention. Often, they're people who don't bother to pay their bills until someone screams at them. They have a FICO score below 500.

Some C and D borrowers have legitimate reasons for their poor rating—they may be trying to cope with a job loss, unexpected bills from an emergency, or some other situation beyond their control. Others just haven't figured out why a good credit rating is essential. And, of course, there are probably some who aren't going to pay whatever they can get away with not paying.

If you have a B, C, or D buyer, use a mortgage broker; don't go directly to a lender. A good mortgage broker has lenders willing to accept higher-risk borrowers. Of course, the loans are made at higher interest and the terms may not be as attractive as they are for A borrowers, but it may be the only way to get the necessary funds.

◼ Recovering from Bankruptcy

Although in certain circumstances bankruptcy is the best option (or perhaps the lesser of the evils), my general advice is to avoid bankruptcy if at all possible. However, if you have a bankruptcy in your past, you can overcome this stain on your credit rating and still become wealthy.

Just consider the following well-known people who have filed, and recovered from, bankruptcy. Film director Francis Ford Coppola filed two Chapter 11 (reorganization) petitions in 1983, another one seven years later in 1990, and still another two years later in 1992—and went on to direct more blockbuster hits. Olympic gold medal winner and world-renowned figure skater Dorothy Hamill filed a Chapter 11 petition in 1996 after a series of financial setbacks that she claimed were the result of years of poor investment advice and mismanagement.

Popular talk show host Larry King declared bankruptcy in 1978 and bounced back to become one of the most recognized names on cable news. After a series of bad investments and declining film roles, actor Burt Reynolds filed a Chapter 11 bankruptcy petition in 1996. And, of course, Donald Trump's financial ups and downs are legendary and include bankruptcies filed by the Trump Castle Casino Resort (1992), the Trump Plaza Hotel & Casino (1992), and the Trump Taj Mahal Casino Resort (1991) in Atlantic City.

◼ When Your Credit History Is Less Than Perfect: What to Do

Lots of things can happen to damage your credit rating. If you have blemishes on your credit report, you have to take care of them as soon as possible. Start by obtaining a copy of your credit report from all three major credit reporting agencies. Remember, it's unlikely that the information they contain will be identical, so check all three. Study each report carefully. Each agency includes instructions on how to read the report and what to do if it contains incorrect information.

Challenge anything that isn't accurate. You can even challenge negative entries that are actually correct and may be successful in getting them removed. If you have positive information that is not in the file, such as accounts that have been paid on time, request that it be added. I explain how to do this in complete detail using easy-to-understand terms with sample letters and forms in my book, *Credit: How to Obtain, Increase, and Preserve Credit* (see resources chapter for details on how to obtain this book).

A few flaws on your credit report do not necessarily mean that you can't obtain credit. Credit is an issue that comes up often among our students, and I have found that many, many people believe they have a credit problem they can't do anything about. The reality is that even the wealthiest of people have late pays and errors on their credit reports. This doesn't stop them from getting loans—and getting those loans on good terms.

If you follow my advice, you'll be able to overcome your credit problems forever. My students tell me their positive stories regularly. Kevin B. says that before he studied my techniques and started his real estate business, he could "barely get a credit card with a meager limit of $500 to $1,000, and now I'm being sent Platinum cards without even applying for them. Too bad I don't need them now." Al L. says that he was able to get many negative items removed from his credit bureau file and substantially upgrade his creditworthiness. Just six weeks after applying my techniques, he was able to get a $10,000 signature loan that, he says, "I wouldn't have had a prayer of getting before."

Warning

By 1850, debtors' prisons were eliminated in the United States, so you're not likely to be sent to jail for your debts. However, there are some circumstances under which you could be jailed for not paying: If you willfully violate a court order, especially an order to pay child support; if you are convicted of willfully refusing to pay income taxes; or if you attempt to conceal yourself or your property to avoid paying a debt for which a creditor has a judgment against you.

■ If It Happens to You

If you are a victim of identity theft, prompt action makes recovering some-what easier—but be prepared for a frustrating, lengthy process.

Immediately contact all your creditors, even the ones not apparently involved in the fraud. They should put a note on your account to be alert for suspicious activity. The ones involved in the fraud need to shut down the fraudulent accounts.

File a police report and then contact the fraud units at all three major credit reporting agencies. Notify the Social Security Administration by calling its fraud hot line at 800-269-0271. File a complaint with the FTC at 877-IDTHEFT or at <www.consumer.gov/idtheft>.

Document everything you do. Keep copies of all correspondence and make notes of telephone calls; get the name and title of everyone you talk to, and write down a brief summary of your conversation. Also, be prepared for some creditors to not believe you. They may ask you to prove that you didn't incur the expenses, and it can be very difficult to prove a negative.

■ How Safe Is Your Credit Rating?

The fastest-growing crime in the United States is identity theft. More than one million people each year fall victim to these clever thieves. With just your name, Social Security number, and birth date, criminals can get credit cards in your name, take out loans, apply for health insurance, buy various products and services, and even get a job under your name. When your credit is maxed out and your reputation ruined, they move on to the next victim, and you could literally spend years cleaning up the mess.

Identity thieves used to get their information by going through trash, but they've gotten more sophisticated in recent years. Some steal mail from your box; others buy information from insiders (store and restaurant employees or clerks at your doctor's office, health insurance carrier, and even your own office) who are willing to sell it. You can't control what other people do with your information, but you can take steps to make it more difficult for someone to victimize you. Here are some tips:

■ *Protect your Social Security number.* Never give the number out unless you have to, and never use it as an ID or account number. Don't carry your card with you. Check your earnings statements once a year; call the Social Security Administration (SSA) at 800-772-1213 to have them sent to you.

■ *Check your credit report* with all three major reporting agencies at least once a year.

■ *Guard your mail.* If you pay bills by mail, take those envelopes to a post office or place them in a locked mail box rather than leaving them in your unsecured home mail box for the letter carrier to pick up. Be sure your incoming mail is picked up promptly after delivery. A post office box is well worth the nominal fee.

■ *Shred documents before discarding.* When throwing away old tax returns, bank statements, or even junk mail that contains personal information, shred those documents first.

■ *Use common sense.* Don't discuss private financial information in public where others can overhear. Pay attention to your billing cycles so you'll notice if a bill doesn't arrive on time and you can follow up on it. Use passwords for ATM cards, debit cards, and other services that are complicated and won't be obvious to someone trying to guess. Memorize your Social Security number so you don't have to carry it around with you. Tell your bank, credit card vendors, health insurance carrier, and other companies and services you do business with not to share your information with affiliates.

You need to pay as much attention to your credit rating as you do to the details of your real estate deals. Understand it, take care of it, and use it to build wealth.

MILLIONAIRE MENTOR Credit Highlights

■ Credit is the privilege of delayed payment extended to a buyer or borrower and is a very powerful wealth-building tool.

■ Your credit rating has a significant bearing on your ability to obtain credit. The better your rating, the easier it is.

- If you have damaged your credit rating, begin immediately to repair and rebuild it.

- Always use credit to buy assets that will increase in value and generate positive cash flow. Never buy depreciating assets on credit.

- When buying investment property, use as little of your own cash as possible; use credit (other people's money) as much as you can.

- Learn how lenders think so you can present yourself and your loan application in the most positive light possible.

- Your credit score is a critical part of your overall credit rating. Know what affects your credit score and how to keep it as high as possible.

- Protect yourself from identity theft by employing commonsense precautions. If you do become a victim of this growing crime, report it to law enforcement, the credit bureaus, and your creditors immediately.

CHAPTER 16

Asset Protection

Got It? Keep It!

Chances are you have assets right now that need protection; and as you begin building your real estate business, your assets will increase substantially and thus make the issue of asset protection critical. The money you make will be money you've earned, and if you want to give it away, that should be your choice. But don't let anyone take it from you.

Many people worry about being sued, a legitimate concern in our increasingly litigious society. The United States has more lawyers per capita than any other country in the world, and they're advertising everywhere—in the telephone directory, on radio and television, on billboards and bus benches—you name it. They're looking for people who want to sue someone, and they can be remarkably creative in finding a cause of action (the reason for the lawsuit). And they look for targets with deep pockets—people with a lot of money to pay a judgment or maybe the willingness to settle out of court for a tidy sum. As you build your own fortune, your pockets are going to get deeper and deeper and that bull's eye on your forehead will get bigger. So let's talk about how you can stay out of the line of fire.

My students often asked how to set up their affairs to avoid getting sued. One way is to stay poor forever. Obviously that's not your first choice, or you wouldn't be reading this book. The reality is that you can't avoid lawsuits. You can take steps to minimize the risk of getting sued, but if you're out there doing business and becoming successful, there's a chance you'll be sued at some point. Perhaps even more than once.

Will the suit have merit? Maybe, maybe not. Under our legal system, anybody can sue anybody else for any reason, and it's up to the judge or the jury to determine whether the plaintiff (the person doing the suing) has a legitimate claim and is entitled to compensation. I think some people file lawsuits for the same reason they buy lottery tickets—they know it's a long shot, but they're hoping to hit the jackpot and figure it's worth a try.

Over the past 25 years, I have owned hundreds of single-family and multifamily residential units as well as a number of commercial properties and tracts of land. That translates to hundreds of tenants, and I have only been sued once in a real estate issue involving liability—and it wasn't even by a tenant. It was an employee in a commercial building I owned who fell on the property. Her name was Sue, and I found out later that she made jokes about being appropriately named. She had fallen at other jobs and sued other employers and landlords. She claimed that she tripped over a clothespin in our parking lot. I believe it was a planned fall and a fraudulent claim; I probably would have fought it on principle, but I turned the matter over to my insurance company (after all, defending lawsuits is part of what insurance premiums go for). Sue was able to scheme about $60,000 out of my insurance company; I understand the company later initiated an investigation against her for fraud, but I never learned the final outcome.

My point of sharing that story is to stress this: Don't allow the possibility of being sued stop you from investing in real estate and building your own fortune. Litigation is just a fact of life in today's business environment. There's no way to predict if, how often, or for how much you'll be sued. Recognize that and prepare for it by using the techniques I'm going to share in this chapter, and then get on with enjoying your businesses successes.

It's important to recognize that the possibility you may at some point be sued and even lose a lawsuit is only part of the reason you need to understand and apply sound asset protection techniques. You want to protect what you've worked so hard to get from other claims; you want to keep your taxes as low as possible; and you want your heirs—not the government—to get your estate when you die.

A problem you've prepared for isn't nearly so damaging as a problem that blindsides you. When you've developed strategies for dealing with assaults on your assets, you'll know what to do when it happens and can stay calm and in control. If you panic, you'll lose control and make stupid mistakes that will cost you dearly. If you prepare for a disaster that never happens, you haven't lost anything. But if you aren't prepared when disaster strikes, you could lose everything.

■ Insurance: Necessary but Not Enough

I've already touched on the importance of having insurance in previous chapters. You need property insurance to replace or repair your buildings if they are damaged as a result of fire, flood, storms, theft, vandalism, or other "covered peril," to use insurance jargon. You need liability insurance to pay the bills if someone is injured on your property. And you may decide to purchase certain other types of business insurance, depending on the specifics of your particular operation.

But you can't buy insurance to cover every possible risk. In fact, when you buy an insurance policy, one of the most important sections to read is the exclusions. You'll probably be shocked at what your general liability policy, for example, *doesn't cover.*

There's also the question of limits. Property and casualty insurance is fairly straightforward: You insure the building for what it would cost to replace it. Liability is a different animal. How much liability coverage do you need? $1 million? $5 million? $100 million? That's a decision only you can make.

Sit down with your insurance agent and your estate planner to determine an overall insurance strategy for you personally and for your business activities. You need adequate insurance, but you don't want to be "insurance poor"—that is, all your profits are eaten up by insurance premiums for coverage you may not ever need. A good insurance agent will help you strike the right balance of coverage and also provide guidance for ways to keep your premiums down. I recommend choosing an agent who has experience working with business owners and other real estate investors. The agent who has been insuring your house and car for years probably doesn't have the experience and knowledge base to help you determine what type of property and liability coverage you need once you begin acquiring investment real estate.

General liability insurance is usually not very expensive, but it's worth the peace of mind it provides. In my early years of investing, I opted for about $300,000 in liability on each of my properties. Eventually, I added an umbrella policy that covered all my properties; in other words, I had $300,000 on each property, but had I been sued and the plaintiff won a judgment for more than $300,000, the umbrella policy would kick in.

What you should keep in mind is this: Although insurance is an important element in risk management, it is *not* asset protection.

■ What Is Asset Protection?

The concept of asset protection is basic, revolving around how you set up the ownership of your assets and who knows about them. The primary goals of a sound asset protection strategy are:

- **Privacy.** You want information about the ownership of your assets to be private, meaning that it isn't available through public resources, such as courthouse records.
- **Control.** You want to maintain control of your assets even when you are being sued or after a judgment is entered against you, your company, or any property or entity that you own or control.
- **Liability protection.** You want to shield your assets from liability claims no matter how large the claim against you.

Privacy is both a goal and a critical element of successful asset protection. The less people know about what you have, the less likely they will try to take it away from you. If someone who wants to sue you can't find any assets, the would-be suer will probably decide not to proceed. Why go to all that trouble if there's nothing to win?

From this perspective, you actually have plaintiffs' attorneys on your side. Many attorneys take cases on a contingency basis, meaning they don't get paid unless they win, and then they get a percentage of the award. So when they consider the case, look at the defendant (you), and find that your assets aren't worth going after, they'll decline the case.

Attorneys don't line up to sue poor people. You can get judgments against poor people all day long, but you'll never see a dime, so what's the point? But attorneys love to sue people with assets, especially accessible, identifiable, unmovable assets like real estate. If you own real estate in your own name, you are almost begging to be sued.

Does this mean you should wear shabby clothes, drive a clunker of a car, live in a slum, and keep the fact that you own certain investment properties a huge secret? Of course not. The key is to own your assets in a way that allows you to control and profit from them but to keep them untouchable by anyone else.

■

SUCCESS
STORIES

You Don't Have to Be in Real Estate to Protect Your Assets

Whether you ultimately decide to invest in real estate or not, understanding and applying sound asset protection strategies will benefit you. My students prove that every day. Because of the nature of these examples, I'm not identifying these individuals, but they all successfully completed and benefited from asset protection training.

A salesperson who earned an average of $600,000 a year was paying about a third of that in local, state, and federal taxes. Our instructors suggested three techniques that reduced his taxes to about 10 percent of what they had been. In five years, his tax savings will top $1 million.

The techniques he used were definitely not "do-it-yourself tips and tricks." He worked closely with our counselors and attorneys, and if you're going to try anything like this, I recommend professional guidance. Here's essentially what he did: He asked his employer to split his wages, paying $50,000 to him reported on a 1099 (which let him keep his benefits) and the balance to the C corporation we recommended he create. He was already flipping a few properties a year, so we advised him to handle those transactions through his corporation, which prevented it from being classified by the IRS as a professional services company. This strategy allowed the corporation to pay tax on net earnings at the corporate rate, which was much lower than his personal rate.

His next step was to transfer ownership of all the real estate he personally held to land trusts, then assign the beneficial interest in each trust to a limited partnership. This let him personally take all the tax savings from the real estate ownership while still giving him significant protection from possible litigation.

His C corporation paid him an annual wage of $100,000. Added to the $50,000 his employer paid him directly, he received a total personal income of $150,000. With his business-related expenses and regular personal deductions, his final tax bill was negligible. In the meantime, his C corporation was making tax-deductible contributions to a defined benefit plan, so he could retire in just a few years in addition to investing in tax-advantaged insurance products. The corporation also created a charitable operating foundation so it could deduct contributions to a charity he actually controlled. After all of this, the corporation will pay a tax of about $15,000, and our student will personally pay about $5,000.

Another student had enjoyed significant success investing in real estate after separating from her husband while the divorce was pending. He left her when she was just getting her real estate business started and hadn't yet made any money. She was concerned that if he found out about her success, his lawyers would try to squeeze money from her that he had no right to. It would be expensive for her to defend herself against his claims, and the outcome would be unpredictable. We counseled her to use legitimate asset protection strategies to hide her income and protect her from litigation.

When another student took home what she learned in our training and began applying it to structure her business, her attorney and CPA objected. They both called our offices to complain, but our instructors were able to demonstrate how the techniques worked, explained the potential tax savings, and showed how the professionals could both help and benefit from this information. They thanked us before hanging up.

■ The Correct Way to Own Property

Real estate investors are particularly vulnerable to claims for two reasons. The first is that real estate ownership is shown in the public records for anyone to find. The second is that any judgment against you, the investor, can become a lien against *all* of your real estate. A judgment of any size could tie up all your real estate until you either get the matter released by the court or pay the judgment. Even if you file an appeal, the judgment will nevertheless place a lien on your property until the appeal is decided. If you still lose after taking all available legal action, you'll have to pay the judgment. If you don't, the lienholder can execute on the judgment, which means he can sell off your real estate as he chooses until the judgment is satisfied. Should that happen, don't expect your property to be sold at fair market value. You wouldn't pay market value for a property sold at a distress sale or judicial sale, would you? Of course not. You would expect to pay 50 to 70 percent of the fair market value. And that's what your properties will probably realize should you end up in a situation where a lienholder forces the sale of your assets.

By owning real estate in your own name, you give up control of your assets and risk losing everything. You might think a logical solution is to buy real estate in the name of your corporation. But if the corporation is sued, the resulting judgment will still place a lien on all the property the corporation owns. You've solved nothing; you've merely transferred the problem.

A very effective way to protect your real estate is to separate the ownership of the property with each property owned by a separate entity. That entity need not be a corporation; in fact, I recommend that it not be. In addition to the cost to set up a corporation, in most states you'll spend at least $500 a year in corporate taxes and accounting fees. That means if you own 20 separate properties, you could spend as much as $10,000 a year to protect them through a corporation. That will eat into your profits, and, in most cases, it's just not practical.

What you need is a manner of ownership that provides for separate ownership of each property with the protection you need but doesn't have all the costs and complications of a corporation. One solution is to own each property in a *separate land trust.*

Did You Know?

If your trust agreement includes a nondisclosure/privacy provision, the trustee of a land trust can't reveal the name of the beneficiary (owner of the trust and therefore of the property in the trust) under most circumstances. This means it would be very difficult for someone just fishing for information to find a "deep pocket" before filing a suit to find out that you own certain property. Also, if the trustee is an attorney, he can invoke the attorney-client privilege and not be forced to reveal the beneficiary's name. Most attorneys who represent their clients in real estate and corporate matters act as trustees of the clients' land trusts and as registered agents of their corporations without additional fees.

■ Creating a Land Trust

To create a land trust, you enter into a land trust agreement with a trustee you choose and then deed the property into the trust. The trust agreement names a trustee, who can be your attorney or even a friend or family member you trust but who preferably doesn't have the same last name as you. The trustee's name appears in the public records, and you don't want someone who may recognize your last name investigate a particular land trust further. The agreement also names a beneficiary, which is you or your company. That company can be either a corporation or a limited partnership—and when I address limited partnerships later on, you'll see why that's a great way to own property. The beneficiary owns the trust that owns the real estate. A land trust is revocable, which means it can be amended or terminated by the beneficiary at any time.

Trustees have to do only what you give them written instructions to do, and you're not going to tell them to do anything at all. This means you can ask your brother-in-law or great aunt or best friend to be the trustee of your land trust; the trustee doesn't have to do any work nor be liable for anything the trust does or for any action that the trustee might take on behalf of the trust. The trustee can resign at any time, and you can fire the trustee if you want. If the trustee quits, is terminated, or dies, you have the right to appoint a new trustee of your choosing.

The beneficiary's job—that is, *your* job—is to direct the trustee, manage and control the property, and get the money. The trust doesn't file a tax return; but the beneficiary must report all income and expenses.

When the land trust is established, you change the title of the property from the previous owner to the trustee as the agent of the trust. Let's say you're buying a 16-unit apartment building. You create a land trust and name it Aspen Apartments Land Trust (the name of the building) and designate your favorite aunt, Mary Poppins, as trustee. When you transfer ownership of the property from the seller, the title lists the new owner as Mary Poppins, trustee of Aspen Apartments Land Trust.

You don't have to record the land trust agreement, and you shouldn't. You just record the deed. Because the property is not titled in your name and the land trust agreement is not recorded (that is, not part of the public records), only you and the trustee know that you own it. And the trust should contain a provision explicitly preventing the trustee from disclosing your ownership.

Each of your land trusts should have a separate name. I've found the easiest way to do this is to simply name the trusts with the address of the property. For example, the house at 123 First Street would be placed in the 123 First Street Land Trust, and the duplex at 456 Maple Street would be in the 456 Maple Street Land Trust.

You can transfer property you currently own to a land trust with no tax consequences, and the only expense is a small filing fee payable to the county. (The exception is Pennsylvania, which taxes transfers both into and out of land trusts and also charges an annual fee for each land trust.) You needn't worry about a due-on-sale clause in your mortgage either. Federal law provides an exception to the due-on-sale clause for the transfer of property into a land trust as long as the real ownership (also known as the "beneficial interest") of the property doesn't change. This means you can transfer your property into a land trust, and the bank can't call the mortgage due.

Even though land trusts are legal in all 50 states and Canada, don't be surprised if your attorney doesn't know what you're talking about when you mention land trusts. Even though you can legally form a trust to do just about anything you want wherever you want, law schools don't teach the specific terms and uses of each type of trust. If a lawyer becomes an expert in trusts or asset protection, or in any other specific area of the law, she does so by continuing her education beyond law school. You'll have to invest some time checking around for a good lawyer who is familiar with land trusts, but the payoff is increased protection and privacy.

■ Recording the Deed

Once you have created a land trust, recording the deed is a standard process that courthouses are accustomed to handling. The property's owner is the *grantor,* and the trustee is the *grantee.* The deed should be signed and notarized. Take the original to the courthouse and keep a copy for your own records.

You will probably have to pay a minimal recording fee, usually no more than $30. In most states (except in Pennsylvania, as explained earlier), no transfer taxes are due when you move a property you own into a trust you own. If the clerk at the courthouse attempts to charge a transfer tax (also known as doc stamps), ask to see a list of exemptions. Moving a property into a trust of which you are the beneficiary is on that list, so politely point that out to the clerk, and you won't be charged the tax.

Benefits of Using Land Trusts

When you transfer each property into a separately named land trust, you have in essence separated the ownership of the properties. All it has cost you are the nominal recording fees and a little time and paperwork. The benefits are numerous and well worth it.

Let's say you haven't done this, and you own ten properties in the name of your corporation. One tenant sues and wins, and the judgment becomes a lien against all the properties the corporation owns. Either you have to pay the judgment or the lienholder can force the sale of your properties until the judgment is satisfied.

But if each of those ten properties is owned by a separated land trust, the outcome would be quite different. The tenant, who happens to live at

456 Maple Street, sues the owner of that property, which is the 456 Maple Street Land Trust, and wins. The judgment becomes a lien against the 456 Maple Street Land Trust and any properties it owns. Because the land trust owns only one property, the tenant has a lien against only one property. Your other nine properties are safe in separate land trusts, and you're free to sell or mortgage them without being forced to pay the judgment. You are in control of your property, and that's just where you want to be.

What, however, if you are sued personally and a judgment is entered against you? If all your real estate is in separate land trusts, the judgment can't become a lien against your property because you personally don't own any property.

When one of my students, who had just learned about land trusts, found out that an abandoned underground fuel tank was in the backyard of a small apartment building he owned, he transferred the property to a land trust. Various business factions in his town were trying to force a sale of the property and called the Environmental Protection Agency, which cited the trustee of the land trust for noncompliance and placed a restraining order on the property. Eventually, the matter was settled, but at no time was the property owner's other 35 properties at risk—and they would have been had he owned the property in his own name.

Smart Thinking

Whenever you pay a professional (attorney, accountant, consultant of any kind) to do something for you, such as setting up a corporation, ask for the document(s) on a disk that the professional has created on your behalf. Be willing to pay a little extra for it. You may be able to use that document again, and having it on the disk will save you time and money.

■ Setting Up Your Companies

Many people first get into real estate almost accidentally. Maybe they inherit a piece of property and decide to keep it rather than sell it. Or they buy a new house and decide to keep the old one as a rental. Then they figure out that they're making money, so they start buying more property. But if they're doing all this in their own name, they're taking a huge risk—and they're probably not getting all the tax benefits they could be.

When you decide to get into business, whether it's real estate investing or something else, it's probably going to be to your advantage to create a company. And the first decision you have to make about that company is its legal structure. You have five basic choices as explained in the following sections.

Sole proprietorship. With this form of ownership, the owner *is* the business, personally liable for all debts and obligations. Income and expenses are reported on Schedule C as part of the owner's personal tax return. When a sole proprietor dies, the business ceases to exist.

Partnership. This is an arrangement whereby two or more people agree to be in business together. The partnership agreement spells out the individual percentage of ownership, responsibilities, restrictions, and requirements of each partner. But from a legal perspective, all the partners are in charge, and all the partners are liable. The partnership files a tax return but doesn't pay taxes; the partners pay taxes individually on their share of profits or deduct their share of losses.

Limited partnership. The Uniform Limited Partnership Act (ULPA) has been adopted in every state except Louisiana as the ULPA or as the Revised Uniform Limited Partnership Act (RULPA). A limited partnership has two types of partners: general and limited. The general partner (typically only one, although there may be more) runs the company, is in charge, and is liable. Limited partners have no control over the operation of the business and no liability for its conduct. This form of ownership is designed to encourage investors to put their money into companies, which is good for the economy; limited partners are risking only their investment. A limited partnership is an excellent asset protection tool for yourself and for any investors you may want to attract into a real estate deal.

Corporation. A corporation is a legal entity that is owned by shareholders. The corporation files a tax return and is liable for its own conduct. The shareholders (it's possible for a corporation to have only one shareholder) elect officers to run the company, but they are not individually liable for anything the corporation does. In general, corporations offer tremendous liability protection and tax advantages.

Limited liability company (LLC). LLCs are a relatively new form of business ownership designed to offer some of the protection of a corporation with the tax advantages of a partnership. Requirements and details vary by state.

The type of real estate investing you do is the deciding factor in what type of company and how many companies you form. At the least, you need two: an entity in which you flip properties and buy for the short term and a different entity in which you buy and hold for the long term. My advice is to put your short-term holdings in a corporation and your long-term investments in a limited partnership. Your other business activities, such as mortgage notes, tax lien certificates, or a property management company (if you have one), should be set up separately as well.

Wealth Secrets

Never buy real estate as a tax shelter—that is, never buy property that will lose money so you can use that loss to offset income from another source. Certainly use every legitimate deduction you can find to reduce and/or eliminate your tax liability, but buy real estate only if the deal will be profitable for you.

■ The Benefits of Incorporating

When you conduct your business affairs as a corporation, you open up a whole new world of opportunities for increasing your net profit through proper tax planning. Operating your business as a corporation makes available to you all the tax advantages giant companies like IBM, General Motors, and AT&T have been using for years. The corporation also protects you from personal liability for problems involving corporate assets or employees.

The corporation was originally conceived to provide business owners with protection from liability. The idea was to encourage people to create and grow businesses by eliminating some of the risk of personal loss. Corporations are owned by shareholders, who are not individually liable for corporate activities. For example, let's say that while shopping in a Home Depot, you trip over something left in an aisle. You're injured, you sue, and you win a judgment. The many thousands of people who own shares of Home Depot stock are not personally liable for that judgment; Home Depot as a corporation is.

If an employee of a corporation causes an accident, the victim can obtain a judgment against the corporation but not against the shareholders. If corporate employees feel they have been discriminated against or otherwise harmed by the company, they can sue and obtain a judgment against the corporation, not against the shareholders. If someone is injured on corporate property, again the liability is with the corporate entity, not the shareholders. When a corporation is sued, the corporate assets are at risk, but the shareholders are safe and secure. So when you create a corporation, even though you may be its sole shareholder, you are not personally liable for what that corporation does.

Of course, to maintain the line between yourself as an individual and the corporation as a separate entity, you must operate the corporation in accordance with the laws of your state; you must keep accurate and appropriate records and you must not commingle corporate and personal funds. If you fail to maintain the corporation as a separate entity, you risk something known as "piercing the corporate veil." That's when a clever attorney shows that the corporation is not in fact separate but rather an extension of yourself, and you can be held responsible for corporate actions. So if you're not sure what you have to do to maintain the integrity of your corporate structure, ask your attorney or your state department of corporations.

Beyond liability, another important reason to incorporate is the many tax advantages you're afforded. One way to benefit from the tax breaks a corporation offers is by creating a solid employee benefits package. Even if your corporation has only one employee (that's you), you can provide a wide range of benefits, and the cost is tax deductible as a business expense. If you have additional employees, the cost of providing their benefits is also tax deductible. However, you can only provide yourself with a limited amount of tax-deductible benefits unless you make those same benefits available to the other employees.

The most important benefit you can provide is a medical expense reimbursement plan, which provides for the payment of *all* medical expenses for employees, their spouses, and dependent children. This means that the corporation pays for medical insurance, copayments, deductibles, prescription drugs, and other expenses not covered by insurance.

If you pay these expenses yourself, the only tax deduction you're allowed is for the part that exceeds 7.5 percent of your adjusted gross income. The corporation, however, can deduct these expenses from the first dollar spent, which means neither you nor the corporation ever pays income tax on the money used by the corporation to pay benefits on your behalf. And because you're going to be paying these expenses anyway, doesn't it make sense for you to allow your corporation to pay them on your behalf and get the tax deduction?

A medical reimbursement plan requires special language and documentation during the formation of the corporation. It is available only if you take the C corporation election, and you must set the plan up correctly to get the deduction. Be sure the attorney you use understands this; don't wait until you file your first corporate tax return to find out it wasn't done properly.

Remember that the corporation can provide more than simply medical coverage. It can pay for life insurance, disability insurance, long-term care insurance, catastrophic illness insurance, and many other types of coverage for you and your family.

The corporation can receive a tax deduction when it pays for a wide range of other expenses, including business use of an automobile, certain education expenses, business use of your home, business travel, and more. These expenses are money you're going to spend anyway. If you pay for these business expenses personally and then deduct them on the Schedule C of your individual tax return, your tax savings won't be nearly as great as they would if your corporation paid for and deducted the expenses.

A third reason to incorporate is to avoid being personally designated as a real estate dealer by the Internal Revenue Service. If you buy property with the intent to sell (flipping), the IRS may classify you as a dealer, which creates a number of tax *dis*advantages. The first is that as a dealer, you can't depreciate any real estate, including your long-term investment property, which greatly increases your taxable income.

Second, instead of reporting rental income on Schedule E of your personal tax return, you must report it on Schedule C. The net income on the Schedule C is then reported on Schedule SE, which is used to figure your self-employment income tax, which can be as much as 15.3 percent of your net income in additional taxes. Self-employment taxes are not normally due on rental income.

Third, you can't take advantage of tax-deferred exchanges under section 1031 of the Internal Revenue Code. This provision allows owners of investment real estate to sell their property, escrow the net proceeds, purchase additional investment property, and avoid paying part or all of the income tax that would otherwise be due.

Finally, as a dealer you can't elect to use the installment method of reporting the sale of real estate. Typically, when you sell a property and receive payments over time instead of the complete purchase price at once, you can choose to report the money you receive as income only when you actually receive it. Without the option to elect the installment method of reporting, you must report the total amount of the sale and pay the full amount of tax due, even if you haven't yet received the money. If you sold a property for $50,000 with $5,000 down and the remainder in payments, you could conceivably owe more in income taxes than the cash you received at the time of the sale.

To avoid being classified as a dealer, buy and sell real estate through your corporation; if the corporation is classified as a dealer, the shareholders aren't affected. If being classified as a dealer hurts the corporation's tax status, you have the option of dissolving that corporation and starting a new one. However, the corporation's tax status is not likely to be affected by the dealer classification because the penalties don't hurt a corporation when it simply buys and sells real estate. You can continue to report rental income on Schedule E or own the rental property in a different entity and receive the appropriate tax advantages.

■ C or S: Making the Corporate Choice

You've probably heard people refer to C and S corporations. These are not different types of corporations—a corporation is a corporation . . . period. The C and S designations refer to subchapters in the Internal Revenue Code that describe how the IRS treats the corporation for tax purposes. The IRS automatically treats every corporation as a Subchapter C unless the shareholders unanimously elect to be treated as a Subchapter S corporation.

A C corporation has no limits on the type of shareholders, the number of shareholders, or the classes or types of stock. An S corporation may have a maximum of 75 shareholders and only one class of stock, which is common voting stock.

A C corporation is a separate taxpayer, which means it pays tax on its net income. You have a variety of tax-planning options available with a C corporation that you don't have with an S corporation. If you are the owner of the corporation (a shareholder) and also an employee of the corporation, you can make certain that the business never pays taxes by spending all the money it earns each year. If profits are still undistributed as you approach the end of your tax year, you can pay yourself those profits as a bonus to reduce the tax liability of the corporation.

Like individuals, corporations fall into various tax brackets, so the tax rate increases as income rises. Many people think corporate tax rates are much higher than individual rates, but this is not necessarily true. In fact, at lower income levels, corporate tax rates are quite reasonable and may even be lower than your personal tax rate. For this and possibly other reasons, you may choose to leave profits in the C corporation.

An S corporation files a tax return to report income but doesn't pay taxes. The shareholders pay taxes on the net profits according to their respective percentage of ownership, much like a sole proprietor or partnership. If the corporation has a net profit that it retains and doesn't distribute, the shareholders pay taxes on the money anyway. If the corporation loses money, those losses are reported on the shareholders' tax returns and can offset other income.

■ Corporations: Not the Only Option

For most people, engaging in business without a corporation is risky to the point of foolishness, and I encourage you to incorporate as soon as possible, whether or not your business is profitable yet. But in addition to your corporation, you will also find circumstances when other business structures are more appropriate for whatever you happen to be doing.

It's not a good idea to have all your assets owned by one entity, such as your primary corporation. But as I've said, forming multiple corporations can become cumbersome and expensive. A very effective and fairly simple way to control and protect your assets is to divide them and own them in limited partnerships.

From an asset protection standpoint, the most important point to know about limited partnerships is that a limited partnership interest can't be attached, can't be taken from you, and can't be sold by a judgment holder.

This differs from the usual treatment of stocks, bonds, mortgages, real estate, beneficial interests, and all other property interests, whether real or personal. Someone who has won a judgment against you can take those assets from you or force their sale. But a judgment holder can't take your limited partnership interest. The courts continually rule that it is against public policy and the ULPA to allow anyone to attach or take a limited partnership interest.

When your privacy is breached or you have to provide details of your assets, simply explain that they are held in limited partnerships. Your first line of defense is keeping information private, which means that people won't try to sue you for what they don't know you have. You'll eventually have to disclose your assets if you're under serious attack. But that's not a problem if the other party can't touch what you have.

In many cases, judgment holders simply give up at this point. But if they have a smart lawyer who knows what to do (and that's a big if—many good attorneys don't know this), they'll get a charging order. This order requires any income that would otherwise be distributed to you as a limited partner be paid to judgment holders until they are paid in full. This is not a problem, and I'll explain why. But first, let's look at how limited partnerships are set up and structured.

As I told you earlier, a limited partnership is composed of at least one general partner and one or more limited partners. The partners can be individuals or corporations. The general partner is often a corporation you control. The limited partners can be yourself, your family members, your business partners, or others. The limited partners can own up to 99 percent of the interest with the general partner owning merely 1 percent. The general partner's interest is freely transferable; the limited partners' interests are not. Usually, the interests of a limited partner can be transferred only with the unanimous consent of all the partners at the time of the proposed transfer.

For income tax purposes, all income and expenses flow through the partnership to the individual partners and are reported on your personal income tax return. You won't suffer any adverse tax consequences by using a limited partnership.

The general partner is in complete control of partnership decisions and is liable for all acts and debts of the partnership. That's why it's a good idea to make the general partner a corporation that owns just 1 percent of the partnership. Remember, employees and shareholders are not liable for corporate conduct, so you can personally control the corporation without risking liability. The limited partners have no control and no liability for either partnership acts or partnership debts. By being a limited partner, you may be subject to a personal attack by a plaintiff, judgment holder, or creditor, but they won't win.

So let's say someone has obtained a judgment against you and has been smart enough to obtain a charging order requiring your income as a limited partner be paid to him until the judgment is satisfied. Don't bother getting out your checkbook. Think about it: Who is in control of the limited partnership and any distributions? The general partner. Who is in control of the general partner? You are. So you completely control the distributions to the limited partners. If you or your spouse is an employee of a corporate general partner, one of you can still receive a salary and have your expenses paid even though you don't pay the judgment.

You may be thinking that a patient judgment holder may just wait and hope to collect in the future. That's not likely because federal income tax law requires partners to pay income taxes on the net income of a partnership even if no money is distributed. So let's say the limited partnership showed a handsome profit and reinvested that money back into the business. As a limited partner, you'd still have to pay income tax on your share of the net profit. But the IRS requires a judgment holder with a charging order to pay income tax on your share of the net income, even if no money is actually distributed or received. So the judgment holder has to pay taxes on your share of the profits, even though he doesn't get any money—and the greater the profit made by the partnership, the more taxes the judgment holder has to pay.

Think about what you've done here: Instead of letting others take your assets, you've placed them in a position of having two bad choices when they find out your assets are in limited partnerships. They can give up and walk away, or they can obtain a charging order and wait for you to receive income, and then they'll pay income taxes on money they're not getting in the meantime. You are in total control.

Smart Thinking

Before you open a bank account in the corporate name, call the bank ahead of time to find out what documents they need. All banks have their own set of requirements and they vary. You don't want to get halfway through the process and realize you're missing a document the bank is going to insist on seeing.

■ The Certainty of Death and Taxes

One of these days, you're going to die. In the meantime, if you're making money, you're going to pay taxes. There's just no getting around it, but you can take steps to minimize those taxes.

Let me make one thing clear: Failing to report income and doing illegal things to avoid paying taxes are crimes, and the penalties are severe. So report all your income and pay your taxes.

At the same time, I'm not suggesting that you pay more taxes than you are required to. The tax code is full of ways for you to legitimately reduce your tax liability. Take advantage of every single opportunity it offers, from how you set up your companies and receive income to how you offset that income with expenses.

You also want to do estate planning to minimize the taxes your estate will have to pay when you die. The most basic part of estate planning is a will that clearly states who your beneficiaries are. But there's more to it than that. Take the time to consult with a lawyer knowledgeable in estate planning so you can set up your holdings in a way that ensures they are distributed according to your wishes and with the least amount of taxes due when you die.

■ In the Final Analysis

We've talked a lot in this chapter about how to avoid paying judgments. Let me say clearly that if you have a legitimate debt, you should pay it. I'm teaching you these asset protection strategies so that people who are not entitled to what you've worked hard to build can't take your money away from you.

Without an asset protection plan, you could be worth $1 million, get sued for $1 million, and lose everything. With a properly structured asset protection plan, you could be worth $1 million, get sued for $1 million, and lose nothing. You might be beaten in a battle or two along the way, but you'll definitely win the war.

MILLIONAIRE MENTOR Asset Protection Highlights

■ There is no way to stop someone from suing you. You can take steps to reduce the likelihood that you'll be sued, but you can't totally prevent it. Don't let the possibility of being sued make you fear becoming wealthy; instead, learn how to protect your assets from lawsuits, taxes, and other claims.

■ You need adequate property insurance and general liability insurance. Consult with an insurance agent for the right amount of coverage for your particular circumstances. But insurance is not asset protection.

■ The primary goals of asset protection are privacy, control, and liability protection.

■ A very effective asset protection strategy for real estate investors is to own each property in a separate land trust.

■ When it comes to the legal structure of your companies, your choices are sole proprietorship, partnership, limited partnership, corporation, and a limited liability company. Corporations and limited partnerships are generally the best structures for liability protection and tax reduction.

CHAPTER 17

Communication and Negotiation

The People Side of the Business

The mechanics of real estate may revolve around land and buildings, but it's really a people business. You buy from, and sell to, people. Your renters are people—even if you're renting commercial property to companies, you're dealing with people. As you grow and expand, you'll be hiring people to work for you. Your Power Team is made up of people. Every deal you do involves people.

Clearly, people are critical to your success as a real estate investor. You may know all there is to know about wholesale buying or foreclosures or options, but if the sellers don't like you or don't understand what you're trying to do, or if the lenders don't have confidence in you, you're going to have a hard time closing deals.

The other side of that coin is that when people like you, trust you, and believe in you, they'll be lining up to do deals with you.

Let me be clear: This isn't about being phony, saying things that aren't true, or being manipulative. This is about honesty, integrity, knowledge, and building relationships that serve everyone.

■ The Art of Communication and Negotiation

"What we have here is a failure to communicate."

Remember that line from the movie *Cool Hand Luke*? Most of the time when there's a conflict in a relationship, it's because the parties involved are failing to communicate. I'm not suggesting that poor communication is the source of all the world's ills, but I do believe that improved communication would definitely solve many problems, from troubled marriages to warring countries. And I can guarantee that good communication is a cornerstone of your success.

The first element of good communication is *active listening*. This isn't new nor is it rocket science. It's simply listening in a way that you really do hear what the other person has said and then showing it. The most common technique is to paraphrase what another has said. Say something like this: "So your point is . . ." or "If I understand you correctly, you're saying . . ." and then repeat the main points in your own words. This not only demonstrates that you were listening, but also gives the other person a chance to correct you if you misunderstood or if the other person misspoke.

When you listen actively, you're focused on what the other person is saying, not on what you're going to say next. You're paying attention to her body language and to what she's *not* saying as well—which is often more important than her actual words.

Once you're sure you've heard the other person accurately, reflect on the implications of what was said. Try saying something like this: "So if you sold this property, you'd be in a position to . . ." or "Buying this house would mean that you'd be able to . . ."

Stay open-minded, objective, and nonjudgmental. Be willing to see someone else's point of view, no matter how different from yours it may be. Things don't have to go the way you originally planned for everyone to still profit from the situation.

Remember that silence can truly be golden. It's the most powerful communication tool you have. Let others finish what they have to say. Don't interrupt, don't try to squeeze your own point in, and don't finish their sentences. You don't know what they're going to say, and even if you do, finishing someone else's sentence doesn't prove how smart you are—it's just annoying.

You may be dealing with people who are uncomfortable talking about their circumstances, especially if they're in a distressed situation like financial difficulties or divorce. They may find it difficult to answer your questions, even though they know you have to have the information to put a deal together. So when you have a sensitive question, such as asking how far behind in the payments they are or if they have a place to go if the foreclosure isn't stopped, ask the question and then be quiet. And stay quiet until you get your answer. The silence may be awkward. It might stretch out for several minutes, and those minutes will seem like hours. But ask—and wait. It's the best way to find out what you need to know.

In addition to listening to others, you need to also *listen to yourself.* You have to be confident, positive, and direct, not obnoxious, overbearing, or competitive. Think whether you would want to do business with someone who speaks and acts as you do. If you wouldn't, you need to make some changes.

Another key element of communication is education—and you're the teacher. Size up the people you're dealing with, understand their needs, and then educate them about the transaction and why what you're proposing is good.

As you speak, use "you" language to shift the focus away from yourself to what is important to the other person. So rather than "I can close in two weeks," say, "The closing can be scheduled any time between the 10th and the 15th. What's a good time and date for you?"

You also want to be totally accepting of everyone who is involved in the transaction, whether or not you agree with all of them. Keep *your* judgment out of *their* decision-making process. This helps them feel safe and comfortable with you, which in turn leads them to being more open and honest about how they feel and what they want.

However—and this is critical—just as important as it is to listen and understand the other person's point of view, it's equally important to clearly state your own position and what you want. After all, there are at least two parties involved in any transaction. You want to reach a conclusion that meets enough of your own needs and of the other person's needs to come to an agreement that will satisfy you both.

I told you about Chuck Hastings in Chapter 6. He says that as important as it is to understand how to put together real estate deals, knowing how to deal with people and what to say to them is what really makes it all happen. He admits that his wife, Sherri, is a better communicator than he is, so she gets the deals started and then he steps in and handles the details.

Words of Wisdom

Don't be intimidated when you're buying from a seasoned real estate investor. It's actually easier to buy from this type of seller than from an individual who is not in the business and is more likely to be emotional about the transaction. Experienced investors know what you're trying to do, and they don't mind if you make money as long as they get a deal they can live with.

■ Communication Mistakes: What *Not* to Do

As important as understanding what contributes to positive communications is recognizing your bad communication habits and working to change them. Listen to yourself to see if you're making any of these communication mistakes—and if you are, work on changing your style.

Arguing. If you like to play devil's advocate or disagree on an issue when your opinion wasn't asked for, you could be alienating others. Someone who is constantly presenting an opposing view—whether it's right or wrong—tends to make others feel uncomfortable, inferior, and uninformed.

Acting the victim. Do you constantly drag up old injuries to gain sympathy? It may make you feel good to get pity from others, but you're putting them in a difficult position and probably even depressing them in the bargain. You may need therapy to let go of the need to be a victim; if so, get it from a professional, not your friends and business associates.

Comparing yourself. When the way you react to what others say is to immediately relate it to something in your own life, it shows that you're not really interested in them. You need to learn to focus more on the other person.

Topping. Even worse than the habit of comparing yourself is the habit of always going one better than the other person. You know the type—if someone got a good deal, he got a better one. If someone went on a five-day cruise, she took a two-week one. If you always have to top someone else's story, you're not communicating, you're alienating.

Judging. People who are frequently critically judgmental about others are often insecure about themselves. Making negative statements about others says much more about you than it does about them—and it's not complimentary.

Gossiping. Similar to judging, people who gossip are frequently insecure and generally can't be trusted with confidences. This is not the reputation you need.

Interrupting. The quickest way to let someone else know you have absolutely no interest in what that person has to say is to constantly interrupt. It's a clear statement that you think only your words have value. Bite your tongue if you have to, but let the other person finish speaking.

■ Negotiating from a Position of Power

To negotiate from a position of power, you don't need a figurative sledge-hammer to beat everyone else into submission. Instead, approach the situation with confidence, secure in the knowledge that you can come up with a solution that will make everyone feel as if they've walked away a winner.

One of the biggest mistakes people make is looking at negotiating as though it must be a win-lose proposition. That's browbeating, not negotiating. And it might get you one good deal, but it won't create the relationships you need to build a fortune.

When your goal is a win-win solution; when everyone involved can benefit from your proposals; and when you're honest, confident, and knowledgeable, you're negotiating from a position of power.

Words of Wisdom

Be totally present in the discussion, which means turning off your cell phone and pager. Shut out as many other distractions as possible— radios, televisions, and the like. Focus 100 percent on what is being said so you can process it and use the information to put together a win-win deal.

■ Real Estate Negotiating Tips

Basic negotiating tips can be applied to any situation, whether you're selling a product, deciding on a movie (when you and your spouse are not in the mood for the same thing), or persuading your fussy toddler to eat his vegetables. But there are some specific techniques that you can use when negotiating real estate deals that work well.

Before you begin negotiating, set limits and stick to them. Know what you're willing to pay and what concessions you're willing to make, and don't go beyond those. This is especially important if the property is one you really want because it could be easy to allow your emotions to override your common sense. To think "Well, it's only $X more" is OK for a luxury consumer purchase if you can afford it, but that type of thinking can mean the difference between profit or loss on a real estate deal. If you can't get the property for a price that allows you to make a profit, walk away. This is also important to keep in mind if you're buying at auctions.

Early in the process, whether you're buying or selling, state clearly that you want to do the deal but the numbers have to make sense. You are an investor, this is your business, and you must make a profit or you won't do the deal. At the same time, say that you also want the other person to be satisfied with the outcome. When you set the goal early on that you want everyone to come away from the closing table a winner, you've established a positive tone for the negotiations.

If the seller rejects your initial offer because it isn't high enough, you can expedite the negotiation process by asking, "What is the very lowest price you would sell this property for?" Most people will answer you honestly. With that number, you can decide how—and if—to continue negotiating.

When a seller asks if you'll increase your offer, your immediate response should be, "My research indicates that I am able to offer $X [whatever your offer was] at this time. I'm not saying your property may not be worth more to somebody else, but I'm willing to offer you $X for your property right now." Then wait for a response. You can always change your offer later.

In your initial offer, ask for things that you don't care if you get. Here's a quote floating around on the Internet: "If you want a kitten, start out by asking for a horse." The technique works just as well in real estate as it does with pets. You might ask for the seller to do some cosmetic work, such as painting, that you really intend to do yourself. Or ask him to leave things that you don't really care about, such as a swing set, area rugs, special light fixtures, non-built-in appliances, or even certain pieces of furniture. This gives the seller something to say no to, and you might even end up with more than what you really wanted. Take a similar approach if you're asking for seller financing. Don't start off with your best offer. If you're willing to pay 10 percent interest with a five-year balloon, offer 8 percent with a seven-year balloon. If you have to go up to the amount you were originally willing to pay, you haven't lost anything and the seller feels as though he's won something in the negotiations. And you may end up getting a better deal. This technique works with every part of your offer.

When you're dealing with first-time buyers or sellers, recognize they are going to feel insecure and apprehensive about the transaction. It may be just another piece of investment property to you, but it's a home to them. Respect their feelings and do what you can to take the mystery out of the process. Give them an outline and timetable of what they can expect to happen as the transaction moves forward. Break it down into simple, easy-to-understand steps, and be sure to do it in a way that isn't condescending. If you sense "first-timer fear," try saying something like "One of the things I like to do in all my transactions is go over what's going to happen and when. You may already know this, but I've found it helpful if we just go through the sequence of events." Then quickly outline what is going to happen and how long it will take. This is also a good way for you to identify any potential problems that may arise with the deal so you can handle them early.

Throughout your negotiations, ask questions to confirm that the other person understands what you're saying and agrees with it. Phrase the questions to elicit a positive response. For example, you can ask, "Does that sound fair (or good) to you?" or a more simple "Fair enough?" Most people will let you know if they don't think it's fair or good, and you'll have a chance to deal with a sticking point before you close the deal.

Words of Wisdom

Help the people you're doing business with make good decisions. Take the time to explain your offer, show them how they can benefit from it, and be sure they understand it.

■ Selling Skills = Relationship Skills

Most people hate the idea of selling. Most industries have gotten beyond the stereotypical image of the loudmouthed, badly dressed, pushy salesperson, but as individuals we still cringe at the idea of having to sell something. Yet the techniques that top professional salespeople use are the same techniques most of us use every day in our relationships.

Listening for $35,000

Kevin Haag, one of my long-term personal Realtors and a member of my Wealth Team, knows the value of good communication skills. Kevin makes sure everybody he knows is aware of what he does for a living. His neighbor was at a garage sale when he heard about a man whose son was facing foreclosure. The neighbor passed the son's name on to Kevin, who called immediately and set up a meeting.

"He was really down, so I just let him talk," Kevin recalls. "About 15 minutes into the conversation, he mentioned a selling price of $30,000 less than I was going to offer." That was good, but it got better. "I casually mentioned that his price was about $5,000 more than I was able to pay. He met my price."

Two major lessons can be learned from this story. The first is the importance of telling everybody you know that you invest in real estate. Tell your friends, your neighbors, your doctor, the people at church, the clerks in stores, the person who does your hair—everybody! If Kevin's neighbor hadn't known what Kevin does, he wouldn't have thought to tell Kevin about the house, and the seller would have faced foreclosure.

The second lesson is to let the seller be the first one to mention a price. You can always increase your offer if the circumstances warrant, but it's hard to reduce it once you've made an offer. "If I had offered a figure first, I would have $35,000 more into that house than I do," Kevin says. "That's a lot of money for talking too much."

Good salespeople find out what their customers need and then demonstrate how their product or service can meet that need better than anything else on the market. They make referrals when appropriate, because they know that an honest referral— "I don't think what we have is what you need, but ABC Company has a product that should work"—is worth a priceless amount of goodwill and future business.

How does that approach transfer to your personal relationships? Simple. When you want others to do something, you show them why it's to their advantage and how they can benefit from it. For example, you want to go to a party Saturday night and your spouse wants to stay home. You don't say, "We're going and that's it." (Well, you might, but if you do, you're not likely to have a very good time.) Instead, you find reasons your spouse would want to go. You might point out that this is a great chance to wear the new outfit that's hanging in the closet. Or that someone your spouse finds extremely interesting will be at the party. Or that if your spouse will go to the party, you'll go to a particular restaurant your spouse wants to try.

Think about a buying experience that was positive when you got what you wanted at a good price, and you told all your friends about it. Think about the techniques the salesperson used. Those are the exact same techniques you should be using every day in every relationship, whether it's business or personal. It's not being manipulative; it's solving problems in a mutually beneficial way.

Of course, certain selling basics that you should always keep in mind are discussed in the following.

Identify the decision maker and decision influencers. Find out who is actually going to make the decision and who that person will listen to in the process. You don't want to waste a lot of time selling to someone who can't make a decision. On the other hand, you shouldn't ignore the decision influencers; if they're on your side, your job is significantly easier.

Know your competition. Who else is doing what you do? Who else can meet the customer's needs with a different product? For example, if you're buying properties in foreclosure, you have to know what the other real estate investors working your area are doing. You also need to understand how to compete against bankruptcy (we talked about that in Chapter 6). If you're buying or brokering discounted notes, you need to know who the other note buyers and/or brokers are. You also need to know about the lenders in the market, because someone interested in selling all or part of a note as the result of an immediate need for cash may also consider keeping the note and just borrowing the money.

Use win-win communication and negotiation techniques. I've already talked about this. Find out what your customer's needs are and be clear about your own goals. Put together a deal that benefits everyone.

Recognize that objections mean opportunity. Always remember that most objections are simply a request for more information. Often, they're a signal that the person really wants to do the deal but just needs reassurance, or something about the transaction isn't completely clear. You have to clarify the objection, agree that the concern has merit, and respond to it.

For example, you've made an offer on a wholesale property, and the seller says, "Your price seems low. I thought I could get more for the house than that." First, clarify the objection. "So you're saying that the only issue you have with this offer is the price; is that correct? Do you have any other questions?" If the seller has other questions, deal with those first, and then address the price issue if it's still a problem. If the seller has no other questions, then deal with the price objection. "I can appreciate that this offer might seem a little low, but as I've said, I'm an investor who specializes in buying run-down properties at below market value. I take them as is, so you don't have to do any of the cleanup or fix-up. You could spend a substantial amount of time and money on that, and by the time you did, your net would be about what it is with what I'm offering. And if you accept my offer, we can close in three weeks."

Watch for smoke screens—they sound like objections, but they're really not. Often a smoke screen is tossed out because people feel they ought to object at least once or twice to strengthen their negotiating position. On the other hand, a smoke screen might be a cover for a true objection, or it could be just a stalling tactic. That's why you must clarify the objection before you respond to it.

Wealth Secrets

You don't have to buy at the seller's price—ever! Always buy at your price, or don't buy.

■ Dealing with Upset or Angry People

No matter how fair and honest you are, there are always situations when you have to deal with someone who is upset or angry. This could be a buyer, a seller, a tenant, a lender, a contractor—anyone. Whether the person is right or wrong, you have to defuse the situation and get things on a productive footing.

If the other person is screaming and ranting, use a technique known as a "pattern interrupt," which means doing something neutral to stop the display of angry behavior. It could be as simple as asking for a drink or if you can close a door or window. You could also ask the person to pause for a moment while you get pen and paper so you can take notes.

When he has put his tirade on hold, ask him to repeat what he was saying so you can write it down. This process usually diminishes some of the anger. When he's finished, read back the points he's made in a neutral tone, taking all the emotion out of what has been said. Ask if you've correctly written down his concerns and if there is anything else. If there is, repeat the process until he has said everything he needs to.

If the anger is directed at you, you don't have to accept the blame. Instead, say something like this: "It was never my intention to make you angry. What can I do to correct the situation?" Then be quiet until you get an answer.

If the anger is directed at someone else, don't participate in criticizing that person. Instead, empathize and find out what you can do. Say "I certainly understand how that could make you so angry. How can I help?"

If you've made a mistake, ask for forgiveness but don't apologize. People expect an explanation with an apology, and that's not necessary. You don't have to explain or excuse; you just have to take responsibility for your actions and do what you can to fix the problem. All you need to say is "Please forgive me, I made a mistake. What can I do to make it right for you?"

When the anger is not justified, don't argue—and don't point out how absurd the other person's position is. Use the technique of writing down his issues and reading them back; in most cases, simply taking the time to listen and make notes is calming enough for you to move beyond the point of anger.

■ How to Build Relationships

Even though most of this book deals with real estate, the book is really about relationships—your relationships with your friends and family, with your teachers and mentors, with your business associates, with clients, and with others. The relationships you create and nurture are critical to your success. Something I've learned is that the more talented and successful people I surround myself with, the wealthier I become. The path to success cannot be traveled alone.

In the first chapter, I told you that I have built my fortune based on three things: the hands I shake, the decisions I make, and the actions I take. By "hands I shake," I mean relationships. I could never have achieved the success I have had I insisted on doing everything by myself.

Relationships are a fundamental building block of your success. You need relationships on a variety of levels, from simple and casual to deep and complex. But never let those relationships be superficial. When you have a genuine interest in other people and you are sincere, it shows and will be reciprocated.

To maintain your relationships, use whatever technique or system works for you. I've known people who keep elaborate computer databases with files on everyone they meet, whereas others have a gift for remembering names, faces, and other details without ever making a written note. However you choose to do it, make it a point to build relationships that will enhance your own life both personally and professionally and allow you to do the same for others.

Words of Wisdom

How you act is how you attract. When you function at a high level— whether it's ethically, morally, or from a professional skills perspective —you attract others who are the same. This provides you the opportunity to build a personal and business network of the best and brightest in addition to providing you and your associates the support you need to succeed.

■ Operating with Integrity

Absolutely nothing is more important in the business world today than trust. Yes, knowledge and skill are important. Having a solid Power Team is important. Building a network that provides you with the connections to make things happen when it's necessary is important. But without trust, the rest is virtually useless.

Trust isn't something you create in a day. It takes time. Trust is earned through honesty, quality, service, and consistent performance over time. How do you achieve that? I'm sure you know, but I'll remind you anyway.

Always be truthful about your intentions. When you lie and people find out—and believe me, they will—they aren't going to believe you the next time.

Maintain an open line of communication. Share information. Encourage feedback. Know the concerns of the people you're dealing with so you can take appropriate action.

If you make a mistake, acknowledge it and fix it. Trying to cover it up or make excuses only compounds the problem. Correct the situation and move on.

Always give people more than they expect. We've all been disappointed when someone promised more than they could—or would—deliver. Underpromising and overdelivering does more than just delight your customers and associates; it clearly demonstrates that you are trustworthy and deserve respect.

Don't be tempted to move into a gray area just because you think you can get away with it and the profits could be substantial. When the stakes are high, your integrity should be even higher.

Finally, remember that trust is a two-way street. Just as you are willing to earn the trust of your associates, so should they be of you. And if they prove untrustworthy, remove them from your network.

I'm not saying that scoundrels don't get rich. Sadly, it happens all the time. But when you build on sand, you never know when the foundation will shift and your house will come crashing down around you. Build on rock—that is, on truth, honesty, and integrity—and you can be confident that your foundation is secure and you can weather any storm.

MILLIONAIRE MENTOR Communication and Negotiation Highlights

■ Strong communication and negotiation skills are essential for success in any business. You may make money on real estate, but you have to deal with people skillfully to do it.

■ Listen actively. Focus on what the other person is saying and respond with comments that make it clear you understood. Avoid being judgmental.

■ While listening for what the other person wants and needs, also be clear about your own position and what you need to make the transaction work.

■ Communication mistakes include arguing, acting like a victim, judging, one-upmanship, gossiping, and interrupting.

■ Key real estate negotiating tips include setting limits and sticking to them; leaving room for negotiation in your initial offer; helping first-time buyers (or sellers) feel secure about the transaction; and asking questions to confirm understanding and agreement.

■ Don't just do deals, build relationships. Relationships are a fundamental building block of your business and your success.

■ Always operate with truth, honesty, and integrity.

The End

For You, the Beginning

This final chapter of *Millionaire Real Estate Mentor* may be the end of the book, but it's just the start of your future.

If you're still working for someone else, the day you quit your job could be one of the most exciting days of your life. But be prepared. Some people recommend that you put that step off as long as possible. After all, they say you have benefits and the security of a paycheck. I say be reasonable and sensible, but as soon as you have reached financial independence, quit your job and go to work making money full-time. Receiving benefits through a job is the most expensive way you can get them, because you're spending your time helping someone else become rich rather than building your own fortune. And the only paycheck that is truly secure is the one you create for yourself.

Once you have achieved financial independence, the next step is wealth. And if you use the techniques in this book, it will come faster and easier than you ever thought possible.

When you're wealthy, will your life be perfect? I doubt it. You'll still have problems—misunderstandings with your spouse and your kids testing their limits and your patience. You may have to cope with your own or your loved ones' health issues. Mechanical things still break down, people let you down, and it'll rain when you were hoping for sunny weather. This is life, and it's not perfect. But it will be a whole lot easier to deal with when you're wealthy. As my good friend Tony Youngs says, "When you're rich, you still have problems, but you arrive at them in style."

So now that you know your options in real estate, what do you do next?

■ Assess Your Market

As you read about the different ways you can invest in real estate, you probably liked some better than others. But before you make a final decision on the types of transactions you want to do, assess your market realistically to make sure the potential is there. For example, if you like the idea of buying foreclosures, be sure there are enough foreclosures in the area where you want to work. Where I live in Cape Coral, Florida, the opportunity for foreclosures is very narrow; but across the bridge in Fort Myers, it's much greater. And in a city like Atlanta, you could work 24 hours a day and still not have time to handle even a fraction of all the foreclosures.

How do you conduct this market assessment? Read the newspaper—the business section, the classified ads, and the legal notices—for a solid sense of the market. Join your local real estate investors club, landlord club, or other similar organization; you'll find out quickly where the members are making their money, because they'll be talking about their deals. Talk to mortgage brokers, lenders, and other investors; they'll be happy to give you their opinion of the market and where the best opportunities are. If you want to shortcut this process, take our training. Our instructors work with you to help you recognize the potential of your specific market.

Wealth Secrets

You are a direct result of the people you spend the most time with, so surround yourself with millionaires and successful people from all walks of life who can help you get where you want to be. Your journey will be faster and easier than you could ever imagine.

Procrastination *Doesn't* Pay

After learning how to buy wholesale property at our training program, Dan Davis spent an entire year putting off the start of his real estate career. "The bottom line was that I was just too scared," he says. He finally decided it was time for action, so "I rolled up my sleeves and went to work." At the end of a year, he owned 31 properties totaling 36 units with a total appraised value in excess of $1 million. The properties were purchased at 65 to 85 percent of their appraised value and generate $3,000 a month in positive cash flow. And his net worth has gone from just the equity in his home (less than $20,000) to $250,000.

"Not bad for someone whose goal was to make a few extra dollars so he could afford to send his daughter to college," he observes. "Needless to say, my goals are different now. A willingness to work, the right information, and someone who will support and mentor you are a combination with only one outcome: success!"

■ Inventory Your Resources and Develop a Plan

The next step is to make an inventory of your resources and put together a plan of action. By resources, I mean financial, informational, and emotional.

Your financial resources include cash, investment accounts, stocks, real estate, and other noncash assets as well as your available credit. Your informational resources are what you know, the people who are potential members of your Power Team, and how you can gain additional knowledge. And your emotional resources include the support you have from family members and friends.

With a clear picture of your market and your resources, you can put together a plan. The plan begins with goals. How much real estate do you want

to own and by what specific date? How much cash flow do you want the properties to generate? To say that you want to "be rich" isn't a goal—it's a fantasy.
To say that within the next two years you want to own 25 residential income-
producing properties with a total of 75 units (a combination of single-family
homes, duplexes, and fourplexes), with a collective appraised value of at least
$2 million, generating $9,000 a month in positive cash flow—now, that's a
goal. It's specific, it's measurable, it's doable, and you can easily put together
a plan to get there.

Some people find it hard to set that initial goal because, as much as
they'd like to be wealthy, there's something deep down inside them that is
telling them they can't. They hear a nagging little voice saying that they
might be able to buy a few pieces of real estate, but they will never be a landlord to hundreds of tenants. They might eventually be able to afford a home
of their own, but it will never be a million-dollar mansion. Here's how to
quiet those sabotaging little voices: Write the goal down, look at it, and ask
yourself, "Is this goal worthy of me?" *not* "Am I worthy of this goal?"

The next step is to take your large goal and break it down into small
steps. You don't have to start thinking how you're going to get to $1 million.
Think how you can make $3,000 or $4,000, and put that in your plan. Then
think how you can make $5,000 or $10,000, and plan for that. Your plan
might start with doing some quick flips of wholesale properties to generate
enough cash to buy a multiunit building. Or you might want to rehab some
distressed properties and either sell them for the immediate cash or put
them in your portfolio as rentals.

If you focus exclusively on the larger goal, you'll never get there. If you
don't own any real estate, or even if you own only your own home, acquiring 75 units in two years seems like a monumental achievement. Do the
math, though, and it means you only have to buy 3.1 units a month—less
than 1 a week. Two duplexes, and you've hit your goal for the month. Could
you do that? Karen Herrera bought 32 units in a single day—and did it with
no money down. I think Karen's a pretty special person, but what she did is
something anyone can do. That's what Whitney Canada students Beverly
Martin and Debbra Greig told me too. In their first month as real estate investors, they closed three deals, made a $50,000, profit, and became the
owners of $350,000 in real estate. They learned the techniques and applied
them, just as you can and will.

Start with putting together the numbers and a few deadlines. You want 50 units in two years? OK, that's 25 units the first year. Two units a month. One unit every two weeks. Plot that out on a calendar.

You've probably already thought about the techniques you want to use, so put them into your plan. How many foreclosures? How many wholesale properties? Once you own them, how many traditional tenants and how many lease option tenants do you want?

Now, think about how you're going to locate these properties, fix them up, and find tenants or buyers for them. I've explained how to check the classifieds, read the legal section, and drive through neighborhoods. Using those recommendations, put together a plan that will fit your goals. Gloria Steinem was right on target when she said, "Rich people plan for four generations. Poor people plan for Saturday night."

Wealth Secrets

Wealthy people don't depend on just one source of income. They have multiple income streams, which is why I've shown you a variety of ways to generate cash and build wealth. Be sure your plan includes applying several of my proven techniques.

■

Knowledge + Determination = Success

Gary S.'s situation looked hopeless. He'd been laid off from his job, the bill collectors were hounding him, and he had a negative net worth of –$48,000. "I have the prettiest wife and kids you've ever seen, and they deserved better," he says.

He wanted to attend my three-day real estate training program and tried to borrow the money from his parents. They said no. They told him he didn't know anything about real estate, he was too stupid to do any deals, and my program was a scam anyway. But his father-in-law was willing to take a chance on Gary's dream and gave him the money for the seminar.

At the end of the training session, Gary hit the ground running. He found seven properties in two weeks, made no-money-down offers on all of them—and was turned down for each one. And in his head, he heard his father's voice saying that he couldn't do this, that it wouldn't work, that it was just a scam.

But Gary was determined. He decided to try lining up bank financing before making another offer on property. He went to 21 bankers and heard "no" 21 times. Then the next banker said something that rang a bell. He said, "I like you, but right now there is nothing I can do." Gary remembered what I'd taught him about banks not always being able to make loans because of the status of their own portfolios, so he said, "I see. Portfolio is a little heavy on one side, is it?" The banker just smiled and told him to try again later.

A few more bankers, a few more no's, and then he found the one he was looking for. Gary recalls, "He said, 'Find something and bring it to me.' I was excited. I found a building appraised at $98,000. I offered $72,000 and asked if the seller would take the rest in a second mortgage to be paid off by 10 percent of the profit from the rent after all expenses. He said yes." That no-money-down deal was just the first of many successful deals for Gary. He now owns more than $250,000 in real estate, all purchased with no cash down; he has his own contracting company and is steadily increasing his holdings.

"I can now provide for my family the way they deserve," Gary says. "And now my mom works for me."

■ Working the Plan

Once you have a plan written down with specific steps and deadlines, put it into action. This may be one of the hardest things for you to do, but it's the only way you'll turn your dreams into reality. That first action step may feel like you're stepping off a cliff, but you're not. You're prepared, you know what you want, and you have a plan to get it. Remember, it takes activity to see results. If you're not doing something, nothing will happen.

Are you worried that something will go wrong? That's normal. But what you have to focus on is implementing your action plan and making things go right. Certainly be prepared for what you'll do if there's a snag, but concentrate on the positives. Looking only at what could go wrong allows you all kinds of excuses to not implement your plan. I see this in some of our students. For whatever reason, they're afraid to try, so they look for all the reasons not to—what if the seller doesn't show up at closing, what if there's more wrong with the property than you thought, what if the tenant moves out before the lease is up, what if a pipe breaks in the middle of the night. Do these things happen? Sometimes. But most of your real estate transactions will go smoothly and yield the profits you want.

Don't think as much about what can go wrong as you do about what can go right. Sure, you need to do worst-case scenario analyses on deals, but know that the worst case rarely happens. Just remember: When you're good at making excuses, it's difficult to excel at anything else.

Words of Wisdom

Don't be nervous about calling in response to classified ads or For Sale signs. Remember, the people who place ads and put up signs want *you to call them. In fact, they've spent money—and in the case of many large-circulation daily newspapers, a substantial amount of money—to get you to call. They have a problem they want to get rid of, and you just might be the solution. So pick up that phone and dial with confidence.*

■ Unseen Support: The Value of a Deep Foundation

From skyscrapers towering over cities to one-story homes in the suburbs, every building has a foundation. The taller the building, the deeper the foundation. If architects used the same foundation for a 20-story highrise as they did for a two-story frame house, construction would likely not make it past the third floor. In fact, in every construction project a tremendous amount of time, energy, and materials are invested in a part of the building that is never seen: the foundation.

Your foundation, that platform on which your future will be built, is *knowledge.* The more knowledge you have, the deeper your foundation. The deeper your foundation, the higher your ultimate reach.

■ Never Stop Learning

One of the most exciting things about this business is that you can do real estate as badly as it can be done and still make money. And when you do it well, there is absolutely no limit to what you can achieve.

The best way to do this or any business well is to begin with knowledge and keep on learning. Start with the resources listed in this book. Then read more books and magazines. Listen to tapes. Watch videos. Attend seminars and high-level education programs. One of our companies, the Whitney Education Group, focuses on training adults for second careers in real estate investing and entrepreneurship. We have 11 training centers across the United States plus centers in Canada and the United Kingdom. Every week, these centers are filled with students who are being trained in a classroom by live instructors, who are also expert investors, and then taken out for practical, hands-on field training. These people understand the value of life-long education, and you've had the privilege of meeting just a few of them in the pages of this book. I urge you to join their ranks and acquire the knowledge on which your success can be built.

Beyond structured education, learn something from every deal, whether it goes through or not. In fact, you'll learn as much, or more, from the deals you lose as you will from the deals you make.

Find a mentor—someone who will work with you one-on-one. In fact, you probably should have more than one mentor. I still have mentors who are experts in different areas to whom I turn often. It's something I feel so strongly about that we created a mentoring program as part of our company. We have more than 30 full-time mentors whose job is to work one-on-one with our students. They'll come to your house, take you by the hand, and walk you through the process of getting started. The resources section of this book outlines some of our programs and tells you how to find out more about them.

Know that with more knowledge comes less fear. And knowledge comes from training and experience. That's why learning should never stop. There is always someone who can teach you something.

Wealth Secrets

Make your growth geometric rather than linear. In other words, don't do it one deal at a time. Have multiple deals going on at once. While you're waiting for the financing on one deal, be looking for the next property. While workers are rehabbing the house you bought last week, close on another house this week. If you've got 4 or 5, or even 10 or 20 deals going on at once, any one of them can fall through without causing you a serious problem.

■ Closing Thoughts

I hope that as you read this book, you were able to see the passion I feel for real estate and for learning. I am a product of my industry. I read a book,

I bought a piece of property, and I made money. So I read more books, bought more properties, and made more money. Then I decided to write my own book. That first book was the springboard to the creation of a company dedicated to offering educational products and programs on building wealth.

Today, my real estate holdings are global in scope. And I have students around the world using my techniques to achieve financial independence, security for the future, and true wealth for themselves and their families. I hope you'll become one of them.

Will you make mistakes along the way? Certainly. Will you have deals that looked like a sure thing but then fell apart at the last minute? Of course. You can't have success without failure. When you think of Babe Ruth and Reggie Jackson, you think of baseball superstars, right? But Babe struck out almost 16 percent of his times at bat, and Reggie Jackson struck out more than 26 percent of his times at bat.

The difference between a successful person and one who is not is that a successful person doesn't let failure turn into a roadblock. Successful people learn from their failures, make changes in their strategy if they need to, and keep moving forward. Successful people don't do everything perfectly; they just do things smart.

You know the definition of insanity: doing the same thing over and over and expecting different results. The definition of smart is doing the same thing enough to develop a ratio of results so you know what to expect and then making changes in your technique to improve your results.

People unknowingly and unwittingly restrict themselves. But trust me when I tell you: You don't have a clue how high is high yet. If you just give yourself a chance, you can accomplish so much more than you ever thought possible.

Yours in success,
Russ Whitney

GLOSSARY

absolute auction An auction with no preset reserve prices; the auctioneer must accept all bids.

acceleration clause Part of an agreement that gives a lender permission, under certain conditions, to demand all the money owed on a loan.

action A suit or judicial proceeding.

ad valorem According to value; a method of taxation using the value of the property being taxed to determine the amount of tax.

agent One who is authorized by another person or company to act in that person's or company's behalf.

allowance A sum of money set aside in a construction contract for items that have not been selected or specified in the contract.

amendment A modification or addition that supplements another written document.

amortization schedule A timetable of mortgage payments over the course of a loan that shows how much is applied to both the principal and interest.

appreciating asset An asset that increases in value, such as real estate.

articles of incorporation A document that creates a corporation under a state's general corporation laws.

assemblage The combining of two or more contiguous properties into one large property; an assemblage often makes the one large property more valuable than the sum of its parts.

assignee One to whom property is assigned or transferred.

assignment A transfer to another of one's interest in a right or property.

assignor One who assigns or transfers property.

available office space Vacant office space available for lease that may not always be ready for occupancy, as it may be under construction, has to be built out to a tenant's specifications, or requires remodeling.

backup bidder The person offering the highest bid prior to the winner.

blanket mortgage A mortgage covering more than one property.

broker A person who, for a commission or fee, brings two or more parties together and assists in negotiating contracts between them.

build-out The space improvements put in place according to a tenant's specifications.

buyer's premium An advertised percentage of the high bid or a flat fee added to the high bid to determine the total contract price to be paid by the buyer.

buying signal A communication from prospects or customers indicating they are strongly considering making the purchase, typically delivered in the form of a question.

bylaws Rules that govern how a corporation may conduct its business.

cause of action A claim for some type of relief.

change order A written document that modifies the plans and specifications and/or the price of a contract.

claim An alleged right to money, property, or other type of relief.

cloud on title The result when a title search finds a claim on a property.

common areas Those areas or portions of a building used by more than one tenant, such as hallways, elevator lobby area, janitorial and maintenance closets/rooms, and restrooms.

communication The process of sending and receiving messages.

Community Development Block Grant Program (CDBG) A federal program that provides eligible metropolitan cities and urban counties with annual direct grants that can be used to revitalize neighborhoods, expand affordable housing and economic opportunities, and/or improve community facilities and services principally to benefit low-income and moderate-income people.

community property Property in which each spouse is considered to own one-half.

concession Giving in, admitting, or yielding to the requests or demands of, or an offering used as an enticement to, an individual or entity; the concession may or may not be of monetary value.

conditions of sale The legal terms that govern the conduct of an auction, including acceptable methods of payment, terms, buyers' premiums, possession, reserves, and any other limiting factors.

contingency fee A fee paid to attorneys to represent clients, which is conditioned on a favorable judgment.

co-signer Any person who signs a loan made to someone else and assumes equal responsibility for repayment.

credit history The record of how an individual has borrowed and repaid debts.

creditor One to whom money is owed by a debtor.

curb appeal The appearance of a house or other building from the curb.

debt Any obligation of one person to pay or compensate another.

debtor One who owes another something or is under obligation to pay money or fulfill some other obligation.

deed in lieu of foreclosure A conveyance of titles to real estate executed in lieu of having the mortgagee foreclose on the property.

deed of trust A document that gives a lender the right to sell property if the borrower can't repay the loan.

defendant In civil proceedings, the party who has been sued or is responding to a complaint; in criminal proceedings, the defendant is the accused.

deficiency judgment Legal action sought by a lender who wants to recover losses on a foreclosure or repossession.

deposit Money given as security for the temporary use of property and to be refunded if the property is left undamaged.

deposition The giving of testimony under oath.

depreciating asset An asset that decreases in value, such as automobiles, appliances, electronics, and furniture.

discount The difference between the face amount of a note or other income stream and the purchase price paid by the funding source.

due diligence The process by which brokers and funding sources assess the risk and authenticity of a deal through gathering and verifying information and documentation related to the transaction.

due-on-sale clause A clause that allows a lender to declare the full amount of the mortgage balance due and payable if any portion of the property is sold by the mortgagor.

earnest money A deposit of money paid by the buyer for real property as evidence of good faith.

easement A right created by an express or implied agreement to make lawful and beneficial use of the land of another.

encumbrance Anything that affects the title of a property or limits its use, such as liens or restrictions.

equity The value or interest an owner has in real property over and above any mortgage debt or other liens against the property.

escalator(s) Term used to describe how a tenant's payment for rent or service shall increase; also the term used to describe a moving staircase.

escrow The system by which money, documents, personal property, or real property are held in trust for others by a disinterested third party until the terms and conditions of the escrow parties are completed or terminated.

eviction The physical expulsion of someone from land through legal proceedings.

Federal Deposit Insurance Corporation (FDIC) A federal agency whose mission is to maintain the stability of, and public confidence in, the nation's financial system; the FDIC insures deposits and promotes safe and sound banking practices.

Federal Home Loan Mortgage Corporation (Freddie Mac) An agency created by the federal government that buys and sells mortgages in the secondary market.

Federal Housing Administration (FHA) A federal agency that insures loans offered by certain commercial lenders.

Federal National Mortgage Association (Fannie Mae) A government-sponsored corporation that buys and sells loans in the secondary market.

federal tax lien A lien of the United States on all property and rights to property of a taxpayer who fails to pay a tax for which he is liable to the federal government.

fee Payment for services rendered or to be rendered.

fire sale price The under-the-market price of a property that is intended to guarantee a quick sale.

fiscal year A period of 12 months not based on a calendar year.

fixed-price contract A contract with a set price for specified work.

forced appreciation Situation when the value of a property goes up as a result of improvements and/or a more profitable use.

foreclosure A legal proceeding to enforce payment of a debt secured by a mortgage that is in default through the sale of the property.

funding source An individual or institution that provides money or funding to transact a cash flow deal; this is the entity that actually buys the real estate note.

general contractor An individual or company that contracts with the owner of a property to perform certain work on the property; a general contractor may use employees or subcontractors to complete the work but is responsible for the execution, supervision, and overall coordination of a project, and may also perform some of the tasks.

Government National Mortgage Association (Ginnie Mae) A federal corporation that insures mortgage-backed securities and offers financing options to homebuyers.

grantor One who conveys by deed a gift or trust.

green note A note created for immediate resale to an investor.

hard money lender A funding source that loans money on real estate based on the value of the property with little consideration to the creditworthiness of the owner; typically, the loans are short term at higher interest and points than those made by conventional lenders and are for 50 to 70 percent of the property's value.

holdover rent An extremely high rent intended as a penalty to a tenant that continues to use, or remain in possession of, a leased premise beyond the lease term.

incorporate An action that involves filing all necessary documents with the applicable department of a state to establish a corporation.

investment-to-value ratio The measure of security of a mortgage holder's position and the likelihood of recouping all investment money in the event of a foreclosure.

joint tenancy A form of ownership in which the property is owned equally by two or more persons who have rights of survivorship.

judgment A legal document stating that a debt is owed by one party in a lawsuit to another.

judgment creditor A creditor who has obtained a judgment against a debtor through which the creditor can obtain the sum due him.

judgment debtor A person against whom there is a legal judgment for repayment of a debt.

judgment lien The result of recording a judgment in land records that places a lien against the debtor's property.

land contract A form of real estate purchase in which the buyer makes installment payments toward the purchase of the property and has use of the property but does not receive title to it until payment is made in full.

lease An agreement by the lessor to temporarily give up possession of property while retaining legal ownership; an agreement by the owner/

landlord to turn over, for all purposes not prohibited by terms of the lease, the specifically described premises to the exclusive possession of the lessee for a definite period and for a consideration called rent.

leasehold improvements The construction, fixtures, attachments, and any and all physical changes and additions made to lease premises whether made by the tenant (with or without the landlord's permission) or on the tenant's behalf by the landlord or a representative (e.g., subcontractor) of the tenant.

lessee One who holds an estate by virtue of a lease; a landlord's tenant.

lessor One who grants a lease to another.

lien A charge, hold, or claim on the property of another as security for some debt or charge.

loan-to-value ratio (LTV) The percentage of the value of a property that a lender is willing to lend against; a measure of how heavily mortgaged a property is and how likely the owner is to default on the debt.

luck Term referring to a situation in which preparation meets opportunity.

manufactured home A factory-built mobile housing unit built after June 15, 1976, that is designed to meet or exceed the Housing and Urban Development code.

manufacturer's specifications The written installation and/or maintenance instructions developed by the manufacturer of a product that may have to be followed to maintain the product's warranty.

market value The price that a piece of property would command on the open market.

mechanic's lien A claim placed on real estate by someone who didn't receive payment for construction work completed on the property.

mixed-income Term describing a residential mix that includes families with various income levels within one development, therefore decreasing the economic and social isolation of public housing families.

mobile home A factory-built mobile housing unit built prior to June 15, 1976, when the Housing and Urban Development code went into effect.

modular home A factory-built housing unit designed to be permanently installed that is certified to meet or exceed state and local building codes.

mortgage note A negotiable promissory note secured by a mortgage on specific real estate property.

mortgage A pledge of real property for the security of a debt whereby the debtor maintains the right to the property.

mortgagee The entity that lends money to purchase real property and identified as the creditor and holder of the mortgage note.

mortgagor The entity that possesses real property and is paying for that property under terms of a mortgage note to a mortgagee, with the property pledged as collateral for the mortgage.

natural appreciation Term referring to the situation when the value of a property goes up with the market.

negotiation dance The process of making offers and counteroffers by the parties involved in a negotiation.

nonverbal communication The process of sending messages without the use of words; includes body language, clothes and accessories, touch, and vocal quality; nonverbal messages usually override verbal ones.

objection A statement of challenge or rejection by a prospect or customer of a feature, benefit, product, or service.

open-ended question A question that cannot be answered with a yes or no and is designed to encourage a prospect or customer to expand on a response.

option A contract that gives the holder a right or option to buy or sell specified property at a fixed price for a limited period.

panelized home Factory-built housing panels designed to be assembled on-site containing doors, windows, and wiring, and built to meet or exceed state and local building codes.

passive income Income from sources other than a job, such as income from rental properties and other investments.

payment borrower A borrower who doesn't care about the price of a house but is only concerned with the down payment required and the monthly cost.

payment schedule A pre-agreed-on schedule of payments to a contractor usually based on the amount of work completed.

payment stream Scheduled periodic payments under the terms of a note but not including a final balloon payment.

permit A government authorization to perform a building process.

plaintiff One who initially brings a lawsuit or files a complaint.

positive cash flow A situation when income from real estate or business exceeds the expenses incurred.

premises Land or a portion of the land and the structures on the land.

private auction An auction not open to the public; bidders are invited by the auctioneer or her employer.

private mortgage insurance (PMI) A type of insurance often required by lenders when the buyer's down payment is less than 20 percent; the goal is to protect the lenders from default when the buyers don't have a strong equity position in the property.

public auction A public sale of land or goods in which the highest bidder wins.

quitclaim deed A document that can be used to both transfer ownership of a property and release a person's claim on a property; a quitclaim deed conveys only that right, title, or interest that the grantor has and doesn't warrant that the grantor actually has any particular title or interest in the property.

recording The placing of any instrument that affects the title of a property in the public records of the county where the property is located.

remodeling contractor A general contractor who specializes in remodeling work.

rent abatement A concession offered by a landlord as an inducement to tenants to lease office space and that provides for a reduction of monthly rent by omitting a required payment for a specific number of months.

rent roll statement A list or account of rents or income on a property.

rent Payment for the use of property.

repossession Seizure or foreclosure; the secured creditor takes possession of a property after the debtor defaults on payments.

reserve auction An auction where items are offered with a minimum price; if the minimum is not reached in bidding, an item is not sold.

return on investment (ROI) The amount of profit generated by an investment before taxes and appreciation.

satisfaction The discharge of an obligation by paying the full amount due on a debt.

sealed bid auction An auction generally conducted by mail; the bids are sent in and opened at the same time, with the highest bidder winning.

seasoned note A note that has a payment history.

secondary market Companies that buy groups of loans from lenders and then sell them to other lenders and investors.

seller financing A type of financing whereby the seller of the property holds all or part of the mortgage (the same as owner financing).

shill A bidder at an auction whose sole purpose is to drive the bidding as high as possible without having the final bid.

specialty contractor A contractor licensed to perform a specialty task such as electrical or plumbing work or asbestos abatement.

spot bid auction Auction similar to a sealed bid but where bidders are present and hand their bids to the auctioneer in an envelope.

stated income loan A loan designed for self-employed borrowers; the lender accepts whatever income the borrower states as truth.

statute An act, rule, or code enacted by a legislature and adopted as law.

subcontractor An individual or company to whom the property's owner, the general contractor, or another subcontractor sublets all or part of a contract; subcontractors typically specialize in one aspect of the construction work.

sublet space Space that is being offered for lease by a tenant rather than a landlord.

subsidy A payment of benefit made where the benefit exceeds the cost to the beneficiary.

take-out buyer Another name for the funding source in a real estate note transaction.

tax deed Deed from a tax collector to a government body after a period of nonpayment of taxes according to statute; deed to a purchaser at a public sale of land taken for delinquent taxes.

tax evasion The fraudulent and willful underpayment of, or nonpayment of, taxes; evasion is distinguished from tax avoidance, whereby proper interpretation or relevant tax law is made to legally minimize tax liability.

tax lien A lien for nonpayment of property taxes that attaches only to the property on which the taxes are unpaid; a federal tax lien may attach to all the property of the one owing the taxes.

tax sale A public auction where property is sold to the highest bidder in order to recover delinquent property taxes.

tenancy by the entirety A form of ownership that exists only between spouses and includes a right of survivorship; neither spouse can encumber or dispose of the property without the other's consent.

tenancy in common A form of ownership in which tenants do not have rights of survivorship and may own unequal shares in proportion to their contribution.

tenant mix Term that refers to how types of tenants are combined in retail property.

tenant placement Term that refers to where tenants are placed in relation to property elements and each other in a retail center.

time and materials contract A contract that specifies a price for different elements of construction or rehab work, such as the cost per hour of labor, overhead, profit, and the like.

title insurance Insurance that indemnifies the owner of real estate in the event that her clear ownership of property is challenged by the discovery of faults in the title.

title search An investigation of documents in the public records office to determine the state of a title.

title Ownership.

underwriting A lender's process to evaluate whether to give a borrower a loan.

upset A term that means the same as *reserve* but used when auctioning real estate that has been foreclosed on; a minimum amount the property must sell for.

warranty deed A document used to transfer ownership of a property that warrants the grantor has the title he claims to have.

wraparound mortgage A type of mortgage whereby the amount of the loan encompasses all liens on the property; the borrower makes the entire payment to the junior lien holder, who then makes the payment on the senior encumbrance.

zoning The mandate of local government through laws and ordinances as to the use and purpose of real property in specified areas or districts as well as any associated limitations or other requirements.

■ RESOURCES

Because no one person has all the answers, I've created this resource list as a starting point for you as you begin your journey to becoming a real estate millionaire.

■ Whitney Education Group, Inc.™, Advanced Training

Intensified Real Estate Training, a dynamic, action-packed three-day program teaching the ins and outs of identifying, negotiating, buying, and managing cash flow in real estate; includes a property tour and negotiations with actual sellers; held weekly in Cape Coral, Florida.

Wholesale Buying, an exciting, high-energy three-day program that covers how to identify wholesale properties, find and negotiate with sellers, financing techniques, and short-term and long-term strategic planning; includes a property tour; held in multiple locations in the United States and internationally.

Foreclosure Training, a reality-based three-day program that explains the foreclosure process and teaches students how to buy properties that are in foreclosure using win-win techniques; this hands-on training includes a property tour as well as a trip to the county courthouse to learn how to research foreclosures and title and property tax information; held weekly in Atlanta.

Investing in Mobile Homes, a three-day program that teaches students to take advantage of one of the most profitable real estate niche markets; topics covered include how to buy, sell, and rent existing mobile homes; how to develop and operate a mobile home park; how to profit from foreclosures and repossessions; regular and unconventional financing; marketing to potential tenants and buyers; and more; held monthly in Fort Myers Beach, Florida.

Purchase Option, an exhilarating three-day program that explains proven purchase option strategies and teaches students how to buy or control property with little or no money down; a unique property tour demonstrates how to apply the techniques in the real world; held monthly in Las Vegas, Nevada.

Property Management and Cash Flow, a motivating, down-to-earth three-day program devoted to effective, profitable property management and building a substantial positive cash flow; training includes a property tour and detailed information on management, marketing, government regulations, tenant relations, maintenance, and more; held monthly in Albany, New York.

Commercial Real Estate Investing, a challenging three-day program that teaches students the fundamentals of buying, managing, and disposing of commercial real estate; a field trip provides the opportunity to view potential investments and do a complete analysis on each; held quarterly in Orlando, Florida; Las Vegas, Nevada; and Honolulu, Hawaii.

Mentor Program, one of the most innovative real estate training programs available; students benefit from four days spent in one-on-one training and practical, real-world application with a mentor handpicked by Russ Whitney and who is a successful real estate investor; conducted weekly in all states in the United States plus the United Kingdom and Canada.

Discount Notes and Mortgages, an energizing three-day program in which industry experts teach how to buy, broker, and sell mortgages and notes at a discount; topics covered include finding notes, locating funding sources, other debt instruments that can be bought or sold at a discount, and using privately held notes to buy and sell real estate; held monthly in Atlanta, Georgia.

Keys to Creative Real Estate Financing, a powerful three-day program that is the real-world equivalent of a postgraduate degree in real estate finance; students learn multiple techniques to finance any deal worth buying; held monthly in Sarasota, Florida.

Asset Protection and Tax Relief, a comprehensive three-day program covering asset protection techniques used by the wealthy; forms of ownership; techniques that save and possibly even eliminate some taxes; and other asset protection and tax relief techniques you can use immediately; held monthly in Orlando, Florida, and Las Vegas, Nevada.

International Finance and Investment, a unique and powerful six-day program focusing on international investing and business, tax issues, international demographics and economic trends, and more—plus the opportunity to visit some of Costa Rica's most breathtaking natural attractions; held quarterly in Rancho Monterey, Costa Rica.

Teach Me to Trade, a comprehensive package of seven training programs designed to show students how to cash in on the stock market with successful trading strategies; the programs begin with a complete foundation of practical technical analysis and move into a range of increasingly sophisticated techniques; students thrill to the exciting experience of standing on the floor of a major stock exchange; more information is available online at <www.teachmetotrade.com>.

■ Whitney Education Group, Inc.™, Software, Publications, and Independent Study Packages

The following educational products can be purchased by calling 800-741-7877 or online at <www.WhitneyEducationGroup.com>.

Building Wealth Live by Russ Whitney; a combination of books, CDs, and videotapes designed to guide the beginning real estate investor through the process of successfully acquiring investment property.

Building Wealth with Notes and Mortgages by Russ Whitney; a two-volume package of books, a CD, and videotape that introduces the discount mortgage industry and takes the student through the process of building wealth with debt instruments.

Business Success System by Russ Whitney; a complete system for starting a new business or fine-tuning an existing one, including business development, marketing, investing, and the Internet.

Communication, Negotiation & Salesmanship by Russ Whitney; proven techniques to increase business and personal success through positive communication, win-win negotiation, and skilled sales techniques.

Credit: How to Obtain, Increase and Preserve Credit by Russ Whitney; contains numerous proven techniques for repairing and strengthening your credit rating.

Millionaire U Video Collection by Russ Whitney; the next best thing to actually attending Russ Whitney's Millionaire U, where you'll learn how to locate and purchase property, negotiate with sellers, obtain financing, inspect property, and much more.

One in a Million 90-Day Challenge by Russ Whitney; the plan and tools to break the chains that have been holding you back.

Property Tax Reduction Manual by Russ Whitney; explains property tax assessments and how to challenge a tax bill to reduce taxes and realize a savings of between 12 and 25 percent.

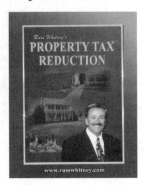

Real Estate and Business Success System Software by Russ Whitney; the ultimate business tool containing contracts, letters and legal forms; real estate analysis; loan prequalification and creative loan analysis; business assessment; business plan creator; legal assistant; and time management.

Wealth Intelligence Network (WIN) by Russ Whitney; membership includes an information-packed monthly magazine, financial hot line, financial management services, merchant accounts, mortgage and insurance services, asset protection assistance, and much more.

■ Associations

Building Owners and Managers Association (BOMA), 1201 New York Ave., NW, Suite 300, Washington, DC 20005; 202-408-2662; www.boma.org

Institute of Real Estate Management, an affiliate of the National Association of Realtors, 430 N. Michigan Ave., Chicago, IL 60611; 800-837-0706; www.irem.org

National Apartment Association, 201 N. Union St., Suite 200, Alexandria, VA 22314; 703-518-6141; www.naahq.org

National Association of Residential Property Managers, P.O. Box 140647, Austin, TX 78714-0647; 800-782-3452; www.narpm.org

National Housing and Rehabilitation Association, 1625 Massachusetts Ave., NW, Suite 601, Washington, DC 20036; 202-939-1750; www.housingonline.com

National Real Estate Investors Association, P.O. Box 1759, Pittsburgh, PA 15230-1759; 888-762-7342; www.nationalreia.com

■ Government Resources

Federal Deposit Insurance Corporation, Washington, DC; 877-ASK-FDIC (877-275-3342); www.fdic.gov

U.S. Department of Housing and Urban Development (HUD), 451 Seventh St., SW, Washington, DC 20410; 202-708-1112; www.hud.gov

U.S. Department of Agriculture (USDA), Rural Housing Service National Office, Room 5037, South Building, Fourteenth St. and Independence Ave., SW, Washington, DC 20250; 202-720-4323; www.usda.gov

Department of Veterans Affairs, Washington, DC 20011; 800-827-1000; www.homeloans.va.gov

General Services Administration, 1800 F St., NW, Washington, DC 20405; 202-501-0084; Office of Property Disposal, 800-473-7836; http://propertydisposal.gsa.gov/property/PropForSale/

Small Business Administration, 409 Third St., SW, Washington, DC 20416; 800-U-ASK-SBA; www.sba.gov

U.S. Army Engineer District, Savannah, Homeowners Assistance Program Branch, P.O. Box 889, Savannah, GA 31402-0889; 800-861-8144; www.sas .usace.army.mil/hapinv/hapinfo.htm

■ Internet Resources

Consumer credit information, www.monitrust.com

Credit score, www.myfico.com

Internal Revenue Service, Real and Personal Property Sales, www.treas.gov/auctions /irs/index.html

National Association of Realtors, www.realtor.org

Public Record Information, www.searchsystems.net

United States Treasury Auctions Page, www.treas.gov/auctions/

USDA properties for sale, www.resales.usda.gov/properties.cfm

■ Whitney Education Group, Inc., Primary Locations

Whitney Education Group, Inc., 1612 E. Cape Coral Pkwy., Cape Coral, FL 33904; 800-741-7877; www.WhitneyEducationGroup.com

Whitney Canada, Inc., Airways Center, 5955 Airport Rd., #260, Mississauga, ON, Canada L4V 1R9; 800-288-8015; www.WhitneyEducationGroup.ca

Whitney UK, LTD., 500 Chiswick High Rd., London, UK, W4 5RG; 020 8956 2242; www.WhitneyEducationGroup.co.uk

Rancho Monterey, Esterillos, Costa Rica; information about development opportunities is available through Whitney Information Network, 1612 E. Cape Coral Pkwy., Cape Coral, FL 33904; 800-741-7877; www.russwhitney.com

Note: Every effort has been made to ensure the accuracy of the information listed; however, please remember that addresses, phone numbers, and Web sites can change without notice.

■ THE WEALTH TEAM

In putting together my training organization, I have assembled a team of the best and brightest minds in real estate investing, asset protection, business start-ups, marketing, and management. These people make up our Wealth Team. Their contributions to this book were substantial and I want you to meet them.

Jim Aviza. As an instructor for Whitney Education Group, Jim Aviza has taught thousands of students the secrets of property management and cash flow. He is also president of Northeast Management and Realty and Northeast Properties, LLC. Over the past two decades, Jim has personally bought and sold hundreds of properties, and he currently owns and manages several hundred residential rental units as well as commercial offices and retail space.

Don Burnham. In his role as a trainer for Whitney Education Group, Don Burnham, using a relaxed but thorough style that students appreciate, teaches on both the fundamental and advanced levels. Don holds a bachelor's degree in business management and a master's degree in education and has been a successful entrepreneur since 1969. He has made millions in the discount buying of real estate and real estate notes, and he enthusiastically shares his techniques in the classroom and through two published books.

Shawn M. Casey. Attorney Shawn M. Casey is widely recognized as a leading financial expert in the fields of asset protection, tax planning, and wealth creation, and is an instructor on those subjects with Whitney Education Group. He shows the average person how to use simple legal strategies to reduce or eliminate taxes, protect assets, and grow personal wealth. Using his own techniques plus those of others on the Whitney team, Shawn has built a personal fortune that puts him well beyond millionaire status.

Robert W. Demes. An economist by education, Robert W. Demes teaches asset protection for Whitney Education Group and is the managing director of Monterey Development in Costa Rica. Robert has more than two decades of experience in international banking, specializing in business relocation and development. In his career, he has designed and constructed more than $40 million in commercial and residential development.

David Gilmore. David Gilmore has been investing in residential and commercial properties since 1979. His practical experience covers all aspects of real estate, including developing, building, sales, and funding. He is a certified instructor for Russ Whitney's Real Estate Training Academy and helped Russ develop the Commercial Real Estate Investing training program. David is a self-made millionaire and has taught countless numbers of students to follow in his footsteps.

Kevin Haag. Kevin Haag owns one of southwest Florida's largest independent real estate offices and has overseen more than $200 million in real estate transactions. As one of Russ Whitney's personal real estate brokers, he is a member of Russ's Power Team and has taught hundreds of Whitney students how to choose, and effectively work with, a real estate agent. With his own real estate holdings in excess of $10 million, Kevin continues to create opportunities for his investors.

Jean Lapointe. Jean Lapointe is a mentor for Whitney Education Group in Canada. He holds real estate licenses in both the United States and Canada and is a Canadian mortgage broker with 15 years' experience in real estate and discount mortgaging. He continues to actively invest in real estate and debt instruments, and he has assisted Canadian students in purchasing more than $55 million in property with creative financing and no-money-down techniques.

Glenn Purdy. Combining expertise in real estate, finance, marketing, and international business, Glenn Purdy brings a wealth of talent and resources to Whitney Education Group. He has been buying real estate since 1988 and has owned property in the United States, Canada, and the United Kingdom. He currently owns and operates seven different businesses and is a dynamic, energetic, and empowering trainer and speaker.

David Shamy. David Shamy is a consultant-speaker for Whitney UK and also a speaker-trainer for Teach Me to Trade in the United States. He received an honorary master's degree in real estate investing from Meta Institute in 1995, has lectured for 23 years, and is the author of 17 books. With a quarter century of experience in real estate investing and a personal portfolio of properties worth millions of dollars, David is exceptionally qualified to train future millionaires to build wealth through real estate.

Jim Shead. Jim Shead is a trainer for Whitney Education Group's Discount Notes & Mortgages and has his own funding company. He is a successful entrepreneur who buys and flips wholesale properties; in addition, he buys, sells, and brokers privately held notes and mortgages.

Larry Simons. With more than a quarter century in the real estate business, Larry Simons has a tremendous amount of knowledge to share with the Whitney students who attend trainings in Cape Coral. Larry owns Home Hunters USA, Inc., a real estate rental, sales, and property management company. A subsidiary, Home Improvement USA, Inc., handles property maintenance and rehab. Larry is also one of Russ's real estate brokers and a member of Russ's Power Team. Larry's real estate holdings include single-family homes, multifamily units, and commercial property.

Gary G. Tharp. Gary G. Tharp is a senior emeritus member of the faculty of the Commercial Investment Real Estate Institute and a popular instructor with Whitney Education Group. He has been investing in real estate since 1966, has received numerous awards for his achievements in the commercial real estate field, and has authored many articles and courses on investment real estate. His own holdings include several office buildings in downtown Orlando.

Pete Youngs. The skill to deliver the highest-quality results at the lowest possible price has earned Pete Youngs building and renovation contracts with such prestigious clients as Publix Distribution Center (servicing Publix Supermarkets), Marriott Hotels, MCI, and the 1996 Olympic Games in Atlanta. As a property rehab specialist for the foreclosure training portion of Whitney Education Group's programs, Pete shows his students how to save up to 75 percent on fix-up and maintenance costs. In partnership with his brother Tony, Pete owns more than 50 properties and practices what he teaches.

Tony Youngs. Specializing in foreclosure properties, Tony Youngs has acquired and helped hundreds of others acquire FHA, VA, HUD, REO, pre-foreclosures and auctioned property all over North America. Tony is a foreclosure specialist for Whitney Education Group, and his students get to tap into a wealth of first-hand, plain-language knowledge and experience presented in a refreshing, down-to-earth style. With his brother Pete, Tony owns more than 50 properties purchased using the foreclosure techniques he teaches.

■ INDEX

A Special Bonus for Readers of
Millionaire Real Estate Mentor:
The Secrets to Financial Freedom Through Real Estate Investing

A **FREE** Subscription to
The Russ Whitney *Building Wealth Newsletter*

This **free** online newsletter is filled with timely and useful tips and techniques on what's new, what's working, and what to avoid, along with proven strategies to improve your real estate and financial success.

It's a tool you'll use now and throughout your investing career to help you make smarter, more profitable investments. And it's **absolutely free**—all you have to do is subscribe. Please accept it along with the best wishes of Russ Whitney and his Wealth Team.

To Get Your FREE Subscription Started Today

Go to <www.russwhitney.com> and Register Online

OR

Fax this form to 1-239-540-6562.

Name _____

Address _____

City _____ **State** _____ **Zip** _____

Phone _____

E-mail _____

THANK YOU!

OR

Call toll-free 1-800-741-RUSS (7877)
and speak to one of our representatives.

A Mentor for Everyone!

For quantity discount information,
please contact Robin Bermel
at 800-621-9621, ext. 4455,
bermel@dearborn.com.

For added visibility, consider
our custom cover service,
which highlights your organization's
name and logo on the cover.

We can also create special books,
booklets, or book excerpts to
fit your specific needs.

Dearborn Trade is an excellent
resource for dynamic and
knowledgeable speakers.

Dearborn™
Trade Publishing
A **Kaplan Professional** Company